G.F.Watts, R.A. pinx.   Walker & Boutall, ph.sc.

William Morris.

aet 37.

THE LIFE OF
WILLIAM MORRIS

BY

J. W. MACKAIL

VOLUME I

NEW IMPRESSION

LONGMANS, GREEN, AND CO.

39 PATERNOSTER ROW, LONDON, E.C.4

FOURTH AVENUE AND 30TH STREET, NEW YORK

BOMBAY, CALCUTTA, AND MADRAS

1920

BIBLIOGRAPHICAL NOTE.

First printed, April 1899; Reprinted, May 1899;
October 1899.

New and cheaper edition, large crown 8vo, 1901.

Reprinted, October 1907; February 1911 ; July 1920.

DIVO PATRI

J. W. M.

M. B.-J.

PREFACE TO FIRST EDITION

THIS biography was undertaken by me at the special request of Sir Edward Burne-Jones. I will not attempt to say how much it owes to his guidance and encouragement, nor how much it has lost by their removal.

When the task of writing the life of Morris was placed in my hands, his family and representatives gave me unreserved access to all the materials in their possession. To them, and more especially to his executors, Mr. F. S. Ellis and Mr. S. C. Cockerell, I owe my best thanks for their friendly help. I am further indebted to Mr. Ellis for the index at the end of the book.

Among the few survivors of Morris's earliest friends, I must express very special obligations to Mr. Cormell Price for generous and ungrudging assistance, and to the Rev. Canon R. W. Dixon. For information as to later years I am greatly indebted to Mr. Philip Webb, Mr. George Wardle, Mr. C. Fairfax Murray, Mr. William De Morgan, and Mr. Emery Walker, who were all long and closely associated with him both in work and in friendship. The partners of the firm of Morris & Co., Messrs. Smith and Mr. J. H. Dearle, have given me access to the early books of the firm and much valuable information with regard to Morris's conduct of the business.

PREFACE

I would take this opportunity of thanking all those others who have communicated letters or other material to me in the course of the work. To Lady Burne-Jones, whose share in the help given me has not been less than that of any one I have named, this is not the place where I can fully express my gratitude.

6, Pembroke Gardens, Kensington.
24th March, 1899.

CONTENTS

VOLUME I

PAGE

CHAPTER VIII

VOLUME II

CHAPTER XII

LIST OF ILLUSTRATIONS
VOLUME I

VOLUME II

The design on the title-page containing William
Morris's motto was made by him in or about 1861 for
quarries of glass in some of the painted windows of the
house he was then building for himself (see Vol. I., pp.
142-144).

That on the back of the cover is a reproduction of
one of the borders designed and cut on wood by him in
1872 for the ornamented edition of "Love is Enough,"
then in contemplation (see Vol. I., pp. 285, 286).

Sed dico, Numquid non audierunt? Et quidem in omnem terram exivit sonus eorum et in fines orbis terræ verba eorum.

Hæc autem omnia in figura contingebant illis: scripta sunt autem ad correptionem nostram, in quos fines seculorum devenerunt.

THE LIFE OF WILLIAM MORRIS

CHAPTER I

WALTHAMSTOW, WOODFORD, AND MARLBOROUGH
1834-1852

POET, artist, manufacturer, and socialist, author of "The Earthly Paradise":—this terse unimpassioned entry in the "Fasti Britannici" sums up, in a form of words which he would himself have accepted as substantially accurate, the life and work of a remarkable man. What place he may finally occupy in the remembrance of the world, how long or how distinctly his unique personality may stand out above the smooth surface of oblivion under which, sooner or later, the greatest names are overwhelmed together with the least, it does not rest with his contemporaries to determine. But those who knew him unite in desiring that some record may descend of one who, in an age of transition and confusion, set a certain ideal before him and pursued it, through the many paths by which it led him, with undeviating constancy; the impulse of whose life had before his death wrought a silent revolution in those arts which he practised and transfigured; and the whole of whose extraordinary powers were devoted towards no less an object than the reconstitution of the civilized life of mankind.

William Morris, the eldest son and third child of William Morris and Emma Shelton, was born at Elm

House, Clay Hill, Walthamstow, on the 24th of March, 1834. His ancestry was on neither side in any way remarkable, and family records in the undistinguished middle class, whether commercial or professional, to which both his parents belonged, are generally scanty in amount and do not go far back. Such facts as have been preserved may be briefly set down, without laying any stress on what is known or what is unknown in the history of the family.

The Morrises were originally of Welsh descent, and their native country was the valley of the upper Severn and its tributaries, where the mixture or antagonism of two races in a country of exceptional natural beauty has bred a stock of fine physical quality, but of no remarkable gift either of intellect or imagination. "The quietest places under the sun," so a local proverb describes that countryside; and so they have been and still are, ever since the Welsh Marches were reduced to outward peace. Morris's grandfather (the first of the family, it is said, who dropped the Welsh Ap from his surname) settled in business in Worcester in the latter part of last century, and throve there as a burgess, "a man excellent in every relation of life, and very religious." He married Elizabeth, daughter of Dr. Charles Stanley, a naval surgeon, who had retired from the service and was in practice at Nottingham. She is remembered and described by her grandchildren—she lived to the age of eighty-five—as a tall fine-looking woman. At Worcester their second son, William Morris, was born on the 14th of June, 1797. About 1820, his father having then removed his business to London, he was entered as a clerk in the firm of Harris, Sanderson & Harris, discount brokers, of 32, Lombard Street. It was a newly-founded London house. The Harrises were Quakers, and between them and the Morrises there was some family connexion. When a

little over thirty, William Morris became a partner in
the firm, which was now known as Sanderson & Co., and
some years afterwards removed its place of business to
83, King William Street. Bill and discount broking, then
even more than now, was a class of business carried on by
a comparatively limited number of persons, whose status
and social consideration approached those of private
bankers. Competition was not keen, and the members
of established firms lived in ease and even opulence.

Mr. Morris married soon after his admission to partnership in the firm. His wife, who long outlived him,
and died in her ninetieth year so recently as 1894, was
the daughter of a Worcester neighbour, Joseph Shelton.
The Sheltons were a family with some history. The line
can be traced back directly to a Henry Shelton, mercer,
of Birmingham, in the reign of Henry VII. The Sheltons
were prosperous merchants and landed proprietors in the
sixteenth and seventeenth centuries, and contributed a
number of members to the Church and the Bar. John
Shelton, Proctor of the Consistory Court of the diocese
of Worcester, Mrs. Morris's grandfather, had a family
in whom a taste for music was very strongly developed.
Two of his sons became singing canons of Worcester
Cathedral and Westminster Abbey; a third, Joseph, was
equally devoted to the art, of which he became a teacher
in Worcester. The families of the Sheltons and Morrises,
between whom there was some distant connexion by
marriage, were intimate with one another, and the marriage of William Morris to Emma Shelton, Joseph
Shelton's youngest daughter, was a natural arrangement.
It was then still customary that one of the members of a
City firm should live at their place of business. Mr. and
Mrs. Morris when married set up house in Lombard
Street, where the two eldest children, both daughters,
were born in 1830 and 1832. The next year they ceased

to live in the City, and took a house at Walthamstow, in the pleasant Essex country overlooking the Lea Valley and within a mile or so of Epping Forest. Like many of his neighbours in what was then a favourite residential neighbourhood for City men, Mr. Morris travelled daily to his business by the stage coach.

The modern outgrowth of London has nowhere had more devastating effects than in Walthamstow proper, where the rows of flimsily-built two-storied houses, in all the hideousness of yellow brick and blue slate, stretch in a squalid sheet over the Lea Valley. Clay Hill, a slight rising ground projecting into the flats from the higher Forest country, is now just on the edge of the brick and mortar wilderness. Looking northward from it, however, one sees the face of the country much as it was sixty years ago : a flattish heavily-timbered valley of the familiar Eastern County type, neither beautiful nor ugly, with the line of the Forest stretching along the horizon to the north-east, towards Chingford and High Beach. Elm House till quite recently remained unchanged; it was a plain roomy building of the early years of this century, the garden front facing south on to a large lawn surrounded by shrubberies and kitchen gardens, with a great mulberry tree leaning along the grass. Within the last twelve months the advancing tide of building has swept over it, and house and garden, like many others in the neighbourhood, have wholly disappeared.

William, the eldest son, was the first of the children born at Elm House. There were six younger children, four boys and two girls.

The Shelton stock was long-lived and of powerful physique. But the Morrises do not seem to have been a very robust family. Both Morris's father and grandfather died comparatively young; and he himself, though he afterwards developed unusual physical strength, was delicate in infancy and early childhood. He had to be kept alive, his mother used to say, by calves' feet jelly and beef tea. Perhaps it was on account of this delicacy that he learned to read unusually young. At four years old he was already deep in the Waverley novels; and he formed as a child, not only the love of reading, but the habit of reading with extraordinary swiftness, only equalled by the prodigious grasp of his memory. The knowledge of books came to him almost by instinct. "We never remember his learning regularly to read," his sisters say, "though he may have had a few lessons from our governess:" and he himself could not remember a time when he was unable to read.

Meanwhile the business of the bill-broking firm, and Mr. Morris's own private commercial undertakings, grew and prospered. He was now a wealthy man; and in 1840, when his eldest boy was six years old, the family left Elm House, and moved across the Forest to Woodford Hall, a large spacious mansion of Georgian date, standing in about fifty acres of park, on the high road from London to Epping. The park was only separated by a fence from the Forest itself; and the estate included about a hundred acres of farm land, sloping down to the little river Roding. Behind lay the pathless glades and thickets of hornbeam and beech which still, in spite of all encroachments, and of the nearer and nearer approach of London, remain in all essentials a part of primæval England, little changed in the course of hundreds, perhaps thousands of years. From the Hall the course of the Thames might be traced winding through the marshes, with white and ruddy-brown sails moving among corn-fields and pastures. The little brick Georgian church of Woodford (since enlarged and modernized), stood alongside of the Hall, which had a private doorway into the churchyard. On the roadside nearly opposite, on a green space now enclosed, were the pound and the stocks. "When we lived at Woodford," Morris wrote to his daughter half a century later, "there were stocks there on a little bit of wayside green in the middle of the village : beside them stood the cage, a small shanty some twelve feet square, and as it was built of brown brick roofed with blue slate, I suppose it had been quite recently in use, since its style was not earlier than the days of fat George. I remember I used to look at these two threats of law and order with considerable terror, and decidedly preferred to walk on the other side of the road ; but I never heard of anybody being locked up in the cage or laid by the heels in the stocks."

The outgrowth of Eastern London had not then overflowed the line of low hills which shut off the Lea Valley. The picture which Morris draws, in "News from Nowhere," of this Essex country in the restored and recivilized England of a distant future, substantially represents the scene of his own boyhood. "Eastward and landward," he says in that description, "it is all flat pasture, once marsh, except for a few gardens, and there are very few permanent dwellings there, scarcely anything but a few sheds and cots for the men who come to look after the great herds of cattle. What with the beasts and the men, and the scattered red-tiled roofs and the big hayricks, it does not make a bad holiday to get a quiet pony and ride about there on a sunny afternoon of autumn, and look over the river and the craft passing up and down, and on to Shooter's Hill and the Kentish uplands, and then turn round to the wide green sea of the Essex marshland, with the great domed line of the sky, and the sun shining down in one flood of peaceful light over the long distance."

The park abounded in wild birds and beasts from the neighbouring Forest. It was an ideal home for a boy with healthy outdoor tastes. There Morris, rambling with his brothers on foot or on Shetland ponies through the Forest, formed his intense love of nature and his keen eye for all sorts of woodland life. He never ceased to love Epping Forest, and to uphold the scenery of his native county as beautifully and characteristically English. The dense hornbeam thickets, which even in bright weather have something of solemnity and mystery in their deep shade, and which are hardly found elsewhere in England, reappear again and again in his poetry and his prose romances. Fifty years later, when the treatment of the Forest by the Conservators had been the subject of much public criticism, he went over the familiar ground and reported on the changes which had been made on it. "I was born and bred in its neighbourhood," he then wrote, "and when I was a boy and young man knew it yard by yard from Wanstead to the Theydons, and from Hale End to the Fairlop Oak. In those days it had no worse foes than the gravel stealer and the rolling fence maker, and was always interesting and often very beautiful.

"The special character of it was derived from the fact that by far the greater part was a wood of hornbeams, a tree not common save in Essex and Herts. It was certainly the biggest hornbeam wood in these islands, and I suppose in the world. The said hornbeams were all pollards, being shrouded every four or six years, and were interspersed in many places with holly thickets. Nothing could be more interesting and romantic than the effect of the long poles of the hornbeams rising from the trunks and seen against the mass of the wood behind. It has a peculiar charm of its own not to be found in any other forest."

In this healthy country life he rapidly outgrew his early delicacy of constitution. The life indoors was equally happy. "When I was a little chap" was a phrase often in his mouth; and these allusions to childhood always implied the remembrance of perfect contentment. Among the little things that impressed themselves on his childish memory are mentioned "a picture of Abraham and Isaac worked in brown worsted," and Indian cabinets, and "a carved ivory junk with painted and gilded puppets in it in a glass case." "Naïf or gross ghost stories, read long ago in queer little penny garlands with woodcuts," long haunted his imagination; and as he grew bigger, he found and revelled in Lane's "Arabian Nights." Among the books of the house there was a copy of Gerard's "Herbal." In studying it as a naturalist, the boy's eyes were led to examine the beautiful drawings, many of which later gave suggestions for his own designs in the flower-work of his earlier wall-papers, and in the backgrounds of designs for glass and tapestry. He continued an eager reader of novels. His eldest sister remembers how they used to read "The Old English Baron" together in the rabbit warren at Woodford, poring over the enthralling pages till both were wrought up to a state of mind that made them afraid to cross the park to reach home. By the time he was seven years old he had read all the Waverley novels, and many of Marryat's, besides others which were then in fashion. Reading can be acquired without regular teaching, but writing cannot; and he did not learn to write till much after the ordinary age. But his innate skill of hand made it easy of acquirement to him when he once took pains; and his handwriting became in later life one of remarkable beauty. The subsidiary art of spelling was always one in which he was liable to make curious lapses. "I remember," he once said, when speaking of his childhood, "being taught to spell and standing on a chair with my shoes off because I made so many mistakes." In later years several sheets of "The Life and Death of Jason" had to be cancelled and re-printed because of a mistake in the spelling of a perfectly common English word; a word indeed so common that the printer's reader had left it as it was in the manuscript, thinking that Morris's spelling must be an intentional peculiarity.

The life of an English country house, even of the second or third order of importance, still retained, sixty years since, much of the self-contained and self-sufficing system of the manor house of earlier times. A certain elaborateness of appliances was combined with what would now be thought a strange simplicity. At some points there were links with the habits of mediæval Eng-land. Woodford Hall brewed its own beer, and made its own butter, as much as a matter of course as it baked its own bread. Just as in the fourteenth century, there was a meal at high prime, midway between breakfast and dinner, when the children had cake and cheese and a glass of small ale. Many of the old festivals were ob-served; Twelfth Night especially was one of the great days of the year, and the Masque of St. George was always then presented with considerable elaboration. Among Morris's toys curiously enough was a little suit of armour, in which he rode on his pony in the park. He and his brothers were keen anglers—this taste re-mained one of his strongest throughout his life—and took the usual boys' pleasure in shooting, not the regular game of seniors, but rabbits and small wild birds. The red-wings and fieldfares which they shot on winter holidays they were allowed to roast for supper. It was one of his childish ambitions to shoot woodpigeons with a bow and arrow. Besides the range of the lawn and park the children had little gardens of their own. He writes in later life of "the beautiful hepatica which I used to love so when I was a quite little boy." "To this day," he once said, "when I smell a may-tree I think of going to bed by daylight;" and the strong sweet smell of balm always brought to his mind "very early days in the kitchen-garden at Woodford, and the large blue plums which grew on the wall beyond the sweet-herb patch." One who shared this outdoor life at Woodford with Morris told me, in a phrase of accurate simplicity, that as a boy he "knew the names of birds." There was, indeed, little that he ever saw of which he did not know the name.

The love of the Middle Ages was born in him. Any slight remnants of mediæval tradition in the daily life of Woodford did not go deep; and it was only some years later that the Oxford movement spread over England, and deepened or replaced the superficial mediævalism brought into fashion by Scott. The religion of the family was of the normal type of a somewhat sterile Evangelicalism, which cursorily dismissed everything outside itself as Popery on the one hand or Dissent on the other. The children were not allowed to mix with dissenters with the single exception of Quakers. But the old Essex churches within reach of Woodford, and their monuments and brasses, were known by Morris at a very early age; and a visit which he made with his father to Canterbury when only eight years old left on his mind an ineffaceable impression of the glory of Gothic architecture. On the same holiday they saw the church of Minster in Thanet. It is characteristic of his extraordinary eye and even more extraordinary memory, that just fifty years later, never having seen the church in the interval, he described it in some detail from that recollection. No landscape, no building, that he had once seen did he ever forget, or ever confuse with another.

Nor were the splendid Essex country houses which

survived from the fifteenth and sixteenth centuries less
known or loved by him than the Essex churches. "Well
I remember as a boy," he wrote in his lecture on The
Lesser Arts of Life, in 1882, "my first acquaintance
with a room hung with faded greenery at Queen
Elizabeth's Lodge by Chingford Hatch in Epping
Forest (I wonder what has become of it now?), and the
impression of romance that it made upon me! a feeling
that always comes back on me when I read, as I often
do, Sir Walter Scott's 'Antiquary,' and come to the
description of the Green Room at Monkbarns, amongst
which the novelist has with such exquisite cunning of
art imbedded the fresh and glittering verses of the
summer poet Chaucer: yes, that was more than upholstery, believe me."

When Morris was nine years old, the casual ministra-
tions of his sisters' governess gave place to a more regular
education. He was sent to a "preparatory school for
young gentlemen" in Walthamstow, kept by the Misses
Arundale. This was a couple of miles off, and he rode
over to it on his pony. A year or two later the Misses
Arundale removed with their school to George Lane,
Woodford, within a few hundred yards of Woodford
Hall. He remained there first as a day scholar, and
afterwards for some time as a boarder, until the death of
his father in the autumn of 1847.

For a number of years before his death Mr. Morris
had held a position of some consequence in the district,
and was a well-known name in the City. In 1843 he
obtained a grant of arms from the Herald's College:
"Azure, a horse's head erased argent between three horse-
shoes or, and for crest, on a wreath of the colours, a
horse's head couped argent, charged with three horse-
shoes in chevron sable." The boy of nine was already
of an age to be keenly interested in heraldry; and what-

ever may have been the reasons which induced Garter and Clarenceux to assign these bearings, they became in his mind something deeply, if obscurely, associated with his life. He considered himself in some sense a tribesman of the White Horse. In the house which he built for himself afterwards the horse's head is pictured on tiles and glass painted by his own hand. To the White Horse of the Berkshire downs, which lies within a drive of his later home at Kelmscott, he made a regular yearly pilgrimage. "Not seldom I please myself," he wrote many years afterwards, "with trying to realize the face of mediæval England; the many chases and great woods, the stretches of common tillage and common pasture quite unenclosed; the rough husbandry of the tilled parts, the unimproved breeds of cattle, sheep, and swine, especially the latter, so lank and long and lathy, looking so strange to us; the strings of packhorses along the bridle-roads, the scantiness of the wheel-roads, scarce any except those left by the Romans, and those made from monastery to monastery; the scarcity of bridges, and people using ferries instead, or fords where they could; the little towns well bechurched, often walled; the villages just where they are now (except for those that have nothing but the church left to tell of them), but better and more populous; their churches, some big and handsome, some small and curious, but all crowded with altars and furniture, and gay with pictures and ornament; the many religious houses, with their glorious architecture; the beautiful manor-houses, some of them castles once, and survivals from an earlier period; some new and elegant; some out of all proportion small for the importance of their lords. How strange it would be to us if we could be landed in fourteenth-century England; unless we saw the crest of some familiar hill, like that which yet bears upon it a symbol of an English tribe, and from which, looking down on the plain where Alfred was born, I once had many such ponderings." In Great Coxwell church, halfway between Kelmscott and the White Horse, are two fifteenth-century brasses of William Morys, "sūtyme fermer of Cokyswell," and Johane his wife—the former with a figure of a man in a short gown, with a pouch hanging at his girdle. The discovery of these monuments gave him extraordinary delight. In spite of his Welsh blood and of that vein of romantic melancholy in him which it is customary to regard as of Celtic origin, his sympathies were throughout with the Teutonic stocks. Among all the mythologies of Europe the Irish mythology perhaps interested him least: for Welsh poetry he did not care deeply; and even the Arthurian legend never took the same hold on his mind, or meant as much to him, as the heroic cycle of the Teutonic race.

The very soil of his birth, "this unromantic, uneventful-looking land of England," he loved with a tempered but deep enthusiasm. "The land is a little land; too much shut up within the narrow seas, as it seems, to have much space for swelling into hugeness; there are no great wastes overwhelming in their dreariness, no great solitudes of forests, no terrible untrodden mountain-walls: all is measured, mingled, varied, gliding easily one thing into another: little rivers, little plains, swelling, speedily-changing uplands, all beset with handsome orderly trees; little hills, little mountains, netted over with the walls of sheepwalks: neither prison nor palace, but a decent home." And in that decent home there had dwelt until the coming of the evil days, " a people rustic and narrow-minded indeed, but serious, truthful, and of simple habits."

A little later, the wealth of the family became immensely increased by one of those chances which occur

a few times in a generation, and give almost a touch of
romance to the routine of commerce. In 1844 a company was formed to work certain veins of copper which
had been discovered near Tavistock. It started on the
modest capital of 1,024 shares of one pound each fully
paid up. Of these Mr. Morris held 272; they had
been assigned to him, it is said, in part payment of a
debt. As soon as working was begun, the lodes were
found to be of extraordinary richness. Copper then was
worth a hundred and sixty pounds a ton: from this
mine, famous under the name of the Devon Great Consols, it could be turned out for a trifling expense in
apparently inexhaustible quantities. Within six months
the shares were changing hands in the market at eight
hundred pounds each. Mr. Morris's holding rose for a
while to the value of over two hundred thousand pounds.
Three quarters of a million tons of copper ore were
yielded by the mine before the gradual exhaustion of the
lodes, and the fall in the price of copper, brought its
prosperity to a close. It still leads a somewhat struggling
existence on the proceeds of the arsenic which, in the
high days of the copper-mining industry, was neglected
as an unimportant by-product. But its earlier fortunes,
and its gradual decline, were not without importance in
determining the course of Morris's life.

Some time before his death Mr. Morris had bought
a nomination to Marlborough College for his son. The
school had been recently founded " in a healthy and
central position," to quote the terms of its prospectus,
" and conveniently accessible from all parts of England,
being only twelve miles from Swindon, which is to be the
great point of junction of the chief lines of railway in the
kingdom." It was at all events in the centre of one of
the most beautiful and romantic parts of England, in a
neighbourhood full of history, and still fuller of pre-

historic records.   A childhood on the skirts of Epping
Forest was fitly followed by a boyhood on the edge of
Savernake.   It is not easy to over-estimate the influence
of these surroundings on the development of a sensitive
and romantic nature, or their share in fostering that passionate love of earth and her beauty which remained a
controlling and sustaining force throughout his life.

Morris was entered at Marlborough College in February, 1848, being then just under fourteen. He remained
there till the Christmas of 1851, the last year of Dr. Wilkinson's rather disastrous head-mastership. During these
early years the school had never outgrown the confusion
amid which it started in 1843, when two hundred boys
from all parts of England were suddenly shot down into
the chaos of a new school with no tradition, little organization, and insufficient funds.   Yet the need for the school
was so great that these numbers kept growing term by
term : within the first three years they doubled, and for
some time afterwards there was an incessant race between
the growth of the school and the progress of the new
buildings.   More than a hundred new boys entered along
with Morris at the beginning of 1848. The Great Western
Railway was then being pushed slowly westward from
Reading.   Until Morris left school, Hungerford, eleven
miles off, remained the nearest station.   The town itself
was the same quiet little place that it is now. Its remote-
ness from any large town, and the weakness of the school
organization generally, resulted in the boys being allowed
much greater individual freedom than was even then
common, or than now exists at any public school. There
was no regular system of athletics.   Cricket and football
were only played by a small number of the boys.   In play
hours the bulk of them used to ramble about the country.
There was no fixed school dress, and no prefect system.
A single large schoolroom served for all the boys under

the fifth form.   For the average schoolboy the effects of
this loose discipline may be doubtful; but for a boy of
strong tastes and exceptional gifts it was not without its
advantages.   Under the elaborate machinery and the
overpowering social code of the modern public school the
type is fostered at the expense of the individual : with a
boy like Morris the strain would have been so great that
something must have snapped.   Even as it was he lived
a rather solitary life; and he left Marlborough with
little regret, and retained little affection for it in later
years.   But his physical and moral strength, both unusually great, saved him from serious bullying, and his
school life was not unhappy.   The self-sufficingness which
always remained one of his most striking characteristics
kept him from being either lonely or discontented.   He
never played either cricket or football.   The weekly
whole holiday of the summer half was spent by him in
long rambles through Savernake Forest and over the
Downs, sometimes in company with other boys of congenial tastes, but if not, quite happy to be alone.   The
pre-Celtic long barrows on the ridges above Pewsey
Vale, the round barrows of which Silbury Hill is the
most imposing example, the stone circles of Avebury, the
Roman villas at Kennet, all became familiar to him;
and the royal castle, as it existed in all its splendour in
the reign of Henry III., was almost as real to him as
the beautiful seventeenth-century building which had replaced it, and which, after so many vicissitudes, had become the home of the new school.

The school library at Marlborough was well provided
with works on archæology and ecclesiastical architecture.
Through these he ranged at will.   His power of assimila-
tion was prodigious; and he left Marlborough, he used
to say afterwards, a good archæologist, and knowing most
of what there was to be known about English Gothic.

This interest in churches was reinforced by another influence which now came for the first time into his life, that of the Anglo-Catholic movement. The college, though not founded by any theological party, had a distinctly High Church character. Blore's chapel, now demolished to make room for a larger and statelier building, was fast rising when Morris came to Marlborough, and a trained choir was formed when it was opened in the following autumn. The older church music appealed to him with a force only less than that of mediæval architecture. The romantic movement, which had originated a generation before, and had received so prodigious an impulse from Scott's novels, was now flooding into the channels of Anglo-Catholicism; and Morris left school a pronounced Anglo-Catholic.

A schoolfellow at Marlborough describes him as "a thick-set, strong-looking boy, with a high colour and black curly hair, good-natured and kind, but with a fearful temper." According to another, he took little or no part in the school games, but was a keen collector of birds' eggs. The restlessness of his fingers, which must always be handling something, was even then very noticeable. He used to seek relief from it in endless netting. With one end of the net fastened to a desk in the big schoolroom he would work at it for hours together, his fingers moving almost automatically. Mr. Fearon, the Secretary to the Charity Commissioners, who entered Marlborough in the same term, remembers him as fond of mooning and talking to himself, and considered a little mad by the other boys. On his walks he invented and poured forth endless stories, vaguely described as "about knights and fairies," in which one adventure rose out of another, and the tale flowed on from day to day over a whole term. The captain of his dormitory, who had a fancy for listening to stories, and exacted them night after night from the other boys, found him an inexhaustible source. His gusts of temper, as violent as they were brief, are what seem to have most impressed him on his contemporaries.

After Mr. Morris's death, Woodford Hall became too large and difficult an establishment for the family. In the autumn of 1848, during Morris's second half at Marlborough, they removed from it to another house, on the road from Woodford to Tottenham, and within half a mile of their old house on Clay Hill. The earliest extant scrap of Morris's writing is a letter to his sister Emma, dated Feast of All Saints (1st November) in this year, asking for details about the new house. "It is now only 7 weeks to the Holidays, there I go again!" the boy's letter ends, "Just like me! always harping on the Holidays I am sure you must think me a great fool to be always thinking about home but I really can't help it I don't think it is my fault for there are such a lot of things I want to do and say and see."

Water House, Walthamstow, the new house to which he returned for the Christmas holidays, and which remained the home of the family till 1856, was one of the same general type as Woodford Hall on a slightly smaller scale; a square, heavy Georgian building of yellow brick, with a certain stolid dignity of outer aspect, and spacious and handsome within. Its principal feature was a great square hall paved with marble flags, from which a broad square staircase, floored and wainscotted with Spanish chestnut, led up to a large upper hall or gallery. In one of the window seats there he used to spend whole days reading, both before and after he went to Oxford. Behind the house was a broad lawn, and beyond it the feature which gave the house its name, a moat of some forty feet in breadth, surrounding an island planted with a grove of aspens. The moat was stocked with pike and perch; there the boys fished, bathed, and boated in summer, and skated in winter. The island, rough and thickly wooded, and fringed with a growth of hollies, hawthorns, and chestnuts, was a sort of fairy land for all the children, who almost lived on it.

In one of those prose romances which Morris, when he had just left college and was full of the romantic melancholy of two-and-twenty, contributed to the Oxford and Cambridge Magazine, is a passage which shows how deeply the country in which these school vacations were spent had sunk into his heart and mingled with his dreams. "I was in the country soon," writes the hero of the story; "people called it an ugly country, I know, that spreading of the broad marsh lands round the river Lea; but I was so weary with my hard work that it seemed very lovely to me then; indeed, I think I should not have despised it at any time. I was always a lover of the sad lowland country. I walked on, my mind keeping up a strange balance between joy and sadness for some time, till gradually all the beauty of things seemed to be stealing into my heart, and making me very soft and womanish, so that at last, when I was now quite a long way off from the river Lea, and walking close by the side of another little river, a mere brook, all my heart was filled with sadness, and joy had no place there at all; all the songs of birds ringing through the hedges and about the willows; all the sweet colours of the sky, and the clouds that floated in the blue of it; of the tender fresh grass, and the sweet young shoots of flowering things, were very pensive to me, pleasantly so at first perhaps, but soon they were lying heavy on me, with all the rest of things created. I noticed every turn of the banks of the little brook, every ripple of its waters over the brown stones, every line of the broad-leaved water flowers; I went down towards the brook, and, stooping down, gathered a knot of lush marsh-marigolds; then, kneeling on both knees, bent over the water with my arm stretched down to it, till both my hand and the yellow flowers were making the swift-running little stream bubble about them; and even as I did so, still stronger and stronger came the memories, till they came quite clear at last, those shapes and words of the past days. I rose from the water in haste, and getting on to the road again, walked along tremblingly, my head bent toward the earth, my wet hand and flowers marking the dust of it as I went."

In an unpublished story written fifteen years later, the description of his hero's boyhood has many passages in it which are unmistakably drawn from his own experience. The dreams which mingle with the healthy life of a boy, the first beginnings of thought, of sentiment, of romance, are touched in these passages from knowledge and vivid recollection. "You know," says the boy in the story, "one has fits of not caring for fishing and shooting a bit, and then I get through an enormous lot of reading; and then again one day one goes out and down to the river and looks at the eddies, and then suddenly one thinks of all that again; and then another day when one has one's rod in one's hand one looks up and down the field or sees the road winding along, and I can't help thinking of tales going on amongst it all, and long so for more and more books." The boy who cannot help thinking of tales going on amongst it all is undoubtedly Morris himself, and Morris as he remained all through his life. Even more strikingly autobiographic perhaps is another touch a little later in the same story: "Even though he half saw it he began to dream about it, as his way was about everything, to make it something different from what it was." This kind of dreaming, the instinct of making everything something different from what it was, was indeed, alike for strength and weakness, of the very essence of his nature.

Another passage from the same story, of vivid and singular truth, might be an actual scene on a summer evening at Water House:

" John ran into the toolhouse and took up a garden fork preparatory to going off to the melon ground where the worm-populated old dung heaps were; for some strange reason that moment and the half hour were one of the unforgotten times of his life, and in after days he could never smell the mixed scent of a toolhouse, with its bast mats and earthy roots and herbs, in a hot summer evening, without that evening with every word spoken or gesture made coming up clear into his memory. It struck on him as he came out of the toolhouse again into the glow of the evening, and all his boyish visions of the great red-finned basking chub and shadowy flitting bleak, and the great water lily leaves spreading over the perch-holes, vanished and left him with that vague feeling of disappointment in life past yet hope of life to come . . . some reflex of the love and death going on throughout the world suddenly touching those who are ignorant as yet of the one and have not yet learned to believe in the other.

" He went off whistling from the gate, just as the low moon was yellowing through the windless summer night, in which the nightingales were beginning to sing now : one may easily imagine that his nervous sentimental mood had vanished before the gardener's talk . . . at any rate that thought was not uppermost in his mind as he startled the blackbirds out of their roosts in the thick leaves; nay, whatever there was of sordid about the story had slipped off him and left a pleasant feeling of life active and full of incident and change going on about him, with I know not what of sweeter, of sweetest, lurking behind it all, and the little pleasures lying ready to his hand, they also were so keenly felt, so full of their own beauty."

Another schoolboy letter to his eldest sister, written when he had been a year at Marlborough, shows the threads of fresh interest that were beginning to mingle in his life.

" April 13th, 1849.

" My dearest Emma,

" I received your dear letter yesterday and I am glad you liked the anthem on Easter Tuesday, we here had the same anthem on Monday and Tuesday as on Sunday it was the three first verses of the 72nd Psalm, In Jewry is God known, his name is great in Israel. At Salem is his tabernacle, and his dwelling at Sion. There brake he the arrows of the bow, the sword, the shield, and the battle. I certainly thought it was very beautiful though I have never heard it in Cathedral and like you could not tell how they would sing it there; but a gentleman (one of the boy's fathers) said on the whole our choir sang better than at Salisbury Cathedral; anyhow I thought it very beautiful the first verse was sung by the whole the second began by one treble voice till at last the base took it up again gradually getting deeper and deeper then again the treble voice again and then again the base the third verse was sung entirely by base not very loud but with that kind of emphasis which you would think befitting to such a subject I almost think I liked it better than either of the other two the only fault in the anthem seemed to be to me that it was too short. On Monday I went to Silbury Hill which I think I have told you before is an artificial hill made by the Britons but first I went to a place called Abury

where there is a Druidical circle and a Roman entrenchment both which encircle the town originally it is supposed that the stones were in this shape first one large
circle then a smaller one inside this and then one in
the middle for an altar but a great many in fact most
of the stones have been removed so I could [not] tell
this. On Tuesday morning I was told of this so I thought
I would go there again, I did and then I was able to
understand how they had been fixed ; I think the biggest
stone I could see had about 16 feet out of the ground in
height and about 10 feet thick and 12 feet broad the
circle and entrenchment altogether is about half a mile ;
at Abury I also saw a very old church the tower was
very pretty indeed it had four little spires on it of the
decorated order, and there was a little Porch and inside
the porch a beautiful Norman doorway loaded with mouldings the chancel was new and was paved with tesselated
pavement this I saw through the Window for I did not
know where the sexton's house was so of course I could
not get the key, there was a pretty little Parsonage house
close by the church.   After we had done looking at the
lions of Abury which took us about ½ an hour we went
through a mud lane down one or two fields and last but
not least through what they call here a water meadow up
to our knees in water, now perhaps you do not know
what a water meadow is as there are none of them in
your part of the world, so for your edification I will tell
you what a delectable affair a water meadow is to go
through ; in the first place you must fancy a field cut
through with an infinity of small streams say about four
feet wide each the people to whom the meadow belongs
can turn these streams on and off when they like and at
this time of the year they are on just before they put
the fields up for mowing the grass being very long you
cannot see the water till you are in the water and floun-

dering in it except you are above the field luckily the water had not been long when we went through it else we should have been up to our middles in mud, however perhaps now you can imagine a water meadow: after we had scrambled through this meadow we ascended Silbury Hill it is not very high but yet I should think it must have taken an immense long time to have got it together I brought away a little white snail shell as a memento of the place and have got it in my pocket book I came back at ½ past 5 the distance was altogether about 14 miles I had been out 3 hours ½ of course Monday and Tuesday were whole holidays. As [you] are going to send me the cheese perhaps you would let Sarah to make me a good large cake and I should also like some biscuits and will you also send me some paper and postage stamps also my silkworms eggs and if you could get it an Italian pen box for that big box is too big for school. I am very sorry I was not at home with you at Easter but of course that was not to be and it is no good either to you or to me to say any horrid stale arguments about being obliged to go to school for of course we know all about that.   Give my best love dearest Emma to all,

> " And believe me
> "Your most affectionate brother
> "WILLIAM MORRIS."

The quickness and precision of eye, the thoroughness which made him go back to Avebury next day to verify what he had learned after his first visit, the contempt for " horrid stale arguments," are all highly characteristic: hardly less so is the interest in church festivals and church music, in which his sister fully shared. They had both been touched by the wave of religious revival. A year later Emma Morris married a young clergyman of pronounced High Church views, the Rev. Joseph

Oldham, who had been curate at Walthamstow from 1845 to 1848. Mr. Oldham was at the time of the marriage curate of Downe in Kent, but very soon afterwards he was appointed to a living in Derbyshire, and William Morris was thus put quite out of reach of his favourite sister. He felt the separation keenly; the brother and sister had been closely intimate in all their thoughts and enthusiasms; and it was to some degree under her influence that the Church was settled on as his own destined profession.

With this career in view, Oxford would naturally succeed to Marlborough, and at Oxford the natural college for a Marlborough boy to go to was Exeter. There was a strong connexion between the West-country school and the West-country college; and several of the Marlborough masters were Exeter men. But Morris was not high up in school, and was more of an expert in silkworms' eggs and old churches than in exact scholarship, while the condition of the school in the last year of Dr. Wilkinson's rule had become deplorable, and culminated in an organized rebellion in November, 1851. It was accordingly arranged that he should leave school that Christmas, and read with a private tutor till he was thought fit to go up for matriculation. The tutor chosen, the Rev. F. B. Guy, afterwards Canon of St. Alban's, was a man of high attainment and character, whose influence over his pupil was great, and with whom in later years Morris kept up a cordial friendship. He was then assistant master of the Forest School at Walthamstow, to the head-mastership of which he succeeded a few years later, and took a few private pupils in his house at Hoe Street. Morris was with him for nearly a year. Mr. Guy was a High Churchman of the best type, a friend and kindred spirit of Dean Church, and a man of wide sympathies and cultivated taste, with an unusually large knowledge of painting and architecture. When " The Life and Death of Jason " was published, he pleased himself by tracing its germs to the days in which they had read the " Medea " together. Under his tuition Morris developed into a very fair classical scholar.

A fellow-pupil, Mr. W. H. Bliss, recalls that time with many incidents of Morris's outdoor tastes, his intense love of nature, and his great bodily strength. In playing singlestick, of which he was very fond, his opponent had to be guarded against Morris's impetuous rushes by a table placed between the two combatants. There were frequent visits to Water House, where they chased the swans and dragged the moat for perch, with a net of Morris's own manufacture. Their walks or rides in the Forest were almost daily, and Morris used to go off there by himself when the other pupils went to take a day's amusement in London. The day of the Duke of Wellington's funeral was thus spent by him in a solitary ride to Waltham Abbey. He had refused, with some touch of his later Socialist feeling, to go to London to see the show. One habit he had even then formed which clung to him through life : that of tilting his chair back, getting his legs twisted round it, and suddenly straightening them out to the strain or collapse of the fabric. Many of his own Sussex chairs, not in his own house alone, bear to this day the marks of this trick of his.

At the beginning of June, 1852, Morris went up to Oxford, and passed the matriculation examination at Exeter. This was with the view of going into residence after the Long Vacation. But the college was then so full that his entry had to be deferred till the Lent term of 1853. He returned to Mr. Guy's meanwhile, and read with him for six months more, going with him for the Long Vacation to Alphington, in Devonshire, and returning to Walthamstow for the remainder of the year.

At the examination in the Hall of Exeter there had sat next him another boy who had come up for the same purpose from King Edward's Grammar School, Birmingham, and was destined to be his most intimate and lifelong friend, Edward Burne-Jones.

CHAPTER II

BETWEEN Oxford of the early fifties and Oxford of the present day there lies a gap which is imperfectly measured by the change, vast as that is, which forty-five years have brought over the whole of England. The home of lost causes and impossible loyalties was on the eve of startling revolutions ; but it still clung to the past with obstinate tenacity, and prided itself on keeping behind the material and intellectual movement of the age. The long struggle which the University had carried on against the intrusion of a railway within ten miles of their sacred precinct typifies a contest which was being carried on, perhaps on neither side with a full understanding of the issues involved, in a much wider and more various field. The opening of the railway line between Oxford and Didcot in June, 1844, and the announcement by Lord John Russell's Government, in May, 1850, of the appointment of the University Commission, are the two great landmarks which separate the old Oxford, the stronghold or sleeping-place of a belated yet still living mediævalism, from the new Oxford, which, for good or bad, has plunged into the modern movement and ranged itself alongside of the modern world.

The Oxford in which Morris and Burne-Jones began their residence at the end of January, 1853, was still in all its main aspect a mediæval city, and the name (in Morris's own beautiful words) roused, as it might have done at any time within the four centuries then ended, "a vision of grey-roofed houses and a long winding street, and the sound of many bells." The railway was there, but had not yet produced its far-reaching effects. From all other sides: down the plunging slope of Headington; along the seven-bridged Bath and Gloucester Road, where it trails through the marshes from the skirts of Cumnor; across the Yarnton meadows; over the low stone hills, with their grey villages, that enfold the valley of the Cherwell, one still approached it as travellers had done for hundreds of years, and saw its towers rise among masses of foliage straight out of the girdle of meadow or orchard. "On all sides except where it touched the railway," writes Sir Edward Burne-Jones, "the city came to an end abruptly as if a wall had been about it, and you came suddenly upon the meadows. There was little brick in the city; it was either grey with stone, or yellow with the wash of the pebble-cast in the poorer streets, where there were still many old houses with wood carving, and a little sculpture here and there." Instead of all the meshes of suburb, hideous in gaunt brickwork and blue slate, that now envelop three sides of Oxford, there were but two outlying portions. These still remain distinguishable among the environing changes: the little faubourgs of St. Clement's beyond Magdalen Bridge, and St. Thomas's beyond the bailey-gate of the Castle, each with its tiny High Street and its inconspicuous corporate life. A few streets of small houses had grown up round the Clarendon Press since its establishment in the remote meadows beyond Worcester. Children gathered violets on the Iffley Road within sight of Magdalen. Within the city the modern rage of building had barely begun. The colleges stood much as they had done since the great building epoch of last century, which enriched Oxford with the church of All Saints, the new buildings of Magdalen, and the façade of Queen's. The University Museum was projected, but not yet begun; beyond the grey garden walls of St. John's and Wadham all was unbroken country, and the large residential suburb and the immense pleasure ground that take their name from Fairfax's artillery parks were meadows and market gardens. The Taylorian Institute and Galleries in Beaumont Street, not then overshadowed by the sprawling bulk of the Randolph Hotel, were the only new buildings in Oxford of any importance. The common street architecture was still largely that of the fifteenth century.

Nor in its inner life did Oxford retain less of an old-world air, and of fashions and ideas that had lingered out of an earlier day. But the continuity of life and thought is measured by decades where that of buildings is by centuries; and the furthest tradition that survived in the colleges was that of the stagnant sterility of the eighteenth century. Routh, who had known Dr. Johnson, still retained the presidency of Magdalen, to which he had been elected before the French monarchy had been abolished by the Revolution. During the second half of his long headship the Oxford movement had come and gone. Reaching its climax about the year 1840, it had begun its decline after the secession of Newman in October, 1845, and though it still continued a force of prodigious importance, other movements were ranging up alongside of it, and it was suffering the law of all mutable things. The very life and expansive force of the movement, which made Oxford a missionary centre for the whole country, had laid Oxford itself open to invasion by the outer world and by new ideas. Reform was everywhere in the air. A formidable Liberal reaction had set in, directed almost equally against the pretensions of the Anglo-Catholic school and the privi-

leges of the old-established system. Congreve had
founded a small but ardent school of Comtists at Wadham. Jowett had become the leading force at Balliol,
and was thought certain of the reversion of the master-
ship. The younger fellows of Oriel were nearly all
advanced Liberals. Oxford had at a thousand points
become inextricably attached to the outer world. The
railway mania of 1846, when gambling in shares became
more exciting than theological controversy, is said to have
completed the work begun by the shock of Newman's
secession. Left to itself, Oxford would have slipped
back into the lethargy out of which it had been so un-
willingly awakened by the Tractarian movement. But
it was too late. The ferment struck roots deep. The
modern city, with its tramways and electric lighting, its
whirlwind of building up and pulling down, its tragi-
comedies of extension and modernization, is the realized
effect of a vast and complex body of influences which
were then seething under the surface. Still the Oxford
of 1853 breathed from its towers the last enchantments of
the Middle Ages; and still it offered to its most ardent
disciples, who came to it as to some miraculous place,
full of youthful enthusiasm, thirsting after knowledge
and beauty, the stony welcome that Gibbon had found
at Magdalen, that Shelley had found at University, in
the days of the ancient order.

The year which had elapsed since Morris left Marlborough had not only loosened his connexion, slight as
that in any case was, with the society of his schoolfellows
and the common routine through which the schoolboy
passes into the undergraduate, but had matured his mind
and widened his knowledge to a degree which represents
the normal growth of many years in an ordinary mind.
"I arrived at Oxford," says Gibbon in the Autobio-

graphy, "with a stock of erudition that might have
puzzled a doctor, and a degree of ignorance of which a
schoolboy would have been ashamed." Morris's book-
knowledge, born of extraordinary swiftness in reading
and an amazing memory, was almost as portentous and
no doubt as incomplete. " Just as in after years, in the
thick of his work," Sir Edward Burne-Jones says, " it
was noticeable how he never seemed to be particularly
busy, and how he had plenty of leisure for expeditions,
for fishing, for amusement, if it amused him ; he never
seemed to read much, but always knew, and accurately ;
and he had a great instinct at all times for knowing what
would not amuse him, and what not to read."

For such a self-centred nature, already accustomed to
take its own views of things, the ordinary college life,
the ordinary undergraduate society, had little attraction.
The numbers of Exeter were then about one hundred and
twenty, and the college buildings were over-full. Even
when Morris and Burne-Jones were allowed to come up
they had to go into lodgings for their first two terms.
No undergraduate was then allowed to spend the night
out of college in any circumstances : and the over-crowd-
ing was met by making freshmen lodge out during the
day, and sleep in the third room of sets belonging to
seniors, on whom they were billeted for this purpose.
This curious and cumbrous arrangement was of course
equally distasteful to senior and freshman, and threw the
latter still more on himself, if he had any tendency that
way.

Notwithstanding its popularity and its increasing
numbers, the internal condition of the college was far
from satisfactory. "There was neither teaching nor discipline," is the sweeping verdict of a contemporary of
Morris who afterwards rose to high academic distinction.
The rector, Dr. Richards, was ill and non-resident.

The only one of the fellows who was at all friendly or encouraging was Ridding, the present Bishop of Southwell, who had brought a more energetic tradition with him from Balliol.   Morris's own tutor contented himself with seeing that he attended lectures on the prescribed books for the schools, and noted him in his pupil-book as " a rather rough and unpolished youth, who exhibited no special literary tastes or capacity, but had no difficulty in mastering the usual subjects of examination."   It is proper to add that this vague supervision was then regarded as sufficient fulfilment of a college tutor's duty, and that his college tutor is the last person in the world to whom an undergraduate thinks of communicating his inner thoughts or his literary enthusiasms.

The undergraduates at Exeter were divided, more sharply than is now the case at any college, into two classes.   On the one hand were the reading men, immersed in the details of classical scholarship or scholastic theology ; the rest of the college rowed, hunted, ate and drank largely, and often sank at Oxford into a coarseness of manners and morals distasteful and distressing in the highest degree to a boy whose instinctive delicacy and purity of mind were untouched by any of the flaws of youth.   Of the average college lecture some notion may be formed from a letter written early in 1854 by one of Morris's intimate friends, who shared many of his tastes.

" As for lectures, I have long since ceased to hope that I should learn anything at them which I did not know before.   Imagine yourself ushered into a large room comfortably provided with chairs and a large centre table. The men take their places round it, and the lecturer, looking up from his easy chair by the fireside, exclaims, ' Will you go on, Mr. —— ? ' The approved crib version

I.   D

is then faithfully given, and meanwhile most other men are getting, by heart or otherwise, Bohn's translation of the next piece.   When No. 1 has concluded, the lecturer asks benignly, ' *Dum* governs two moods, doesn't it ? ' ' Yes.' ' It governs the subjunctive sometimes, doesn't it ?' ' Yes.' ' Is *qui* ever used with the subjunctive? It is, isn't it ?' ' Yes.' 'Very well, *very well*, Mr. ——. Will you go on, Mr. —— ? ' ' Haven't read it.' ' Oh, never mind then ; you go on, Mr. ——, will you ? ' and when the crib has been deposited in the hands of a neighbour, in order that any requisite emendations may be whispered into the man's ear, the lecture proceeds. At some awful blunder, up jumps the lecturer, and after a long yawning pause, mildly breaks forth, ' Well, yer know, I should *hardly* think you'd take it in that way, yer know.   Mr. ——, will you just translate that passage ? ' (Another crib version is given.) ' *Precisely* so, precisely so ; quite right, quite right, Mr. ——.' And so we gradually limp through a page or two which none of the men has bestowed ten minutes upon, and leave the room for another exhibition of crib-repetition."

The wit here is not untouched with malice ; but the sketch shows the impression made by the routine of college lectures on a sensitive, enthusiastic boy who had come to Oxford full of hopes and longings, and prepared to find in it the realization of all his school dreams. The effect was such as Morris himself at all events never got over : to the end of his life the educational system and the intellectual life of modern Oxford were matters as to which he remained bitterly prejudiced, and the name of " Don " was used by him as a synonym for all that was narrow, ignorant, and pedantic.

Morris and Burne-Jones made each other's acquaintance within the first two or three days of their first term. At first sight each found in the other a kindred and com-

plemental spirit.   Within a week they were inseparable
friends, with that complete and unreserved friendship
which is the greatest of all the privileges that Oxford
life has to bestow.   " We went almost daily walks together," Sir Edward writes.   " Gloomy disappointment
and disillusion were settling down on me in this first
term's experience of Oxford.   The place was languid and
indifferent; scarcely anything was left to shew that it
had passed through such an excited time as ended with
the secession of Newman.   So we compared our thoughts
together upon these things and went angry walks together
in the afternoons and sat together in the evenings reading.
From the first I knew how different he was from all the
men I had ever met.   He talked with vehemence, and
sometimes with violence.   I never knew him languid or
tired.   He was slight in figure in those days; his hair
was dark brown and very thick, his nose straight, his
eyes hazel-coloured, his mouth exceedingly delicate and
beautiful.   Before many weeks were past in our first term
there were but three or four men in the whole college
whom we visited or spoke to.   But at Pembroke there
was a little Birmingham colony, and with them we con-
sorted when we wanted more company than our own.
In a corner of the old quadrangle there, on the ground
floor, were the rooms of Faulkner, learned in mathematics
and the physical sciences, not so learned in theology,
since, in spite of great distinction and University scholar-
ships, he was once plucked because he included Isaiah in
the number of the twelve apostles.   Dixon, an old schoolfellow of mine and the only poet in our school, had
rooms at the top of the same staircase, and upon the
opposite side of the quadrangle lived Fulford, our senior
by about two years, a man then full of energy and enthusiasm.   But our common room was invariably Faulkner's, where about nine of the evening Morris and I

would often stroll down together, and settle once for all how all people should think."

It was among this Birmingham group, Fulford, Burne-Jones, Faulkner, and Dixon, together with Cormell Price and Harry Macdonald, who came up to Oxford from King Edward's School a little later, that Morris mainly spent his time: and it was they who, together with Godfrey Lushington of Balliol, and Vernon Lushington and Wilfred Heeley of Trinity College, Cambridge, joined him three years later in originating and carrying on the Oxford and Cambridge Magazine. The two Lushingtons were a few years senior to the rest of the group: the acquaintance with them was formed through Heeley, who was also a King Edward's School boy. He was a man of brilliant parts and amiable nature, whose career in India was cut short by an early death. With this Birmingham group Morris, from his first term at Oxford, was much more closely intimate than with his old Marlborough acquaintance. Such of these last as were at Exeter were, with the exception of W. F. Adams, now Vicar of Little Faringdon, and for many years a neighbour of Morris at Kelmscott, in completely different sets; and for the others, the isolation of one college from another was too great for ordinary school acquaintance to be long kept up without some farther attachment of congenial tastes. Mr. Bliss, Morris's fellow-pupil at Walthamstow, tells me that he dined with him at Magdalen now and then, and that they used to play fives together at the racquet-courts. But this was almost a solitary exception to the self-centred isolation in which the small group habitually lived. Within the group, Fulford, from his two years' seniority, and his superabundant volubility and energy, at first took a position of some dominance. He was one of those minds which reach a precocious maturity and quickly exhaust themselves. He had left King Edward's School with an immense reputation among his schoolfellows, which his subsequent performances did little to justify. By the time he left Oxford his friends had already taken his measure, and sighed over an extinct brilliance. But in this circle of undergraduates, distracted among a thousand divergent interests of theology, social problems, art, literature, and history, his genuine and exclusive devotion to pure literature powerfully helped to keep that interest prominent; and Morris's own first essays, both in prose and verse, though from the first moment he far outstripped his model, to some degree owed their origin to Fulford's influence.

Within, and yet above or apart from the rest of this group, the two Exeter undergraduates lived in undivided intimacy and unremitting intellectual tension. In the Michaelmas term of 1853 they moved into rooms in college. Morris's rooms were in the little quadrangle affectionately known among Exeter men as Hell Quad, with windows overlooking the small but beautiful Fellows' garden, the immense chestnut tree that overspreads Brasenose Lane, and the grey masses of the Bodleian Library. There the long nights set in to crown the long days. On the first night of one of their terms in college, after Burne-Jones had arrived late from Birmingham, and had supper, "presently Morris came tumbling in," he wrote home next day, "and talked incessantly for the next seven hours or longer." The two read together omnivorously. At first it was chiefly in theology, ecclesiastical history, and ecclesiastical archæology. Morris early started the habit of reading aloud to Burne-Jones—he could not bear to be read aloud to himself—which continued throughout their lives. Among the works thus read through were Neale's "History of the Eastern Church," Milman's

had lately been renovated by Butterfield ; and the beautiful painted roof had been executed by Hungerford Pollen, a former fellow of the college. The application of colour to architecture was then a startling novelty, and young architects were making it their business to learn painting. Morris's study of " The Builder " newspaper, which he took in regularly, alternated with the study of mediæval design and colouring in the painted manuscripts displayed in the Bodleian. One of these, a splendid Apocalypse of the thirteenth century, became his ideal book. Forty years later he went to Oxford to spend a day in studying it, and looked over it with greater knowledge but unimpaired satisfaction. He was constantly drawing windows, arches, and gables in his books ; and even in his letters of this time, where the pen had paused, there comes a half unconscious scribble of floriated ornament. Burne-Jones had already found in drawing from nature a relief from the burden of theological perplexities, and spent whole days in Bagley Wood making minute and elaborate studies of flowers and foliage. Morris's rooms were full of rubbings which he had taken from mediæval brasses. But the great pictorial art of Italy and Flanders was as yet unknown to either. "Of painting," writes Sir Edward Burne-Jones, " we knew nothing. It was before the time when photographs made all the galleries of Europe accessible, and what would have been better a thousand times for us, the wall paintings of Italy. Indeed it would be difficult to make any one understand the dearth of things dear to us in which we lived ; and matters that are now well known to cultivated people, and commonplaces in talk, were then impossible for us to know." Giotto, Angelico, Van Eyck, Dürer, names which a little later became of capital importance to Morris, were then wholly unknown to him. The reproductions of the Arundel Society were just beginning to be issued; but at present all that he knew of Pre-Raphaelite Italian art was from one or two pictures in the Taylorian Museum, and the rude woodcuts in Ruskin's Handbook to the Arena Chapel at Padua. Among the most immediately stimulating of the books which he and Burne-Jones fell in with at Oxford was a translation of Fouqué's "Sintram," prefixed to which was a woodcut copy of Dürer's engraving of the Knight and Death. Poorly executed as it was, this fired their imagination, and hours were spent in poring over it.

The romances of Fouqué, which supplied Morris with the germ of his own early tales, became known to him through another book which exercised an extraordinary fascination over the whole of the group, and in which much of the spiritual history of those years may be found prefigured, "The Heir of Redclyffe." In this book, more than in any other, may be traced the religious ideals and social enthusiasms which were stirring in the years between the decline of Tractarianism and the Crimean War. The young hero of the novel, with his over-strained conscientiousness, his chivalrous courtesy, his intense earnestness, his eagerness for all such social reforms as might be effected from above downwards, his high-strung notions of love, friendship, and honour, his premature gravity, his almost deliquescent piety, was adopted by them as a pattern for actual life : and more strongly perhaps by Morris than by the rest, from his own greater wealth and more aristocratic temper. Yet Canon Dixon, in mentioning this book as the first which seemed to him greatly to influence Morris, pronounces it, after nearly half a century's reflection and experience, as " unquestionably one of the finest books in the world."

The following reminiscences, contributed by Canon Dixon, of the early years of the " set " as they then called themselves, before this name was replaced by that of the " brotherhood," draw a vivid picture of the life lived among them.

" I matriculated at Pembroke College, Oxford, in June, 1851, and began residence in the October term following, leaving behind me in the Birmingham School Edward Burne-Jones, Edwin Hatch, and Cormell Price.

" At Pembroke I found two Birmingham School men, whom I had known distantly at the school, Richard Whitehouse and William Fulford. As soon as I came up, Fulford called on me, after I had been solitary two or three days. I can still hear his step running up the stairs : and his greeting as he came in. He was a very little fellow, very strong and active, very clever, and immensely vivacious. We immediately fell upon poetry : and he read me a poem, ' In Youth I died,' which afterwards appeared in the Oxford and Cambridge Magazine. He asked me to breakfast next morning : and at his rooms then I met another man of Birmingham, though not of Birmingham School, Charles Joseph Faulkner. We three became very intimate. Faulkner was rather younger than I, though he had been in residence at least one term when I first knew him. His rooms were on the same staircase as mine : his at the bottom on one side, mine at the top on the other, in the northeast corner of Pembroke old quad.

" Fulford this term and after became extremely intimate with me. He was at least a year beyond my standing : but I could not find that he had any intimates before I came. He seemed to have had no set. However, he, Faulkner, and I soon made up a small set, and were constantly together. Fulford had great critical insight, and extraordinary power of conversation. His literary principles were early fixed. He was absolutely devoured with admiration for Tennyson. Shakespeare he knew, and could speak of as few could. Keats the same. (I introduced Keats to him: he had never heard of him before.) Shelley the same. He never changed much from the first three of these.

" Faulkner was, of course, wholly different : a great mathematician, who carried everything in Oxford. I suppose he must have had an original mind in mathematics, though he never made a noted discovery. He was not particularly of literary taste, I think, except so far as it must belong to a powerful mind.

" Next term, I think it was, Burne-Jones came up to Exeter: and William Morris was a freshman of the same term and college. Calling on Burne-Jones, we all became directly acquainted with Morris; and in no long time, composed one set. Jones and Morris were both meant for Holy Orders: and the same may be said of the rest of us, except Faulkner: but this could not be called the bond of alliance. The bond was poetry and indefinite artistic and literary aspiration : but not of a selfish character, or rather, not of a self-seeking character. We all had the notion of doing great things for man : in our own way, however: according to our own will and bent.

" At first Morris was regarded by the Pembroke men simply as a very pleasant boy (the least of us was senior by a term to him) who was fond of talking, which he did in a husky shout, and fond of going down the river with Faulkner, who was a good boating man. He was very fond of sailing a boat. He was also extremely fond of singlestick, and a good fencer. In no long time, however, the great characters of his nature began to impress us. His fire and impetuosity, great bodily strength, and high temper were soon manifested: and were sometimes astonishing. As, *e.g.*, his habit of beating his own head, dealing himself vigorous blows, to take it out of himself. I think it was he who brought in singlestick.

I remember him offering to ' teach the cuts and guards.'
But his mental qualities, his intellect, also began to be
perceived and acknowledged. I remember Faulkner
remarking to me, ' How Morris seems to know things,
doesn't he?' And then it struck me that it was so. I
observed how decisive he was: how accurate, without
any effort or formality : what an extraordinary power of
observation lay at the base of many of his casual or in-
cidental remarks, and how many things he knew that
were quite out of our way; as, *e.g.*, architecture. One
of the first things he ever said to me was to ask me to
go with him to look at Merton tower.

" At this time Fulford had a sort of leadership among
us. This was partly due to his seniority : partly to his
intense vivacity : partly to his Tennysonianism, in which
we shared with greater moderation, and in different ways.
It is difficult to the present generation to understand the
Tennysonian enthusiasm which then prevailed both in
Oxford and the world. All reading men were Tenny-
sonians : all sets of reading men talked poetry. Poetry
was the thing : and it was felt with justice that this was
due to Tennyson. Tennyson had invented a new poetry,
a new poetic English : his use of words was new, and
every piece that he wrote was a conquest of a new
region. This lasted till ' Maud,' in 1855 ; which was
his last poem that mattered. I am told that in this
generation no University man cares for poetry. This is
almost inconceivable to one who remembers Tennyson's
reign and his reception in the Sheldonian in '55. There
was the general conviction that Tennyson was the greatest
poet of the century : some held him the greatest of all
poets, or at least of all modern poets. In my time at
Oxford there were two other men who, without touching
him, obtained an immense momentary vogue, which
has never been equalled since, perhaps, unless by Swin-

burne, or by Morris himself. These were Alexander
Smith, whose 'Life Drama' was in every one's hands,
and caused an immense sensation ; and Owen Meredith
(Lytton), in the 'Clytemnestra' volume containing 'The
Earl's Return.' Morris was delighted with this, especially with the incident of the Earl draining a flagon
of wine, and then flinging it at the head of him that
brought it.

"Now Fulford was absorbed in Tennyson. He had
a very fine deep voice, and was a splendid reader of
poetry. I have listened entranced to his reading of 'In
Memoriam.' He read Milton even better : I suppose
because there was more to read. His reading of 'Paradise Lost,' Book I., I shall never forget. He had a fine
metrical ear, which helped it. No one can tell how
Milton lends himself to a good reader. He was also
writing much at this time, and would often read his
pieces to us. No doubt many of them had a Tennysonian
ring, but they were not mere imitation, they were too
sincere for that. I should like to add here, as my friend
is dead, and in his life never gained fame or profit from
literature, that Fulford's influence was for good. He
loved moral beauty first of all things, and would not
have it put second in poetry or art.

"I have said that we accepted Tennyson in our own
ways. The attitude of Morris I should describe as
defiant admiration. This was apparent from the first.
He perceived Tennyson's limitations, as I think, in a
remarkable manner for a man of twenty or so. He
said once, 'Tennyson's Sir Galahad is rather a mild
youth.' Of 'Locksley Hall' he said, apostrophising the
hero, 'My dear fellow, if you are going to make that
row, get out of the room, that's all.' Thus he perceived
a certain rowdy, or bullying, element that runs through
much of Tennyson's work : runs through 'The Princess,'

' Lady Clara Vere,' or 'Amphion.'   On the other
hand, he understood Tennyson's greatness in a manner
that we, who were mostly absorbed by the language,
could not share.   He understood it as if the poems represented substantial things that were to be considered
out of the poems as well as in them.   Of the worlds that
Tennyson opened in his fragments, he selected one, as
I think the finest and most epical, for special admiration,
namely, ' Oriana.'   He offered the suggestion, and with
great force, that the scenery of that matchless ' ballad'
is not of Western Europe, but South Russian, or Crimean.
He held that ' the Norland whirlwinds' shewed this :
and he had other reasons.   It was this substantial view
of value that afterwards led him to admire ballads, real
ballads, so highly.   As to Tennyson, I would add that
we all had the feeling that after him no farther development was possible : that we were at the end of all things
in poetry.   In this fallacy Morris shared.

  " I spoke of a leadership by Fulford.   In reality,
neither he nor any one else in the world could lead
Morris or Burne-Jones.

  " At this time, Morris was an aristocrat, and a High
Churchman.   His manners and tastes and sympathies
were all aristocratic.   His countenance was beautiful in
features and expression, particularly in the expression of
purity.   Occasionally it had a melancholy look.   He
had a finely cut mouth, the short upper lip adding greatly
to the purity of expression.   I have a vivid recollection
of the splendid beauty of his presence at this time.

  " It was when the Exeter men, Burne-Jones and he,
got at Ruskin, that strong direction was given to a true
vocation—' The Seven Lamps,' ' Modern Painters,' and
' The Stones of Venice.'   It was some little time before I
and others could enter into this : but we soon saw the
greatness and importance of it.   Morris would often

read Ruskin aloud. He had a mighty singing voice, and chanted rather than read those weltering oceans of eloquence as they have never been given before or since, it is most certain. The description of the Slave Ship, or of Turner's skies, with the burden, ' Has Claude given this ? ' were declaimed by him in a manner that made them seem as if they had been written for no end but that he should hurl them in thunder on the head of the base criminal who had never seen what Turner saw in the sky.

" About this time, 1854-5, we started weekly Shakespearean readings in one another's rooms. Fulford, Burne-Jones, and Morris were all fine readers : so was Crom Price, who had come up three or four terms after us, to Brasenose. We used to draw lots for the parts. I remember Morris's Macbeth, and his Touchstone particularly ; but most of all his Claudio, in the scene with Isabel. He suddenly raised his voice to a loud and horrified cry at the word ' Isabel,' and declaimed the awful following speech, ' Aye, but to die, and go we know not where,' in the same pitch. I never heard anything more overpowering. As an incident not in Shakespeare, I may mention that in the reading of ' Troilus and Cressida,' when Thersites ends his catalogue of fools with the remark, ' And Patroclus is a fool positive,' and Patroclus asks, ' Why am I a fool ? ' Morris exclaimed, with intense delight, ' Patroclus wants to know why he is a fool ! '

" Among those of the set who took part in these readings I would mention two other Birmingham School and Pembroke men ; the Rev. James Merrick Guest, still happily surviving in retirement near the School which has been the scene of his life ; and the late deeply lamented Dr. Hatch, the theologian, whose noble spirit was not fully known among us."

Morris's first Long Vacation, that of 1853, was spent in England, largely in going about visiting churches. It included a short visit from Burne-Jones at Walthamstow: it is characteristic of Morris himself and of the terms on which undergraduates live, in a world almost wholly of their own, that Burne-Jones up till then had no idea whether Morris was rich or poor, and whether he lived in a little house or a big one. In the Long Vacation of 1854 he made his first journey abroad, to Belgium and Northern France. This journey was one of profound interest: it introduced him to the painting of Van Eyck and Memling, who remained to him ever after absolute and unapproached masters of painting, and to what he considered the noblest works of human invention, the churches of Amiens, Beauvais, and Chartres. From this Long Vacation also he brought back to Oxford photographs of Albert Dürer's engravings, and an increased hatred of the classicists and (for their sake) of the classics. In Paris the Musée Cluny and the galleries of the Louvre enriched his knowledge of mediæval art in its noblest forms. At Rouen his desires were satisfied to the full.

"Less than forty years ago," he writes in one of the frankly and beautifully autobiographic passages of "The Aims of Art," "I first saw the city of Rouen, then still in its outward aspect a piece of the Middle Ages: no words can tell you how its mingled beauty, history, and romance took hold on me; I can only say that, looking back on my past life, I find it was the greatest pleasure I have ever had: and now it is a pleasure which no one can ever have again: it is lost to the world for ever. At that time I was an undergraduate of Oxford. Though not so astounding, so romantic, or at first sight so mediæval as the Norman city, Oxford in those days still kept a great deal of its earlier loveliness: and the memory of its grey streets as they then were has been an abiding influence and pleasure in my life, and would be greater still if I could only forget what they are now—a matter of far more importance than the so-called learning of the place could have been to me in any case, but which, as it was, no one tried to teach me, and I did not try to learn."

As deep a love, and one that to the end of his life kept all its first freshness and passion, he felt for the common country of Northern France, the soil out of which sprang those radiant cities and glorious churches. The very smell " of beeswax, wood-smoke, and onions " that greets a traveller on landing, gave intense pleasure to his senses ; and more than his own Essex lowlands, more than the "glittering Kentish fields " or the long rolling ridges of the Wiltshire downs, he loved "the French poplar meadows and the little villages and the waters about the Somme, and the long roads among them I longed to be following up more than I can tell."

The year which followed was one of even increased moral and imaginative tension, and launched him on the paths which he followed throughout his life. In March he came of age, and came into the uncontrolled disposition of something like £900 a year. This control over great wealth—for such it was for the Oxford circle in which he moved and to his own simple habits—brought with it at once an increased sense of anxious responsibility and a greater boldness in choosing his own course and following it. The Crimean War was in progress, and the awakening effect it had on English public life—eloquently attested by Tennyson's " Maud," by Kingsley's " Two Years Ago," and by the whole general tendency for years afterwards of English poetry and fiction—made the younger generation feel all the excitement of a new era beginning. Socialism in a

I. E

hundred forms—monastic, or industrial, or aristocratic
—was in the air. The aspirations of " The Heir of
Redclyffe," which two years before had been so vague
and elusory, took definite shape in schemes of elaborate
self-culture and social regeneration. The terrible cholera
autumn of 1854 seemed the climax of a period of physical and moral stagnation from which the world was
awaking to something like a new birth.

" Till late that night I ministered to the sick in that
hospital ; but when I went away, I walked down to the
sea, and paced there to and fro over the hard sand: and
the moon showed bloody with the hot mist, which the
sea would not take on its bosom, though the dull east
wind blew it onward continually. I walked there pondering till a noise from over the sea made me turn and
look that way; what was that coming over the sea?
Laus Deo ! the WEST WIND : Hurrah ! I feel the
joy I felt then over again now, in all its intensity. How
came it over the sea? first far out to sea, so that it
was only just visible under the red-gleaming moonlight,
far out to sea, while the mists above grew troubled, and
wavered, a long level bar of white ; it grew nearer
quickly, it rushed on toward me fearfully fast, it gathered
form, strange, misty, intricate form—the ravelled foam
of the green sea; then oh! hurrah ! I was wrapped in
it,—the cold salt spray—drenched with it, blinded by it,
and when I could see again, I saw the great green waves
rising, nodding and breaking, all coming on together ;
and over them from wave to wave leaped the joyous
WEST WIND ; and the mist and the plague clouds
were sweeping back eastward in wild swirls ; and right
away were they swept at last, till they brooded over the
face of the dismal stagnant meres, many miles away from
our fair city."

So Morris wrote, with some vague but hardly concealed second meaning, in the first of the series of prose romances which were the outcome of this year. It was the discovery, sudden and seemingly unlooked for, of creative power in himself, a natural outlet in words for all his inward thoughts, loves, aspirations, which lifted the cloud away.

That winter Morris and Burne-Jones had moved to new sets of rooms, next to one another, in the Old Buildings of Exeter, then overlooking Broad Street across a little open space with trees, and not long afterwards pulled down and replaced by the dreary modern front towards Broad Street, which opened the disastrous era of rebuilding among the Oxford colleges. "They were tumbly old buildings," Sir Edward Burne-Jones says, "gable-roofed and pebble-dashed. Little dark passages led from the staircase to the sitting rooms, a couple of steps to go down, a pace or two, and then three steps to go up: your face was banged by the door, and then inside the room a couple of steps up to a seat in the window, and a couple of steps down into the bedroom. Here one morning, just after breakfast, he brought me in the first poem he ever made. After that, no week went by without some poem." The story may be continued in Canon Dixon's words.

"One night," he writes, "Crom Price and I went to Exeter, and found him with Burne-Jones. As soon as we entered the room, Burne-Jones exclaimed wildly, ' He 's a big poet.' ' Who is? ' asked we. ' Why, Topsy '— the name which he had given him." This name, given from his mass of dark curly hair, and generally unkempt appearance, stuck to Morris among the circle of his intimate friends all his life. It was frequently shortened into " Top."

"We sat down," Canon Dixon continues, "and heard Morris read his first poem, the first that he had ever

written in his life.   It was called ' The Willow and the
Red Cliff.'   As he read it, I felt that it was something
the like of which had never been heard before.   It was
a thing entirely new : founded on nothing previous : perfectly original, whatever its value, and sounding truly
striking and beautiful, extremely decisive and powerful
in execution.   It must be remembered particularly that
it was the first piece of verse that he had ever written :
there was no novitiate : and not a trace of influence ;
and then it will be acknowledged that this was an un-
precedented thing.   He reached his perfection at once ;
nothing could have been altered in ' The Willow and the
Red Cliff' ; and in my judgment, he can scarcely be said
to have much exceeded it afterwards in anything that he
did.   I cannot recollect what took place afterwards, but
I expressed my admiration in some way, as we all did ;
and I remember his remark, ' Well, if this is poetry, it is
very easy to write.'   From that time onward, for a term
or two, he came to my rooms almost every day with a
new poem."

   This first poem, which produced so profound an impression on its hearers, never went beyond the circle of
its earliest audience.   Morris destroyed his own manuscript of it in a general massacre which he made, soon
after the publication of " The Defence of Guenevere," of
the early poems which he did not choose to be included
in that volume.   " It was a dreadful mistake to destroy
them," Canon Dixon says.   " But he had no notion whatever of correcting a poem, and very little power to do so."
This incapacity or impatience of correction remained
characteristic of Morris as a literary artist.   The manuscripts of his longer poems show little alteration from
the first drafts.   When he was dissatisfied with a poem,
he wrote it afresh, or wrote another instead of it.   The
Prologue to " The Earthly Paradise," " The Story of the

Wanderers," was originally written, and still exists, in a four-lined stanza. Something in the detail or proportion of the narrative dissatisfied him, and instead of remodelling the poem he deliberately wrote the whole tale anew in couplets, so as not to be fettered by the earlier version.

The loss of the poems thus committed to the flames in 1858 is one never wholly to be replaced. Like the poems in "The Defence of Guenevere," and in some cases even more strongly, they appear to have had that evanescent and intangible grace of a new beginning in art, the keen scent and frail beauty of the first blossoms of spring, which is more moving and more penetrating than even the full flower of a mature summer. Such, in their time, had been the troubled and piercing charm of the Virgilian Eclogues, of the early Florentine or Sienese paintings, of Tennyson's marvellous volumes of 1830 and 1832. Since the "old Butcher's Book torn up in Spedding's rooms in 1842 when the Press went to work with, I think, the last of old Alfred's best," so long and so vainly lamented by FitzGerald, there has perhaps not been a loss more to be deplored. One fragment is preserved by a precious chance in a letter written from home to Cormell Price, the youngest and the best-beloved among the brotherhood, in the Easter Vacation of 1855.

"Clay Street,
"Walthamstow, Essex.
"Tuesday in Holy Week.

"My dearest Crom,

"Yes, it's quite true, I ought to be ashamed of myself, I am ashamed of myself : I won't make any excuses: please forgive me. As the train went away from the station, I saw you standing in your scholar's gown, and looking for me. If I hadn't been on the other side, I think I should have got out of the window to say good-bye again . . . Ted will shew something to criticize, or stop, I may as well write it for you myself; it is exceedingly seedy. Here it is.

'Twas in Church on Palm Sunday,
Listening what the priest did say
Of the kiss that did betray,

That the thought did come to me,
How the olives used to be
Growing in Gethsemane.

That the thoughts upon me came
Of the lantern's steady flame,
Of the softly whispered name.

Of how kiss and words did sound
While the olives stood around,
While the robe lay on the ground.

Then the words the Lord did speak
And that kiss in Holy Week
Dreams of many a kiss did make:

Lover's kiss beneath the moon,
With it sorrow cometh soon:
Juliet's within the tomb:

Angelico's in quiet light
'Mid the aureoles very bright
God is looking from the height.

There the monk his love doth meet:
Once he fell before her feet
Ere within the Abbey sweet

He, while music rose alway
From the Church, to God did pray
That his life might pass away.

There between the angel rows
With the light flame on his brows,
With his friend, the deacon goes:

Hand in hand they go together,
Loving hearts they go together
Where the Presence shineth ever.

Kiss upon the death-bed given,
Kiss on dying forehead given
When the soul goes up to Heaven.

Many thoughts beneath the sun
Thought together; Life is done,
Yet for ever love doth run.

Willow standing 'gainst the blue,
Where the light clouds come and go,
Mindeth me of kiss untrue.

Christ, thine awful cross is thrown
Round the whole world, and thy Sun
Woful kisses looks upon.

*   *   *

Eastward slope the shadows now,
Very light the wind does blow,
Scarce it lifts the laurels low;

I cannot say the things I would,
I cannot think the things I would,
How the Cross at evening stood.

Very blue the sky above,
Very sweet the faint clouds move,
Yet I cannot think of love.

" There, dear, perhaps I ought to be ashamed of it, don't spare me. I have begun a good many other things, I don't know if I shall ever finish them, I shall have to show them to Ted and to you first : you know my failing. I have been in a horrible state of mind about my writing ; for I seem to get more and more imbecile as I go on. Do you know, I don't know what to write to you about ; there are no facts here to write about ; I have no one to talk to, except to ask for things to eat and drink and clothe myself withal ; I have read no new books since I saw you, in fact no books at all.

" The other day I went ' a-brassing ' near the Thames on the Essex side ; I got two remarkable brasses and three or four others that were not remarkable : one was a Flemish brass of a knight, date 1370, very small ; another a brass (very small, with the legend gone) of a priest in his shroud ; I think there are only two other shrouded brasses in England. The Church that this last brass came from was I think one of the prettiest Churches (for a small village Church) that I have ever seen ; the consecration crosses (some of them) were visible, red in a red circle ; and there was some very pretty colouring on a corbel, in very good preservation : the parson of the parish shewed us over this Church ; he was very civil and very, very dirty and snuffy, inexpressibly so, I can't give you an idea of his dirt and snuffiness."
[The rest of the letter is lost.]

A week later he writes again, with reference to some criticism which Price had made on the poem.

" It was not at sermon-time that I thought of the ' Kisses,' but as the second lesson was being read : you know the second lesson for Palm Sunday has in it the history of the Betrayal. I say, isn't *tomb* a very fair rhyme for *soon* by the way? the rhymes you call shady, I should like to be able to defend: I think I could do it *viva voce* but can't by letter. . . . It is very foolish, but I have a tenderness for that thing, I was so happy writing it, which I did on Good Friday: it was a lovely day, with a soft warm wind instead of the bitter north east wind we had had for so long. For those bad rhymes, I don't like them, though perhaps I don't feel them hurt me so much as they seem to do you; they are make-shifts, dear Crom: it *is* incompetency; you see I must lose the thought, or sacrifice the rhyme to it, I had rather do the latter and take my chance about the music of it; perhaps I may be able in the course of time to rhyme better, if my stock of thoughts are not exhausted, and I sometimes think they mayn't all be gone for some time.

"I have read a little Shelley since I saw you last; I like it very much what I have read; ' The Skylark ' was one : WHAT a gorgeous thing it is! utterly different to anything else I ever read: it makes one feel so different from anything else: I hope I shall be able to make you understand what I mean, for I am a sad muddle-head : I mean that most beautiful poetry, and indeed almost all beautiful writing makes one feel sad, or indignant, or—do you understand, for I can't make it any clearer; but ' The Skylark ' makes one feel happy only; I suppose because it is nearly all music, and that it doesn't bring up any thoughts of humanity: but I don't know either.

"I am going a-brassing again some time soon: to Rochester and thereabouts, also to Stoke D'Abernon in Surrey."

With the letter from which these extracts are given were sent two other newly-written poems, mainly notice-

able as showing an influence that might not be otherwise
suspected in him, that of Mrs. Browning. She was then
at the height of her popularity, and ranked by many
critics as the first of living English poets. That noble
passion for truth, purity, and freedom which burns
through all her writings, which even now lightens and
kindles the tangled wildernesses of " Aurora Leigh,"
was enough then to excuse all her shortcomings. It
even threw a positive fascination over her extraordinary
mannerisms and floundering technique. Less than a
month before his death, when talking of early days,
Morris said that his first poems were imitations of Mrs.
Browning. This was, perhaps, a little over-stated, but
it expressed a real truth. The slovenly rhymes of his
earlier poetry may probably be traced to her influence :
and it was through her poetry that he became acquainted
a little later with that of her husband, to whom he frankly
owned his obligations, and of whom in succeeding years
he wrote as " high among the poets of all time, and I
scarce know whether first or second in our own."

One other unpublished poem of this year survives. It
is of a higher technical quality than those just mentioned,
and of the same delicate and refined spiritual beauty. It
is here transcribed textually from his own manuscript :
in the second line of the first stanza the word *leaves* is
obviously a slip of the pen for some other word, probably
ground.

BLANCHE.

Broad leaves that I do not know
Grow upon the leaves full low
Over them the wind does blow.

Hemlock leaves I know full well
And about me is the smell
That doth in the spring woods dwell.

And the finch sings cheerily,
And the wren sings merrily,
But the lark sings trancedly.

Silv'ry birch-trunks rise in air
And beneath the birch-tree there
Grows a yellow flower fair.

Many flowers grow around
And about me is the sound
Of the dead leaves on the ground.

Yea, I fell asleep last night
When the moon at her full height
Was a lovely, lovely sight.

I have had a troubled dream
As I lay there in the beam
Of the moon a sudden gleam

Of a white dress shot by me
Yea the white dress frighted me
Flitting by the aspen tree.

Suddenly it turned round
With a weary moaning sound
Lay the white dress on the ground

There she knelt upon her knees
There, between the aspen trees
O! the dream right dreary is.

With her sweet face turned to me
Low she moaned unto me
That she might forgiven be.

O ! my lost love moaned there
And her low moans in the air
Sleepy startled birds did hear

O ! my dream it makes me weep,
That drear dream I had in sleep
At the thought my pulses leap

For she lay there moaning low
While the solemn wind did sough
While the clouds did over go

Then I lifted up her head
And I softly to her said
Blanche, we twain will soon be dead

Let us pray that we may die
Let us pray that we may lie
Where the softening wind does sigh

That in heaven amid the bliss
Of the blessed where God is
Mid the angels we may kiss.

We may stand with joined hands
Face to face with angel bands
They too stand with joined hands.

Yea, she said, but kiss me now
Ere my sinning spirit go
To the place no man doth know.

There I kissed her as she lay
O ! her spirit passed away
'Mid the flowers her body lay.

What a dream is this of mine
I am almost like to pine
For this dreary dream of mine.

O dead love thy hand is here
O dead Blanche thy golden hair
Lies along the flowers fair.

I am all aweary love
Of the bright blue sky above
I will lie beside thee love.

So over them over them ever
    The long long wind swept on
And lovingly lovingly ever
    The birds sang on their song.

Such were the first beginnings. But his discovery
that he could write prose came hard on the heels of his
discovery that he could write poetry, and for some little
time prose was the vehicle in which he could express
his thoughts and imaginations with greater freedom.
The prose romances which he began to write in the
summer of 1855, and went on writing for about a year,
are as remarkable as his early poetry, and have a strength
and beauty which is quite as rare. But during this year
he and Burne-Jones read through Chaucer. He found,
in the poet whom he afterwards took for his special
master, not merely the wider and sweeter view of life
which was needed to correct the harsh or mystical
elements of his own mediævalism, but the conquest of
English verse as a medium boundless in its range and perfect in its flexibility. Thenceforth prose was abandoned,
and, with the exception of one curious and unsuccessful
experiment, verse remained for thirty years the single
form of his production in pure literature.

The secularization of mind, the widening of interest

and outlook beyond the limits prescribed by Anglo-Catholic ideals, towards which the influence of Chaucer and Browning, like two great windows letting in the air and the day, contributed so potently, was coming fast over him in this third year at Oxford—the time in the lives of so many men which is decisive of their whole future. Art and literature were no longer thought of as handmaids to religion, but as ends to be pursued for their own sake, not indeed as a means of gaining livelihood, but as a means of realizing life. More and more it became evident that the taking of Orders, with a direct view to which both Morris and Burne-Jones had gone up to Oxford, was irreconcilable with such a life as they now proposed to themselves. And the idea of common organized effort by the whole group towards a higher life, which for long had been eagerly planned, gradually shifted from the form of a monastic to that of a social brotherhood.

There was a time, early in Morris's undergraduate days, when he had seriously thought of devoting the whole of his fortune to the foundation of a monastery. Such ideas were widely in the air. The community at Littlemore was a centre of influence and a place of pilgrimage, as familiar to all Oxford as the spire of St. Mary's. Similar communities had sprung up in other parts of the country. Some seven years before, Street, the great architect of the revived Gothic, then a young man of twenty-six, had been deeply engaged with a scheme for the foundation of an institution, combining the characters of a college, a monastery, and a workshop, for students of the theory and practice of religious art. Such a community had been actually founded in Rome, a generation earlier, by the German painters Cornelius and Overbeck. That group of religious artists, a curious anticipation of the Pre-Raphaelite Brotherhood, had lived in a Roman palace under a sort of monastic rule; and though the community had ceased to exist about the time when the Tractarian movement in England began, some tradition of it survived to kindle the imagination of younger men. Street had been living in Oxford since 1852 as architect to the diocese, had restored many of the Oxford churches, and was building the great church of SS. Philip and James in the northern outskirts of the city, one of the earliest and purest examples of a return to the architecture of the thirteenth century. Morris did not yet know him personally : but this early project of his, and similar schemes of others, had obtained a large currency.

The earliest distinct allusion to the scheme which, never realized in its original intention, bore fruit of unexpected growth in the Oxford and Cambridge Magazine and the firm of Morris & Company, comes in a letter from Burne-Jones, dated 1st of May, 1853, to a schoolfellow still in Birmingham, but preparing to go up to Oxford. The time-honoured observances which still make May-Day morning hideous in Oxford with the blare of countless whistles and horns seem then to have been resumed with added spirit in the evening, and wound up in scenes resembling those of the Fifth of November. "Ten o'clock, evening," he writes. "I have just been pouring basons of water on the crowd below from Dixon's garret—such fun, by Jove:" and then goes on, "I have set my heart on our founding a Brotherhood. Learn 'Sir Galahad' by heart; he is to be the patron of our Order. I have enlisted one in the project up here, heart and soul." A few months later he writes again, "We must enlist you in this Crusade and Holy Warfare against the age;" the crusade then definitely including celibacy and conventual life.

The last allusion to this scheme in its original conception is in another letter written by Burne-Jones to the same correspondent from Birmingham on the 16th of October, 1854, at the end of the Long Vacation. Term had been postponed for a week on account of the cholera epidemic. "You were surprised no doubt," he writes, "at the postponement of term. It made me very angry, for I was sick of home and idleness and longed with an ardent longing to be back with Morris and his glorious little company of martyrs—the monastery stands a fairer chance than ever of being founded; I know that it will be some day."

But this assurance lacks its old ring of conviction. By the end of that year the religious struggle which seemed for a while likely to land both Morris and Burne-Jones in the Roman Church was practically over, and with this clearing of the air social ideals rose to a more important place, and the monastic element began to fade away from the ideas of the Brotherhood. Price and Faulkner brought to Oxford actual knowledge of the inhuman conditions of human life in the great industrial areas; their special enthusiasms were for sanitation, for Factory Acts, for the bare elements of a possible life among the mass of their fellow-citizens. "Things were at their worst," the former writes, "in the forties and fifties. There was no protection for the mill-hand or miner—no amusements but prize-fighting, dog-fighting, cock-fighting, and drinking. When a little boy I saw many prize-fights, bestial scenes : at one a combatant was killed. The country was going to hell apace. At Birmingham School a considerable section of the upper boys were quite awake to the crying evils of the period; social reform was a common topic of conversation. We were nearly all day-boys, and we could not make short cuts to school without passing through slums of shocking squalor and misery, and often coming across incredible scenes of debauchery and brutality. I remember one Saturday night walking five miles from Birmingham into the Black Country, and in the last three miles I counted more than thirty lying dead drunk on the ground, nearly half of them women." Such surroundings impressed indelibly on those who lived in them the ground truth that all true freedom, all living art, all real morality, even among the limited class who are raised out of the common level by wealth or circumstance, finally depend upon the physical and social conditions of life which exist for the mass of their fellow-creatures. It was not till long afterwards that this view of the matter took full hold of Morris, the country-bred boy, the easy liver and born aristocrat. But its influence was already sufficient to insure him against the belief that salvation lay in dreams of the past or in isolation from the common life of the world.

Another influence during this year tended in the same direction. Morris and several others of his set used to go pretty regularly to fence, box, and play singlestick at Maclaren's Gymnasium in Oriel Lane. Singlestick was Morris's own chief delight. "In defence," writes a friend, " he was unskilful, vehement and iron-handed in attack. I bore for years after discolorations that were due to his relentless onsets." Maclaren once said that Morris's bills for broken sticks and foils equalled those of all the rest of his pupils put together. Between them and Maclaren himself, a man in the prime of life, cultivated and full of enthusiasm, a mutual intimacy and liking sprang up, and grew into a warm friendship. Three or four times in the term they would go and dine with him at Summertown, where they saw their own enthusiasms combined with the charm of a simple family life. There could be no better corrective for the narrowing influence of college monasticism. This larger life was reinforced by their outdoor tastes and their remote-

ness from the little circle of occupations in which so
many Oxford men become hopelessly shut up. For
men who did not spend their afternoons in rowing or
cricket, a walk in cap and gown up Headington or round
Christ Church meadows, discussing questions of theology,
would seem from records of Oxford life in that period to
have been the normal occupation of an undergraduate's
afternoon. Morris's daily pursuits had a range which
would not now be remarkable, but was then almost un-
exampled. The Tractarian impulse survived in the
practice, to which he and Burne-Jones adhered for a long
time, of going to sing plain-song at the daily morning
services in St. Thomas's Church. With Dixon and
Price, they belonged to the Plain-Song Society, which
practised regularly in the Music-Room in Holywell. It
included among its members men of very varied tastes
and ideals : zealous churchmen and freethinking anti-
quarians ; moderate Anglicans like Liddon and Oakley,
votaries of the Eastern Church like Neale and Palmer ;
Street and Woodward the architects, Dyce the painter.
Long afternoons were passed on the upper river and
among the ruins (more extensive then) of Godstow, or
in expeditions to old churches, ranging from Dorchester
to Woodstock, or in the glades of the Wytham woods.
Evenings of excited talk and reading slid into the long
nights in which Morris poured forth the results in prose
and verse of his newly-discovered creative power ; and
all the while, as the old ideals melted away before larger
enthusiasms, the mistress art of architecture, with all else
—music, painting, the whole range of forms and colours
and sounds—swept up into its train, took a continually
deeper and more dominating hold. So passed the spring
and summer days of 1855, while Tennyson at Farringford
was putting the last touches to " Maud," and the English
cannon thundered before Sebastopol.

CHAPTER III

In the summer term of 1855, the Brotherhood, as they now began to call themselves, came up to Oxford full of ideas and enthusiasms that could no longer be suppressed, and that demanded some active outlet. The primitive or monastic ideals of the previous year were fading away before a wider knowledge and a more quickened intelligence. The serious employments of mature life lay still seemingly far ahead, and meanwhile the art of literature made its first appeal to them with all the charm and potency which, in those susceptible years and amid those romantic surroundings, it so inexhaustibly renews over minds full of the first ardour of knowledge and the earliest consciousness of manhood. The newly discovered power and delight of original imaginative writing, and their dissatisfaction with the current tone of thought on all matters deeply affecting human life, alike urged them to some literary enterprise in which imagination and criticism should find harmonious expression. To find some united and organized method of bringing their beliefs and enthusiasms before the world, to join actively in the crusade of which Carlyle, Ruskin, and Tennyson were the accepted leaders, became the first object of their ambition; and their plans now took definite shape in the resolution to found and conduct a magazine of a really high order. It was not to be one of the ephemeral productions, blossoms of the they facetiously term them; the bit of a hill that the Cathedral stands on is very jolly however, green fields and gardens and many trees, all dotted about with quaint old houses, and bits of the old conventual buildings; there are several gorgeous bits about the Church too, and outside happily it has been hardly touched, which makes the exterior much more beautiful and interesting than the interior.

" I saw the Exhibition the other day and liked the Procession of Cimabue better than I thought I should have done, as I said to Ted, I wish I hadn't seen Ruskin's Pamphlet before seeing the picture, for I don't know now what effect his commendation may have had upon me. Millais's Picture is indeed grand, how gorgeously the dawning is painted ! I had been sitting up late the night before, and saw the dawn break, through the window in our hall, just as it might have been there, minus the smoke. There was a very sweet little picture by Collins in the Octagon room, called ' The Good Harvest of '54,' did you notice it ? I think Maclise's picture about as bad as possible, fancy the brute spoiling one of the best scenes in your favourite comedy, don't you hate him therefore ? I saw Dyce's ' Christabel' and thought the face very sweet; but Ruskin says the face is a copy; certainly it doesn't help me at all to the understanding of Coleridge's Poem.

" I saw that same day an impression of Albert Dürer's S. Hubert, and very nearly bought it but couldn't afford it, the same being 6 guineas ; I think I should have done so though if I wasn't living in hope of getting a photograph of it; the photographs represent the engravings much better than I thought they did, looking very much like impressions whose paper is yellow by age, only somewhat darker: what a splendid engraving that S. Hubert is ! O my word! so very, very gorgeous.

" I bought some engravings from Fra Angelico's picture in the Louvre, I am afraid only pretty good; will you have them? they represent the picture fairly I think on the whole, only the loss of colour makes of course a most enormous difference, where the colour is so utterly lovely as in the original—well, I hope you will like them. I have just been doing them up into a parcel whose clumsiness is something absolutely glorious, it is so clumsy. O this steel pen!—tell me if they reach you safely. Well, good-bye. I have forgotten what else I had to say to you, though I know I had plenty.

" Yours most lovingly,

" TOPSY."

The names, and some of the work, of the Pre-Raphaelite school were by this time becoming known to Morris and his companions, though the artists themselves were still unknown to them. In the summer term at Oxford he and Burne-Jones had seen Mr. Coombe's collection at the Clarendon Press, which included two pictures by Holman Hunt and Rossetti's water-colour of Dante drawing the head of Beatrice. During the Easter vacation, in the " very pretty old-fashioned house on Tottenham Green " belonging to Mr. Windus, they had seen for the first time pictures by Millais and Madox Brown. A copy of " The Germ " had also about the same time fallen into their hands; and from " Hand and Soul " and " The Blessed Damozel," which they read and re-read for ever, Rossetti rose to a first-rank place in their list of heroes.

. On the 19th of July, Morris, Burne-Jones, and Fulford started on their tour in France, crossing from Folkestone and going straight to Abbeville. " We meant it to be really a walking tour," Sir Edward Burne-Jones writes, " for cheapness' sake: not that we walked far, but started with fine ideas of economy, necessary for me and conceded by him, who never said whether he had, or had not, money. We went to Abbeville, and there I drew, and to Amiens, and to Beauvais, he falling lame at Amiens, filling the streets with imprecations on all boot-makers; but he bought a pair of gay carpet-slippers, and in these he walked from Clermont to Beauvais, about 18 miles. But from this point, as he was footsore, we tried no more walking, but went everywhere by rail or diligence. We took a volume of Keats with us, and no other book : he knew everything about every place we went to. There was a little quarrel as to whether we should go to Paris or not, for though we wanted to go to Chartres, which lay south of it, he would have had us skirt the city, even by two days' journey, so as not to see the streets of it. But I wanted to see the pictures in the Louvre, and Fulford wanted to see Paris, and after all there was the Hotel Cluny to pacify him with. He had told me that Notre Dame would be a sight miserable to look at, for the sculptures were half down and lying in careless wrecks under the porches. He was fidgetty in Paris, and after three days we hurried away and went straight to Chartres."

On the 25th of July Fulford wrote from Chartres : "On the morning after arrival at Paris we went first to the Sainte Chapelle ; thence to the Beaux Arts depart-ment of the Exposition : conceive our delight to find no less than seven Pre-Raphaelite among the English pictures: three by Hunt, including the Light of the World, three by Millais, one by Collins. They seemed to be entirely unappreciated, except the Order of Re-lease, which attracted a great many from time to time. In the evening to the Opera, to hear Alboni in Le Prophète. Jones was enraptured; Morris seemed a good deal bored. Yesterday to the Louvre. We have moved again, to Morris's great delight : he has been dying to leave Paris and get to Chartres."

Another letter from Morris to Price, at the end of the three weeks' trip, gives the rest of its history.

" Avranches, Normandy,
" August 10th, 1855.

" Dearest Crom,

" I haven't quite forgotten you yet, though I have been so long writing, but the fact is, I am quite uncomfortable even now about writing a letter to you, for I don't know what to say ; I suppose you won't be satisfied with the names merely of the places we have been to ; and I scarcely think I can give you anything else. Why couldn't you come, Crom ?   O ! the glories of the Churches we have seen ! for we have seen the last of them now, we finished up with Mont S. Michel yesterday and are waiting here (which is a very beautiful place however,) till Saturday evening or Sunday morning when we shall go back to Granville and take steamer for Jersey and Southampton.   Crom, we have seen nine Cathedrals, and let me see how many non-Cathedral Churches ; I must count them on my fingers ; there, I think I have missed some but I have made out 24 all splendid Churches ; some of them surpassing first-rate English Cathedrals.

" I am glad that Fulford has lightened my load a little bit, by telling you what we did as far as Chartres : so I won't begin till after we left that place : Well, Crom, you must know that we had thought that we should be forced to go back to Paris to get to Rouen and that we should be obliged to go by railway all the way, which grew so distasteful to us after a bit, that we made efforts, and found that we could get across the country with very little railway indeed ; so we went ; I enjoyed the journey very much, and so did the others I think, though Ted's eyes were bad, as they have been all the time whenever the sun has been out: we went the greater part of the way in a queer little contrivance with one horse the greater part of the way. Behold our itinerary. We started from Chartres quite early (six o'clock) with drizzling rain that almost hid the spires of the Cathedral, how splendid they looked in the midst of it! but we were obliged to leave them, and the beautiful statues, and the stained glass, and the great, cliff-like buttresses, for quite a long time I'm afraid—so we went for about 20 miles by railroad to a place called Maintenon, where we mounted the quaint little conveyance and went off, with the rain still falling a little, through the beautiful country to Dreux, for a distance of about 17 miles; there was plenty to look at by the road, I almost think I like that part of the country better than any other part of the lovely country we have seen in France; so gloriously the trees are grouped, all manner of trees, but more especially the graceful poplars and aspens, of all kinds; and the hedgeless fields of grain, and beautiful herbs that they grow for forage whose names I don't know, the most beautiful fields I ever saw yet, looking as if they belonged to no man, as if they were planted not to be cut down in the end, and to be stored in barns and eaten by the cattle, but that rather they were planted for their beauty only, that they might grow always among the trees, mingled with the flowers, purple thistles, and blue cornflowers, and red poppies, growing together with the corn round the roots of the fruit trees, in their shadows, and sweeping up to the brows of the long low hills till they reached the sky, changing sometimes into long fields of vines, or delicate, lush green forage; and they all looked as [if] they would grow there for ever, as if they had always grown there, without change of seasons, knowing no other time than the early August. So we went on

through this kind of country till we came to Dreux, and
the rain had cleared up long before we reached it, and it
was a bright sunny day.   Some distance from Dreux the
country changed very much into what I will tell you
afterwards, but a great part of Picardy and the Isle of
France seemed to be a good deal the same kind of
country, and the land between Rouen and Caudebec,
along the side of the Seine, was much like this, so much
so, that I think I had it in my mind a good deal just now;
perhaps it is even lovelier than this, the hills are much
higher, but I scarcely think the flowers are so rich, or
perhaps, when we went through it, the flowers had gone
off a good deal.   Well, we had to stop at Dreux about
an hour and we saw the church there, a very good one,
flamboyant mostly, but with an earlier apse very evilly
used, and with a transept front very elaborately carved
once, now very forlorn and battered, but (Deo gratias)
not yet restored : there is a delightful old secular tower
at Dreux too, and that is flamboyant also, with a roof
like the side of a cliff, it is so steep.   So we left Dreux,
and set our faces as though we would go to Evreux ; we
were obliged to undergo about half an hour's ride in the
railway before we got there, to my intense indignation.
We had only a very short time to stay at Evreux, and
even that short time we had to divide (alas ! for our
Lower Nature) between eating our dinner and gazing on
the gorgeous Cathedral: it is an exceedingly lovely one,
though not nearly so large as most of the Cathedrals we
saw, the aisles are very rich flamboyant, with a great
deal of light canopy work about them ; the rest of the
Church is earlier, the nave being Norman, and the choir
fully developed early Gothic ; though the transepts and
lantern are flamboyant also by the way : there is a great
deal of good stained glass about the Church.   When we
left Evreux we found that the country had changed al-

together, getting much more hilly, almost as glorious in
its way as the other land perhaps, but very different; for
it is a succession of quite flat valleys surrounded on all
sides by hills of very decent height with openings in them
to let out the river, the valleys are very well wooded,
and the fields a good deal like the other ones I have described, quite without hedges, and with fruit-trees growing all about them; so we kept going on, first winding
up a long hill, then on a table land for a greater or less
time, then down into the glorious lake-like valley, till
at last we got to Louviers; there is a splendid church
there, though it is not a large one; the outside has a
kind of mask of the most gorgeous flamboyant (though
late) thrown all over it, with such parapets and windows,
it is so gorgeous and light, that I was utterly unprepared
for the inside, and almost startled by it; so solemn it
looked and calm after the fierce flamboyant of the outside; for all the interior, except the Chapels, is quite
early Gothic and very beautiful; I have never, either
before or since, been so much struck with the difference
between the early and late Gothic, and by the greater
nobleness of the former. So after we had looked at the
Church for a little time we mounted the omnibus to go
to the railway station where we were to take train to
Rouen—it was about 5 miles I should think from
Louviers to the station. What a glorious ride that was,
with the sun, which was getting low by that time, striking all across the valley that Louviers lies in; I think
that valley was the most glorious of all we saw that day,
there was not much grain there, it was nearly all grass
land and the trees, O! the trees! it was all like the
country in a beautiful poem, in a beautiful Romance such
as might make a background to Chaucer's Palamon
and Arcite; how we could see the valley winding away
along the side of the Eure a long way, under the hills:

but we had to leave it and go to Rouen by a nasty, brimstone, noisy, shrieking railway train that cares not twopence for hill or valley, poplar tree or lime tree, corn poppy or blue cornflower, or purple thistle and purple vetch, white convolvulus, white clematis, or golden S. John's wort; that cares not twopence either for tower, or spire, or apse, or dome, for it will be as noisy and obtrusive under the spires of Chartres or the towers of Rouen, as it is [under] Versailles or the Dome of the Invalides; verily railways are ABOMINATIONS; and I think I have never fairly realised this fact till this our tour: fancy, Crom, all the roads (or nearly all) that come into Rouen dip down into the valley where it lies, from gorgeous hills which command the most splendid views of Rouen, but we, coming into Rouen by railway, crept into it in the most seedy way, seeing actually nothing at all of it till we were driving through the town in an omnibus.

"I had some kind of misgivings that I might be disappointed with Rouen, after my remembrances of it from last year; but I wasn't a bit. O! what a place it is. I think Ted liked the Cathedral, on the whole, better than any other church we saw. We were disappointed in one thing, however, we had expected Vespers every afternoon, we found they were only sung in that diocese on Saturday and Sunday. And weren't they sung, just. O! my word! on the Sunday especially, when a great deal of the psalms were sung to the Peregrine tone, and then, didn't they sing the hymns?

"I bought the Newcomes at Rouen, Tauchnitz edition, it is a splendid book. Well Crom, I can't write any more, I am fairly run down; I am tired too, and have got to pack up as well, which is always somewhat of a bore; when I see you (which I hope will be soon) I will tell you about the rest. Ah me! if only you had been here, how I have longed for you! so very, very much. This is a seedy letter to send to such a fellow as you are, Crom, please forgive me, and be jolly when I see you. Shall I see you at Birmingham?

"Your most loving

"TOPSY."

Even to so intimate a friend, however, this letter keeps silence as to the great event of the journey. The careless freedom of that summer holiday, with the glories of the world lying all about the fair land, among the sweet breath and colour of the fields, broke down the last hesitations. Walking together on the quays of Havre late into the August night, Morris and Burne-Jones at last took the definite decision to be artists and to postpone everything else in this world to art. It was decided that night that neither should proceed to take Orders; that the Oxford life should be wound up as quickly as possible; and that thereafter Burne-Jones should be a painter, and Morris an architect. From the art which he then chose for his own the former never swerved or wavered. Morris did not graduate as a professional architect, nor in all his life did he ever build a house. But for him, then and always, the word architecture bore an immense, and one might almost say a transcendental, meaning. Connected at a thousand points with all the other specific arts which ministered to it out of a thousand sources, it was itself the tangible expression of all the order, the comeliness, the sweetness, nay, even the mystery and the law, which sustain man's world and make human life what it is. To him the House Beautiful represented the visible form of life itself. Not only as a craftsman and manufacturer, a worker in dyed stuffs and textiles and glass, a pattern designer and decorator, but throughout the whole range

of life, he was from first to last the architect, the master-
craftsman, whose range of work was so phenomenal and
his sudden transitions from one to another form of productive energy so swift and perplexing because, himself
secure in the centre, he struck outwards to any point of
the circumference with equal directness, with equal precision, unperplexed by artificial subdivisions of art,
and untrammelled by any limiting rules of professional
custom.

In the prose romance, written a few months after he
took this momentous decision, which has been already
noted as containing many fragments of half-conscious
autobiography, the hero describes himself in the following significant words: " Ever since I can remember,
even when I was quite a child, people have always told
me that I had no perseverance, no strength of will ; they
have always kept on saying to me, directly and indirectly,
' Unstable as water thou shalt not excel ; ' and they have
always been quite wrong in this matter, for of all men I
ever heard of, I have the strongest will for good and
evil.   I could soon find out whether a thing were possible or not to me ; then if it were not, I threw it away
for ever, never thought of it again, no regret, no longing for that, it was past and over to me ; but if it were
possible, and I made up my mind to do it, then and there
I began it, and in due time finished it, turning neither to
the right hand nor the left till it was done.   So I did
with all things that I set my hand to.   Love only,
and the wild restless passions that went with it, were
too strong for me, and they bent my strong will, so
that people think me now a weak man, with no end to
make for in the purposeless wanderings of my life."

Two other great disturbing forces there were which
came at long intervals into his life.   One was the tem-
porarily overpowering influence of Rossetti, that master-

ful personality which swayed every one who approached it out of his own orbit. The other was more impersonal and more impalpable, the patient revenge of the modern or scientific spirit, so long fought against, first by his aristocratic, and then by his artistic instincts, when it took hold of him against his will and made him a dogmatic Socialist. Apart from these influences and their effects, he continued as he began ; the rare instance of a man who, without ever once swerving from truth or duty, knew what he liked, and did what he liked, all his life long.

A few days after returning from France, Morris rejoined Burne-Jones at Birmingham. There also were Fulford and Price, and Heeley had just returned after passing his examination for the Indian Civil Service. Dixon was at home at Liverpool, reading Carlyle's " French Revolution " and pondering over the difficulties of original composition. Three weeks were spent at Birmingham in furious reading and talking, and in the further incubation of the magazine. The following extracts from a diary kept by Price's younger sister are not without quiet humour :

" Aug. 22. Fan (an elder sister) was invited over to Jones' to meet Morris. Fulford also was there. F. says Morris is very handsome.

" Aug. 23. Fulford, Morris, and Jones came over to tea and supper. Morris *is* very handsome.

" Aug. 27. Crom, Edward, and Morris went to Dudley Castle : came here to tea and supper, and Fulford later on. Fulford read ' The Palace of Art ' ' Vision of Sin ' and ' Oenone.' Morris also read, but he is a queer reader.

" Sept. 2. Edward and Morris came to tea and supper. We had great fun : Morris got so excited once that he punched his own head and threw his arms about frantically."

From Price's own diary an extract has also been preserved.

"Sept. 7. Ted, Top, and Fulford came over to tea and supper. Had much talk with Top about architecture and organization of labour. Discussed the tone of reviews in general, and 'Blackwood' in particular. It is unanimously agreed that there is to be no shewing off, no quips, no sneers, no lampooning in our Magazine."

(Aytoun's unsympathetic review of "Maud" in Blackwood's Magazine for that month had been the last drop in the cup of their indignation against the tone of current literary criticism. "Maud" had been hailed by the set with unalloyed enthusiasm.)

"Sept. 9. Saw Ted and Topsy. Talked chiefly about the review. Politics to be almost eschewed : to be mainly Tales, Poetry, friendly Critiques, and social articles."

During this visit to Birmingham Burne-Jones took Morris to Cornish's, the bookseller's shop in New Street, where, in accordance with the leisurely eighteenth century practice that still lingered in provincial towns, customers were allowed to drop in and read books from the shelves. There Burne-Jones had passed " hundreds of hours " in this employment; and there lately he had found and begun to read a copy of Southey's edition of Malory's " Morte d'Arthur," a work till then unknown to either of the two, and one which Burne-Jones could not afford to buy. Morris bought it at first sight, and it at once became for both one of their most precious treasures: so precious that even among their intimates there was some shyness over it, till a year later they heard Rossetti speak of it and the Bible as the two greatest books in the world, and their tongues were unloosed by the sanction of his authority.

The resolution to become an architect, once taken, was put into effect without delay. After the visit to Birming-

ham, Morris at once began to read hard for his Final
Schools and to place himself in communication with Mr.
Street with a view of entering his office in Oxford as
soon as possible. On the 29th of September he writes
to Price from Walthamstow :

" I went to Malvern the day after I parted from you,
it is certainly a very splendid place, but very much spoiled
by being made into a kind of tea gardens for idle people.
The Abbey bells rang all the day for the fall of Sebastopol, and when I went by railway to Clay Cross the next
day, they had hoisted flags up everywhere, particularly on
the chimneys at Burton—at Chesterfield they had a flag
upon the top of their particularly ugly twisted spire—at
Clay Cross, by some strange delusion, they had hoisted
all over the place the *Russian* tricolour (viz., horizontal
stripes of blue, red, and white,) thinking, honest folks,
that it was the French flag; they have no peal of bells
at Clay Cross, only one bell of a singularly mild and
chapelly nature, said bell was tolled by the patriotic
inhabitants ALL day long, the effect of which I leave you
to imagine. My life is going to become a burden to me,
for I am going, (beginning from Tuesday next) to read
for six hours a day at Livy, Ethics, &c.—please pity me."

A week later he writes again in a more serious tone :

" Thank you very much for taking so much interest
in me—but make your mind easy about my coming
back next term, I am certainly coming back, though I
should not have done so if it had not been for my Mother;
I don't think even if I get through Greats that I shall
take my B.A., because they won't allow you not to sign
the 39 Articles unless you declare that you are ' extra
Ecclesiam Anglicanam ' which I'm not, and don't intend
to be, and I won't sign the 39 Articles. Of course I
should like to stay up at Oxford for a much longer time,
but (I told you, didn't I ?) I am going, if I can, to be an

architect, and I am too old already and there is no time
to lose, I MUST make haste, it would not do for me,
dear Crom, even for the sake of being with you, to be a
lazy, aimless, useless, dreaming body all my life long, I
have wasted enough time already, God knows; not that
I regret having gone to Oxford, how could I ? for I
should be a very poor helpless kind of thing without Ted
and you.   Didn't I tell you that I meant to ask Street of
Oxford if he would take me ?   I intended to tell you, if I
didn't; if that could happen, it would be glorious, for then
I need not leave Oxford at all.   Ah well, may it be so ! "

At home the change in his plan of life caused indeed
disappointment and almost consternation.   It had always
been taken for granted that he was to enter the Church.
The feelings with which Colonel Newcome received
Clive's intimation that he was going to be a painter were
still those of nearly the whole of the wealthier middle
class.   Bohemia was a strange foreign kingdom.   To be
a painter was barely respectable ; even to be an architect
—a profession in which there was at all events definite
office work and possibility of wealth and honour—was
to cut oneself away from the staid traditions of respect-
ability.   Mrs. Morris at first hardly credited the project
announced to her ; and it was not until he was safe at
Oxford and among his friends again that he ventured to
lay his intentions clearly before her.   Term was half over
when the following letter, written after deep thought
and with an unsurpassable delicacy of tenderness, set the
matter before her as fixed beyond recall.

                         " Ex: Coll: Oxon.
                                " Nov. 11th, 1855.
    " My dear Mother,
          " I am almost afraid you thought me scarcely in
earnest when I told you a month or two ago that I did

not intend taking Holy Orders; if this is the case I am afraid also that my letter now may vex you; but if you have really made up your mind that I was in earnest I should hope you will be pleased with my resolution. You said then, you remember, and said very truly, that it was an evil thing to be an idle objectless man; I am fully determined not to incur this reproach, I was so then, though I did not tell you at the time all I thought of, partly because I had not thought about it enough myself, and partly because I wished to give you time to become reconciled to the idea of my continuing a lay person. I wish now to be an architect, an occupation I have often had hankerings after, even during the time when I intended taking Holy Orders; the signs of which hankerings you yourself have doubtless often seen. I think I can imagine some of your objections, reasonable ones too, to this profession—I hope I shall be able to relieve them. First I suppose you think that you have as it were thrown away money on my kind of apprenticeship for the Ministry; let your mind be easy on this score; for, in the first place, an University education fits a man about as much for being a ship-captain as a Pastor of souls: besides your money has by no means been thrown away, if the love of friends faithful and true, friends first seen and loved here, if this love is something priceless, and not to be bought again anywhere and by any means: if moreover by living here and seeing evil and sin in its foulest and coarsest forms, as one does day by day, I have learned to hate any form of sin, and to wish to fight against it, is not this well too? Think, I pray you, Mother, that all this is for the best: moreover if any fresh burden were to be laid upon you, it would be different, but as I am able to provide myself for my new course of life, the new money to be paid matters nothing. If I were not to follow this occupation I in truth know not what I should follow with any chance of success, or hope of happiness in my work; in this I am pretty confident I shall succeed, and make I hope a decent architect sooner or later; and you know too that in any work that one delights in, even the merest drudgery connected with it is delightful too. I shall be master too of a useful trade; one by which I should hope to earn money, not altogether precariously, if other things fail. I myself have had to overcome many things in making up my mind to this; it will be rather grievous to my pride and selfwill to have to do just as I am told for three long years, but good for it too, I think; rather grievous to my love of idleness and leisure to have to go through all the drudgery of learning a new trade, but for that also good. Perhaps you think that people will laugh at me, and call me purposeless and changeable; I have no doubt they will, but I in my turn will try to shame them, God being my helper, by steadiness and hard work. Will you tell Henrietta that I can quite sympathise with her disappointment, that I think I understand it, but I hope it will change to something else before long, if she sees me making myself useful; for that I will by no means give up things I have thought of for the bettering of the world in so far as lies in me.

"You see I do not hope to be great at all in anything, but perhaps I may reasonably hope to be happy in my work, and sometimes when I am idle and doing nothing, pleasant visions go past me of the things that may be. You may perhaps think this a long silly letter about a simple matter, but it seems to me to be kindest to tell you what I was thinking of somewhat at length, and to try, if ever so unsuccessfully, to make you understand my feelings a little: moreover I remember speaking somewhat roughly to you when we had conversation last on this matter, speaking indeed far off from my heart because of my awkwardness, and I thought I would try to mend this a little now; have I done so at all?

"To come to details on this matter. I purpose asking Mr. Street of Oxford to take me as his pupil: he is a good architect, as things go now, and has a great deal of business, and always goes for an honourable man; I should learn what I want of him if of anybody, but if I fail there (as I may, for I don't know at all if he would take a pupil) I should apply to some London architect, in which case I should have the advantage of living with you if you continue to live near London, and the sooner the better, I think, for I am already old for this kind of work. Of course I should pay myself the premium and all that.

"My best love to yourself, and Henrietta, and Aunt, and all of them:

"Your most affectionate son
"WILLIAM.

"P.S. May I ask you to show this letter to no one else but Henrietta."

This term at Oxford was the busiest and happiest of all. The Brotherhood had grown into a close union of minds and hearts, an intimate fellowship in all projects and ideas and enthusiasms. To such a period of common youth and hope, the isolation of later life must turn backward with deep gratitude, yet with such a passionate sense of loss as one might have who found himself alone in a strange world. "Forsooth," says John Ball in his sermon at the village cross, "he that waketh in hell and feeleth his heart fail him shall have memory of the merry days of earth, and how that when his heart failed him there he cried on his fellow, and how that his fellow heard him and came."

Morris passed in the Final Schools without difficulty : the negotiations with Street were successful, and it was arranged that he should be formally articled at the beginning of the year. The set were for the last time all together; Fulford, who had taken his degree a year before and had for a time been teaching in a school at Wimbledon, having returned to Oxford, and Heeley being also there for a considerable part of the term. During this term, too, Morris found a new occupation for his busy fingers. A volume of poems by William Allingham, entitled " Day and Night Songs," had just appeared, containing a woodcut from a drawing by Rossetti. Writing to his mother in this year Rossetti speaks of " Allingham's new Collection of Poems, where there are some illustrations by Hughes, one by Millais, and one which used to be by me till it became the exclusive work of Dalziel, who cut it. I was resolved to cut it out, but Allingham would not, so I can only wish Dalziel had the credit as well as the authorship." To Allingham himself he wrote of it with equal dismay, speaking of a " stupid preconceived notion about intended ' severity ' in the design " on the part of the engraver, " which has resulted in an engraving as hard as a nail, and yet flabby and vapid to the last degree." Severity, in the noblest sense, the design possesses as one element of its beauty. Both Morris and Burne-Jones pored over it continually. The latter wrote of it as " I think the most beautiful drawing for an illustration I have ever seen " : and Morris at once set to work at drawing on wood and cutting the designs himself.

Entries in Price's diary show the progress of the magazine meanwhile.

" Nov. 6. After Hall to Faulkner's where I helped Top to concoct a letter to the publishers.

" Nov. 17. Evening to Dixon's : Solemn conclave as

to the form title &c. of the coming Mag. Ultimately decided on 72 pages monthly.

" Nov. 22. Ground at a prospectus with Top: in the evening to Pembroke and go on with the prospectus, Fulford joining in and doing lion's share."

The publishers were Messrs. Bell and Daldy; and the first number of " The Oxford and Cambridge Magazine, conducted by Members of the two Universities," appeared on the 1st of January, 1856. Twelve monthly numbers duly appeared. At the end of the year the financial drain, Morris's own engrossment in other occupations, and the rapidly divergent interests of the principal contributors, led to its discontinuance. The price of each number was a shilling. But this moderate sum was found too high for the amount of matter by some purchasers, and was thought to have injured the circulation. Each number consists of from 60 to 72 pages in double column, and the contents are classified as Essays, Tales, Poetry, and Notices of Books. The financial responsibility was undertaken wholly by Morris, the only one of the projectors who could easily do so ; though Dixon, out of more limited means, was anxious to help. At first Morris had the general control which, in default of more specific arrangements, follows the control of the purse. But the details of publishing were little to his taste, and as a corrector of proofs he was not very competent. Before the second number appeared the editorship had been formally assigned to Fulford, to whom Morris paid a salary of £100 a year for the performance of that duty. Towards the end of the Christmas Vacation Burne-Jones writes to Price, " Topsy has surrendered active powers as editor to Fulford, who is now to be autocratical master of the magazine, with full powers to accept or reject or modify anything or everything submitted to his imperial jurisdiction—it will be a good thing for all of us, and a great relief to Topsy." The results of this arrangement on the fortunes of his venture are uncertain. On the one hand, the magazine became greatly overweighted with Fulford's own compositions both in prose and verse; yet without his energy, it may be doubtful whether the task of getting out a number somehow on the first of every month would ever have been accomplished. There was some idea, which however did not take effect, of having illustrations after the precedent set by Fraser's Magazine, and by the Pre-Raphaelite "Germ." An elaborately facetious drawing of "Faulkner's Improved Sewerage," designed by Burne-Jones for an article on Sanitation by Faulkner, is still extant: and Fulford writes in March, "I expect Edward will have an illustration in the Magazine in April." It was only the expense which stood in the way. As it was, the deficit on the year's accounts was several hundred pounds, all of which came out of Morris's pocket. The only illustrations issued in connexion with the magazine were two photographs of the medallion portraits by Woolner of Carlyle and Tennyson; and these were printed and sold separately.

The venture received slight, though not unfavourable, notices in the press; 750 copies of the first number were printed, and a further supply of 250 copies had to be added. But a large number of these were presentation copies, and the circulation of the succeeding numbers slowly fell off. At the end of the year there was a large stock of unsold copies on the publishers' shelves. But encouragement came from valued sources. Ruskin praised it warmly, and gave some sort of promise, which however was not carried out, to contribute to it. Fulford writes on the 9th of January, " Ruskin has sent a most jolly note to Jones, promising to write for us when he has time, which won't be at present. But he is very despondent: he thinks people don't want honest criticism; and he has never known an honest journal get on yet." Among the contents of the January number was the first of a series of three articles on Tennyson's poetry by Fulford. He sent a copy to Tennyson and received a cordial acknowledgment.

"I find," Tennyson wrote to him, "in such of the articles as I have read, a truthfulness and earnestness very refreshing to me: very refreshing likewise is the use of the plain 'I' in lieu of the old hackneyed unconscientious editorial 'we.' May you go on and prosper. As to your essay on myself, you may easily see that I have some difficulty in speaking; to praise it, seeming too much like self-praise."

After the editorship was placed in Fulford's hands, Morris's own connexion with the management was confined to writing cheques; but he contributed articles, in prose or verse, to every number except those for June and November. "Topsy and I," Fulford writes in September, "are the only ones of the set that write at all regularly. Ted won't write." In deference to the wishes of certain contributors, I have thought it right not to give a full list of authors, which would otherwise be of no inconsiderable interest : the more so as all lists hitherto published are inaccurate in important particulars. Generally, however, it may be stated that two-thirds of the whole contents came from members of the Oxford Brotherhood. Beyond these, Wilfred Heeley was an important contributor to the earlier numbers; but he was married in September and went out to India soon afterwards, and so ceased to have connexion with it. Of the other writers, the only ones responsible for more than a single article were Vernon Lushington, who had now left Cambridge and was studying law at the Temple ; his brother Godfrey, recently elected Fellow of Oriel ; and Bernard Cracroft, of Trinity College,

Cambridge, who, like Vernon Lushington, was studying
for the Bar, and afterwards became a statist and jurist
of some distinction. He was one of the regular contributors to the Westminster Review under Mill, and
the author of "Essays on Reform" and various other
politico-social works. To these names, however, must
be added that of Dante Gabriel Rossetti. Three of
his best-known poems appeared in the later numbers of
the magazine: "The Burden of Nineveh" in August;
"The Blessed Damozel" in November; and "The Staff
and Scrip" in December. "The Blessed Damozel," a
poem which, even more than the others, Rossetti kept
perpetually retouching, is here printed with many variant
readings, both from its original form in "The Germ"
and from the later versions in the successive editions of
his published volume of poems. The other two, which
also vary materially in text from their later forms, were
printed here for the first time.

There is little in the Oxford and Cambridge Magazine
which may not be read, even at this distance of time,
with much interest: but except these poems of Rossetti's,
Morris's own contributions represent, on the whole,
that part of its contents which is of permanent value.
"Topsy has got the real grit in him and no mistake.
But we shall all go to Heaven. Now I call that rather
good, a whole natural history in two sentences." So
wrote one of the Brotherhood, in a flash of real insight,
when seven numbers of the magazine had appeared.
These contributions consist of eight prose tales, five
poems, an article on Amiens Cathedral and another on
two engravings by Alfred Rethel, and a review of
Browning's recently published "Men and Women."
The article last named is, I believe, the single instance
in which Morris ever voluntarily took the *rôle* of a
reviewer; and together with an article on Rossetti's

volume of poems of 1870, which, much against his will, he wrote for the "Academy," it represents the sum of his formal contributions to literary criticism.

The full list is as follows: the poems being distinguished by having their titles printed in italic.

January: The Story of the Unknown Church. (A tale.)
              Winter Weather.
February: The Churches of North France. No. 1. Shadows of Amiens.
March: A Dream. (A tale.)
              " Men and Women." By Robert Browning.
April: Frank's Sealed Letter. (A tale.)
May: *Riding Together.*
July: Gertha's Lovers. (A tale.) c. 1—3.
              Hands.
August: " Death the Avenger and Death the Friend."
              Svend and his Brethren. (A tale.)
              Gertha's Lovers, c. 4, 5.
September: Lindenborg Pool. (A tale.)
              The Hollow Land. (A tale.) c. 1, 2.
              The Chapel in Lyonness.
October: The Hollow Land, c. 3.
              Pray but One Prayer for Me.
December: Golden Wings. (A tale.)

" These early poems," Canon Dixon writes to me, " seem to me to be lifted out of poetry: to have, besides poetry, a substance of visible beauty of one particular kind: to be poetry without any notion of being poetry, or effort, or aim at it." Four of them were included two years later in " The Defence of Guenevere," and require no further notice here; they are " Riding

Together," "The Chapel in Lyonness," "Pray but One Prayer for Me" (there entitled "Summer Dawn"), and the Prince's Song in "Rapunzel," here printed separately under the title of "Hands." The fifth was omitted from that volume for some forgotten reason, perhaps because it was thought too like the famous "Riding Together." But to that poem it forms so perfect a pendant, and it is in itself of such strong and delicate beauty, that it claims rescue from oblivion.

> We rode together
> In the winter weather
>   To the broad mead under the hill;
> Though the skies did shiver
> With the cold, the river
>   Ran, and was never still.
>
> No cloud did darken
> The night; we did hearken
>   The hound's bark far away.
> It was solemn midnight
> In that dread, dread night,
>   In the years that have pass'd for aye.
>
> Two rode beside me,
> My banner did hide me,
>   As it drooped adown from my lance;
> With its deep blue trapping,
> The mail over-lapping,
>   My gallant horse did prance.
>
> So ever together
> In the sparkling weather
>   Moved my banner and lance;
> And its laurel trapping,
> The steel over-lapping,
>   The stars saw quiver and dance.

We met together
In the winter weather
    By the town-walls under the hill;
His mail-rings came clinking,
They broke on my thinking,
    For the night was hush'd and still.

Two rode beside him,
His banner did hide him,
    As it drooped down strait from his lance;
With its blood-red trapping,
The mail over-lapping,
    His mighty horse did prance.

And ever together
In the solemn weather
    Moved his banner and lance;
And the holly trapping,
The steel over-lapping,
    Did shimmer and shiver, and dance.

Back reined the squires
Till they saw the spires
    Over the city wall;
Ten fathoms between us,
No dames could have seen us
    Tilt from the city wall.

There we sat upright
Till the full midnight
    Should be told from the city chimes;
Sharp from the towers
Leapt forth the showers
    Of the many clanging rhymes.

'Twas the midnight hour,
Deep from the tower
  Boom'd the following bell;
Down go our lances,
Shout for the lances!
  The last toll was his knell.

There he lay, dying;
He had, for his lying,
  A spear in his traitorous mouth;
A false tale made he
Of my true, true lady;
  But the spear went through his mouth.

In the winter weather
We rode back together
  From the broad mead under the hill;
And the cock sung his warning
As it grew toward morning,
  But the far-off hound was still.

Black grew his tower
As we rode down lower,
  Black from the barren hill;
And our horses strode
Up the winding road
  To the gateway dim and still.

At the gate of his tower,
In the quiet hour,
  We laid his body there;
But his helmet broken,
We took as a token;
  Shout for my lady fair!

We rode back together
In the winter weather
    From the broad mead under the hill;
No cloud did darken
The night; we did hearken
    How the hound bay'd from the hill.

In the article on Amiens Cathedral, which appeared in the February number, the intense love and wonderful knowledge Morris had of the Middle Ages, and of those glorious French Gothic churches which were always to him the crown and flower of the whole world's architecture, expressed themselves in what is perhaps even yet the noblest and most loving tribute ever paid to the great Cathedral. It was not written without violent struggles. "I am to have a grind about Amiens Cathedral this time," he writes from home on the 11th of January, "it is very poor and inadequate, I cannot help it; it has cost me more trouble than anything I have written yet; I ground at it the other night from nine o'clock till half past four a.m., when the lamp went out, and I had to creep upstairs to bed through the great dark house like a thief." The praise of Amiens has been written by many different pens; but no one has ever written on it with such white heat of enthusiasm and such wealth of detailed insight. Every word of what he writes comes straight from his heart. "I thought," he says, with simple and unashamed modesty, "that even if I could say nothing else about these grand churches, I could at least tell men how I loved them. For I will say here that I think these same churches of North France the grandest, the most beautiful, the kindest and most loving of all the buildings that the earth has ever borne."

This article is headed "The Churches of North France.

No. 1." It would seem that Morris had meant to write a series of articles on these churches, but there is no trace of his having begun a second. Indeed, after the first few months, his contributions to the magazine appear to be mainly poems and tales written during the previous year; his work at Street's office, together with all the rest of his activities, preventing him from giving the laborious days and nights to writing which would have been necessary. For the essay on Amiens has neither the fluent grace nor the uncertain touch of the tales; it is wrought as if with chisel strokes, precise and yet passionate. The prose tales, on the other hand, were written very swiftly, poured out, as it were, from a brain overloaded and saturated with its pent-up stores of imagination. The only one which bears internal traces of labour or effort is the one entitled "Frank's Sealed Letter," in which for once, and with very faint success, he tried to write a story of modern life. In common with the unfinished and unpublished modern novel which he wrote many years afterwards, it gives the curious impression of some one writing about a kind of life which he only knows from books, with a strange sort of inverted antiquarianism. Put him in the thirteenth century and he is completely and conspicuously at his ease; the pictures rise, the narrative flows, as though he had seen and heard all he describes. But once in the nineteenth, his imagination is clogged and half crippled. On the imaginative side he was far behind, and far before, his own time: he belongs partly to the earlier Middle Ages, and partly to an age still far in the future. The stories of "The Unknown Church" and "Lindenborg Pool" have what may be called a semi-historical setting; they are placed, that is, in a definite European country and in a more or less definite epoch. But in the other five tales, the flower of Morris's early

I.   H

work, the world is one of pure romance. Mediæval
customs, mediæval buildings, the mediæval Catholic religion, the general social framework of the thirteenth or
fourteenth century, are assumed throughout, but it would
be idle to attempt to place them in any known age or
country. The world of fantasy in which they are set
is like and yet unlike that of the second cycle of prose
tales which began more than thirty years later, when he
abandoned the semi-historical setting of "John Ball"
and "The House of the Wolfings" and returned to a
world of pure romance in the story of "The Roots of the
Mountains" and the series of stories which followed it.
Both worlds are vaguely mediæval, but the men and
women who move in these earlier tales are less strong
and more passionate; and the world itself is more opulent,
more Southern, reminding one often of Provence or Italy
rather than of the rich but temperate Northern lands
dwelt in by the men of Burgdale or Upmeads or Utter-
hay. The Muse of the North had not yet become to
him what it was in later years, "Mother, and Love, and
Sister all in one," as he calls it in a poem written about
ten years after this. The tale of "Lindenborg Pool" is
indeed suggested by a story in Thorpe's "Northern
Mythology," and "The Hollow Land" is headed by a
few lines from the Niebelungenlied; but the atmosphere
is throughout that of the French romances, not that of
the Scandinavian epic. Another likeness between the two
cycles of stories is the skilful interweaving of prose and
verse, afterwards adopted by him as a conscious literary
method in "The House of the Wolfings" and "The
Well at the World's End." Among these early romances
are several exquisite lyrical fragments. One of these,
the song sung by Margaret in "The Hollow Land,"
has passed from mouth to mouth among many lovers of
poetry who never read the romance itself :

Christ keep the Hollow Land
  All the summer-tide;
Still we cannot understand
  Where the waters glide;

Only dimly seeing them
  Coldly slipping through
Many green-lipp'd cavern mouths,
  Where the hills are blue.

The first verse of another fragment in the same story, a
Christmas carol heard sung in the snow by a sentinel of
Queen Swanhilda's, was perpetually repeated among his
friends; nor is it easy to forget after a single hearing:

Queen Mary's crown was gold,
  King Joseph's crown was red,
But Jesus' crown was diamond
  That lit up all the bed
          Mariæ Virginis.

Ships sail through the Heaven
  With red banners dress'd,
Carrying the planets seven
  To see the white breast
          Mariæ Virginis.

These romances have never been reprinted. Their
author in later years thought, or seemed to think, lightly
of them, calling them crude (as they are) and very young
(as they are). But they are nevertheless comparable in
quality to Keats's " Endymion ": as rich in imagination,
as irregularly gorgeous in language, as full in every vein
and fibre of the sweet juices and ferment of the spring.

Towards the end of the Christmas Vacation of 1855-6,
when the first number of the magazine had just been

launched on the world, Burne-Jones went for a few days
to London ; and there an event took place which had
momentous consequences in the year which ensued on
his own life and that of Morris.   The story shall be
given in his own words.

" Just after Christmas, I went to London, to visit my
aunt.   I was two and twenty, and had never met, or
even seen, a painter in my life.   I knew no one who
had ever seen one, or had been in a studio, and of all
men who lived on earth, the one that I wanted to see
was Rossetti.   I had no dream of ever knowing him,
but I wanted to look at him, and as I had heard that he
taught at the Working Men's College in Great Ormond
Street, a little University set up by Denison Maurice,
where men skilled in science or history gave lectures
and their services of evenings, I went to the college one
day to find out how it would be possible that I should
set eyes upon him.   I was told that there was to be a
monthly meeting that very evening, in a room in Great
Titchfield Street, and that, by paying threepence, any
one could get admittance, including tea, and hear the
addresses on the condition of the college, and the advance
of studies, which were delivered by the different pro-
fessors ; so without fail I was there, and sat at a table
and had thick bread and butter, but knowing no one.
But good fellowship was the rule there, that was clear ;
and a man sitting opposite to me spoke at once to me,
introducing himself by the name of Furnivall, and I
gave my name and college, and my reason for coming.
He reached across the table to a kindly-looking man,
whom he introduced to me as Vernon Lushington, to
whom I repeated my reason for coming, and begged
him to tell me when Rossetti entered the room.   It
seemed that it was doubtful if he would appear at all,
that he was constant in his work of teaching drawing at

the College, but had no great taste for the nights of
addresses and speeches, and as I must have looked down-
cast at this, Lushington, with a kindness never to be
forgotten by me, invited me to go to his rooms in
Doctors' Commons a few nights afterwards, where
Rossetti had promised to come. So I waited a good
hour or two, listening to speeches about the progress of
the College, and Maurice, who was President, spoke of
Macaulay's new volume, just out, blaming much the
attack on George Fox in a true Carlylese spirit which
was very pleasing, and then Lushington whispered to
me that Rossetti had come in, and so I saw him for the
first time, his face satisfying all my worship, and I
listened to addresses no more, but had my fill of looking; only I would not be introduced to him. You may
be sure I sent a long letter about all this to Morris at
Walthamstow, and on the night appointed, about ten
o'clock, I went to Lushington's rooms, where was a company of men, some of whom have been friends ever
since. I remember Saffi was there, and a brother of
Rossetti's. And by-and-bye Rossetti came and I was
taken up to him and had my first fearful talk with him.
Browning's 'Men and Women' had just been published a few days before, and some one speaking disre-
spectfully of that book was rent in pieces at once for his
pains and was dumb for the rest of the evening, so that
I saw my hero could be a tyrant, and I thought it sat
finely upon him. Also, another unwary man professed
an interest in metaphysics; he also was dealt with firmly;
so that our host was impelled to ask if Rossetti would
have all men painters, and if there should be no other
occupation for mankind. Rossetti said stoutly that it
was so. But before I left that night, Rossetti bade me
come to his studio next day. It was at the top of the
last house by Blackfriars Bridge, at the north-west corner

of the bridge, long ago pulled down to make way for
the Embankment; and I found him painting at a water-
colour of a monk copying a mouse in an illumination.
The picture was called 'Fra Pace' afterwards, and
belongs now to Mrs. Jekyll. He received me very
courteously, and asked much about Morris, one or two
of whose poems he knew already, and I think that was
our principal subject of talk, for he seemed much interested about him. He showed me many designs for
pictures; they tossed about everywhere in the room:
the floor at one end was covered with them and with
books. No books were on shelves, and I remember
long afterwards he once said that books were no use to
a painter except to prop up models upon in difficult
positions, and that then they might be very useful. No
one seemed to be in attendance upon him. I stayed
long and watched him at work, not knowing till many a
day afterwards that this was a thing he greatly hated,
and when, for shame, I could stay no longer, I went away,
having carefully concealed from him the desire I had to
be a painter.'

After this vacation, Burne-Jones returned to Oxford,
more confirmed than ever in his resolution of becoming
a painter at once. During the Lent term he continued
to read for the Final Schools; but at Easter he went up
to London permanently, and left college without taking
a degree. Meanwhile Morris had, on the 21st of
January, signed his articles with Street and begun work
in Street's office in Beaumont Street, living himself in
lodgings in St. Giles's, in a house opposite St. John's.
Street's senior clerk was then Philip Webb, a man a few
years older than Morris. Between them there arose a
close and lifelong friendship. When Webb left Street's
office in 1859 his place was taken by Norman Shaw. It
is hardly too much to say that the work of these three

men has, in the course of a generation, revolutionized
domestic architecture throughout England.

Morris plunged with his usual ardour and thoroughness into his new profession. His single holiday for
several months was on the day when he took his
Bachelor's degree. The evenings during term were, as
before, spent with the old set, who were still in residence,
with the exception of Fulford, now installed in London
as editor of the magazine and literary man. " Edward
says," writes Miss Price in February, " that Fulford
has become very serious." Browning's " Bishop Blou-
gram," published in the previous year, was one of the
poems which were eagerly discussed by the set about
this time. Emigration to Australia or New Zealand
was then greatly in the air as a sort of gospel. Madox
Brown's picture, " The Last of England," painted between the years 1852 and 1855, marks the culmina-
tion of the movement. It already appears strongly
marked in the conclusion of Clough's " Bothie of Tober-
na-Vuolich," published in 1848. Woolner had actually
gone to Australia in 1852, and Tennyson had had serious
thoughts of accompanying him. The arousal caused by
the Crimean War united with other causes to check the
impulse; and work for the elevation and sweetening of
life in England took the place in the ideals of younger
men that had for a few years been occupied by the somewhat fantastic dreams of an Antipodean Golden World.

In his spare time, besides the poems and stories which
he went on pouring forth, Morris was beginning to
practise more than one handicraft—clay-modelling, carving in wood and stone, and illuminating. A page of
his illumination is extant, done in this year. It shows
great certainty and mastery in colour, but not the complete grasp of the art which he had acquired a year later ;
the drawing is uncertain, and the writing not good. His

eye for colour was always perfect, and his knowledge
with regard to it amazing. There is a singular instance
of this in a passage in " The Hollow Land." " As the
years went on," says the Son of the House of the Lilies,
" and we grew old, we painted purple pictures and green
ones instead of the scarlet and yellow, so that the walls
looked altered." That this is what actually happens
from the yellowing of the crystalline lens of the eye in
advanced life was only discovered by specialists many
years later. How did Morris know, or divine it?

From the day he put on his Bachelor's gown, he
ceased the practice, then still enforced on all undergraduates, of shaving the moustache. From that time
forward he never touched a razor ; and now also he
began, partly as a symbol of his profession, partly from
mere disinclination to take unnecessary trouble, to wear
his hair long, as was then the fashion among artists. His
hair remained through life of extraordinary beauty, very
thick, fine and strong, with a beautiful curl that made it
look like exquisitely wrought metal, and with no parting. It was so strong that he afterwards used to amuse
his children by letting them take hold of it and lifting
them by it off the ground. His general appearance at
this time—the massive head, the slightly knitted brow,
the narrow eyeslits and heavy underlids, the delicately
beautiful mouth and chin only half veiled by the slight
beard—are given with great fidelity in a photograph of
about this period which is reproduced here, and which
also shows the characteristic hands—broad, fleshy, and
rather short, with a look about them of clumsiness and
ineffectiveness which was absolutely the reverse of the
truth. It was a perpetual amazement to see those hands
executing the most delicately minute work with a swiftness and precision that no one else could equal. Another
portrait of him at this time of his life exists which many

people have seen without knowing it. In Rossetti's drawing of Lancelot leaning over the barge of the Lady of Shalott, in the illustrated Tennyson published in 1857 by Moxon and often since reprinted, Lancelot's head was drawn from Morris and was an admirable likeness. In spite of the imperfection of the woodcutting, which in this, as in the other illustrations that Rossetti contributed to the volume, drove him almost to despair, in spite, too, of the cap which almost conceals the forehead and hair, this head remains, by the account of his early friends, an exact portrait of the man they knew.

After Burne-Jones went to London at Easter, and began painting under the friendly guidance of Rossetti, Morris used to go up almost every week to spend the Sunday with him at his lodgings in Chelsea. He used to arrive on Saturday in time to see pictures at the Academy or elsewhere, and go to a play with Burne-Jones and Rossetti in the evening. After the play—if Rossetti's imperious impatience of bad acting or bad plays allowed them to sit it out—they would go with him to his rooms on the Embankment overlooking Blackfriars Bridge, and sit there till three or four in the morning, talking. All Sunday the talking, varied by reading of the "Morte d'Arthur," went on in the Chelsea lodging, Rossetti often looking in upon the other two in the afternoon. On the Monday morning, Morris took the first train down to Oxford to be at Street's again when the office opened. During these months Rossetti's influence over him grew stronger and stronger. His doctrine that everybody should be a painter, enforced with all the weight of his immense personality and an eloquence and plausibility in talk which all who knew him in those years describe as unparalleled in their experience, carried Morris for a time off his feet. Much, no doubt, of the daily work in an

architect's office was in itself uninteresting, or even distasteful to him ; and if the statement in Street's " Life,"
that, while his headquarters were at Oxford, he " restored
most of the Oxford churches," be taken in anything like
a literal sense, the work must sometimes have been such
as Morris, with his clear views on the subject of restorations, could not assist in with any comfort, or look
forward to without an alarm almost amounting to disgust as the future business of his own life. He became
an ardent pupil, as he was already a keen admirer, of the
Pre-Raphaelite school. Rossetti introduced him to Madox
Brown and Holman Hunt, and painting rose for a time
almost, if not quite, to the first place in his interest.
On one of his visits to London he fell in love with, and
bought, Mr. Arthur Hughes's beautiful " April Love,"
which was exhibited at the Royal Academy that year,
together with Hunt's " Scapegoat," Millais's " Autumn
Leaves," and Wallis's " Death of Chatterton."

At the end of this summer, Street removed his headquarters from Oxford to London, and Morris came up
with him. In August he and Burne-Jones took rooms
together in Upper Gordon Street, Bloomsbury, a neighbourhood convenient to both as being close both to
Street's office in Montague Place and to the various drawing schools known under the generic name of Gandish's
in the neighbourhood of Fitzroy Square. Some extracts
from a letter written from Oxford in July may show the
ferment working in his brain.

" I have seen Rossetti twice since I saw the last of
you ; spent almost a whole day with him the last time,
last Monday, that was. Hunt came in while we were
there, a tallish, slim man with a beautiful red beard,
somewhat of a turn-up nose, and deep set dark eyes :
a beautiful man. . . . Rossetti says I ought to paint,
he says I shall be able ; now as he is a very great

man, and speaks with authority and not as the scribes, I *must* try. I don't hope much, I must say, yet will try my best—he gave me practical advice on the subject . . . So I am going to try, not giving up the architecture, but trying if it is possible to get six hours a day for drawing besides office work. One won't get much enjoyment out of life at this rate, I know well, but that don't matter : I have no right to ask for it at all events—love and work, these two things only. . . . I can't enter into politico-social subjects with any interest, for on the whole I see that things are in a muddle, and I have no power or vocation to set them right in ever so little a degree. My work is the embodiment of dreams in one form or another. . . .

" Yet I shall have enough to do, if I actually master this art of painting : I dare scarcely think failure possible at times, and yet I know in my mind that my chances are slender ; I am glad that I am compelled to try anyhow ; I was slipping off into a kind of small (very small) Palace of Art. . . . Ned and I are going to live together. I go to London early in August."

The double life which he proposes to himself in this letter was actually carried on for some time, Morris working at Street's office in the day and going with Burne-Jones to a life school in Newman Street at night. But it of course proved to be impossible as a continuance. A visit to the Low Countries which he made during the autumn with Street brought him back fired with new enthusiasm for painting ; and before the end of the year he finally quitted the office. It was after this visit that he adopted, or modified, for his own use, the motto " Als ich kanne " of John Van Eyck.

" Topsy and I live together," writes Burne-Jones in August, " in the quaintest room in all London, hung with brasses of old knights and drawings of Albert

Dürer. We know Rossetti now as a daily friend, and we know Browning too, who is the greatest poet alive, and we know Arthur Hughes, and Woolner, and Madox Brown—Madox Brown is a lark! I asked him the other day if I wasn't very old to begin painting, and he said, ' Oh, no! there was a man I knew who began older; by the bye, he cut his throat the other day,' so I ask no more about men who begin late. Topsy will be a painter, he works hard, is prepared to wait twenty years, loves art more and more every day. He has written several poems, exceedingly dramatic—the Brownings, I hear, have spoken very highly of one that was read to them; Rossetti thinks one called ' Rapunzel ' is equal to Tennyson: he is now illuminating ' Guendolen ' for Georgie. . . . The Mag. is going to smash—let it go! the world is not converted and never will be. It has had stupid things in it lately. I shall not write again for it, no more will Topsy—we cannot do more than one thing at a time, and our hours are too valuable to spend so."

CHAPTER IV

THE formal abandonment of architecture as a profession
which took place under Rossetti's influence at the end
of 1856 was not felt either by Morris himself or by his
friends to be a light matter. Rossetti, now as always
perfectly unscrupulous in his means towards an end
which he believed to be of primary importance, probably did not look beyond the immediate interests of his
own art. For him, at that time, English society was
divided into two classes. The duty of the one class was
to paint pictures, and it included all those who were
competent to do so. The duty of the other class was
to buy the pictures so painted. This amazingly simple
scheme of life he enforced with all the power of his be-
witching personality. To an immense power of humour
and sarcasm, and a dazzling eloquence, he added gifts
even more potent: an intelligence of sympathy towards
the ideas or work of other artists, which Sir Edward
Burne-Jones in recent years described as unequalled in his
experience; a boundless generosity in helping on younger
men who would be guided by him; and behind all these
qualities, a certain hard intellectual force against which
very few of those who came under its influence were
able to make a stand. When Morris was introduced to
Rossetti he was already known among his friends, and
must have already known himself, to be a poet. Yet in

Rossetti's judgment, even poetry, of which he was himself so eminent a master, was to be subordinated to painting whenever that was possible. In 1854 he had written
to Allingham, "I believe my poetry and painting prevented each other from doing much good for a long
while, and now I think I could do better in either, but
can't write, for then I sha'n't paint." It was a theory
of his, expounded with copiousness and vehement conviction, that English poetry was fast reaching the ter-
mination of its long and splendid career, and that Keats
represented its final achievement. English painting, on
the other hand, he regarded as in its dawn. To the
enthusiasm of the Pre-Raphaelites all possibilities seemed
to lie before them in their newly-revived art; and Rossetti
made it his business to preach and proselytize for this
new art as the one thing then and there needful. Writing to William Bell Scott in February, 1857, he says,
"Two young men, projectors of the Oxford and Cambridge Magazine, have recently come to town from Oxford and are now very intimate friends of mine. Their
names are Morris and Jones. They have turned artists
instead of taking up any other career to which the University generally leads, and both are men of real genius.
Jones's designs are models of finish and imaginative detail,
unequalled by anything unless, perhaps, Albert Dürer's
finest works; and Morris, though without practice as
yet, has no less power, I fancy. He has written some
really wonderful poetry, too." But the poetry was to
his mind in the second place. "If any man has any
poetry in him," he said to Burne-Jones again and again
that summer, "he should paint, for it has all been said
and written, and they have scarcely begun to paint it."
The feeling which Morris had shared with his contemporaries at Oxford, that Tennyson represented the end of
all things in poetry, no doubt received a powerful stimu-

lus or revival from this doctrine of Rossetti's; and perhaps the curious view which he always continued to hold of writing poetry as a recreation, an enjoyment to be taken in the intervals of some manual work, was in some measure due to the persistence of this influence.

To his mother, at all events, who had so short a time before been reluctantly reconciled to his becoming an architect, the change of profession came as a severe shock: the more so, that with characteristic vehemence, he did not prepare her mind for it, but announced it with a nervous suddenness while he and Burne-Jones were on a visit to Walthamstow. She never quite forgave Burne-Jones for what she naturally thought was mainly his doing. On Morris himself the resolution had an unsettling, and for a time, almost a disastrous effect. For the two years or so during which he worked hard at painting, he was moody and irritable; he brooded much by himself, and lost for the time a good deal of his old sweetness and affectionateness of manner. Rossetti's conquest of a mind so strong and so self-sufficing was, while it lasted, complete in proportion to the strength which was subdued. He became not only a pupil, but a servant. Once, when Burne-Jones complained that the designs he made in Rossetti's manner seemed better than his own original work, Morris answered with some vehemence, "I have got beyond that: I want to imitate Gabriel as much as I can." The new gospel was carried down to those of the set who still remained at Oxford, and they were all put to drawing or modelling as if their life depended on it.

When Morris ceased to be all day at Street's office, the lodgings in Upper Gordon Street became inadequate for both him and Burne-Jones to work in. They were also rather expensive. Burne-Jones was poor; and Morris, while he was under Rossetti's guidance, had to buy pictures as well as paint them. "Yesterday," runs an entry in Madox Brown's diary for the 24th of August, 1856, "Rossetti brought his ardent admirer Morris of Oxford, who bought my little Hayfield for £40." Just then the rooms at 17, Red Lion Square, which Rossetti and Deverell had occupied in the early days of the Pre-Raphaelite Brotherhood, happened to be vacant; and at Rossetti's suggestion, they removed there. It was a first-floor set of three rooms : the large room in front looked north, and its window had been heightened up to the ceiling to adapt it for use as a studio; behind it was a bedroom, and behind that another small bedroom or powdering closet. Till the spring of 1859 this was their London residence and working place, and it is round Red Lion Square that much of the mythology of Morris's earlier life clusters. From the incidents which occurred or were invented there, a sort of Book of the Hundred Merry Tales gradually was formed, of which Morris was the central figure. A great many of these stories are connected with the maid of the house, who became famous under the name of Red Lion Mary. She was very plain, but a person of great character and unfailing good humour, with some literary taste and a considerable knowledge of poetry. She cooked and mended for the new lodgers, read their books and letters, was anxious to be allowed to act as a model, and neglected all her other duties to stand behind them and watch them painting.

The rooms in Red Lion Square were unfurnished : and from this trifling circumstance came the beginnings of Morris's work as a decorator and manufacturer. The arts of cabinet-making and upholstery had at this time reached the lowest point to which they have ever sunk. Ugliness and vulgarity reigned in them unchecked. While he lived in furnished rooms it was easy to accept things as they were; but now, when furniture had actually

to be bought, it became at once clear that nothing could
be had that was beautiful, or indeed, that was not actively
hideous.　Nor was it possible even to get so simple a
thing as a table or chair, still less any more elaborate
piece of furniture, made at the furnishing shops from a
better design.　It was this state of things which drove
Morris and Webb to take up the designing and making
of objects of common use on their own account, and
which led, a few years later, to the formation of the
firm of Morris & Company.　For the moment, however,
all that was possible was that Morris should make rough
drawings of the things he most wanted, and then get a
carpenter in the neighbourhood to construct them from
those drawings in plain deal.　Thus the rooms in Red
Lion Square were gradually provided with "intensely
mediæval furniture," as Rossetti described it, "tables
and chairs like incubi and succubi."　First came a large
round table "as firm, and as heavy, as a rock": then
some large chairs, equally firm, and not lightly to be
moved, "such as Barbarossa might have sat in."　Afterwards a large settle was designed, with a long seat below,
and above, three cupboards with great swing doors.
"There were many scenes with the carpenter," Sir Edward Burne-Jones says: "especially I remember the
night when the settle came home.　We were out when
it reached the house, but when we came in, all the passages and the staircase were choked with vast blocks of
timber, and there was a scene.　I think the measure-
ments had perhaps been given a little wrongly, and that
it was bigger altogether than he had ever meant, but set
up it was finally, and our studio was one-third less in
size.　Rossetti came.　This was always a terrifying
moment to the very last.　He laughed, but approved."
Not only so, but he at once made designs for oil paintings to be executed on the panels of the cupboard doors

I.　　　　　　　　　I

and the sides of the settle. The design for the central panel, Love between the Sun and Moon, was only executed later; but the painting of the two others was completed during this winter: and these panels, afterwards removed from the cupboard, are now known as the Meeting of Dante and Beatrice in Florence, and their Meeting in Paradise. On the backs of two of the large heavy chairs he also painted subjects from Morris's own poems; these panels, one representing Guendolen in the witch-tower and the Prince below kissing her long golden hair, and the other the arming of a knight, from the Christmas Mystery of " Sir Galahad," are also extant. The theory that furniture should mainly exist to provide spaces for pictorial decoration was carried in these chairs to an extreme limit. But the next piece of furniture required for the rooms was a wardrobe; and this covered by Burne-Jones in the spring of 1857 with paintings from " The Prioress's Tale " in Chaucer, remained to the last the principal ornament of Morris's drawing-room in London, and is familiar to all his later as well as his older friends.

Morris himself worked hard at drawing and painting all that spring. His wonderful faculty of pattern designing had already come to him, and with it a unique sense for justness in colour, fed on admiring study of the best early mediæval work, especially in illumination. " In all illumination and work of that kind," Rossetti writes just before Christmas, 1856, " he is quite unrivalled by anything modern that I know." In the drawing and modelling of animate forms he never could become proficient. The human figure was too much for him, and even with birds or animals in his designs he felt difficulty. So it remained afterwards. The animals in his wall-papers were, as a rule, drawn by Webb, and the figures in his tapestries by Burne-Jones; and many

years later, when designing the borders for the Kelmscott Chaucer, he expressed his regret at not being able
to fill them with Chaucer's favourite birds. Such figures
as he designed, of which there are a number both in
illuminations and in stained glass, are obviously faulty
in drawing.

In June, Rossetti, writing to W. Bell Scott, mentions
Morris as then busy painting his first picture. Its subject,
taken from the " Morte d'Arthur," was the recognition
of Tristram by the dog in King Mark's palace. This,
like the few other pictures he completed, was in oil.
The only recorded instance of his painting a picture in
water-colour was three or four months later, when he
was on a visit to Dixon at Manchester to see the famous
Art Treasures Exhibition of 1857. While staying there
he painted a water-colour of " The Soldan's Daughter in
the Palace of Glass." The Soldan's daughter was seated
in a heavy wooden armchair, probably studied from one
of those at Red Lion Square, and the palace was in all
shades of bluish glass. To the pictures in the Manchester Exhibition he seemed to pay little attention, but
studied the collection of carved ivories minutely. The
visit ended with a very characteristic scene. " When he
was to go," Canon Dixon says, " we both, I think, mis-
read the Railway Guide, and drove to the station when
there was no train; and there was nothing for it but to
wait till next day. I was made aware of this by a fearful cry in my ears, and saw Morris ' translated': it lasted
all the way home ; it then vanished in a moment ; he was
as calm as if it had never been, and began painting in
water-colours." It was during this visit to Manchester
that he wrote the " Praise of My Lady," with the lovely
Latin burden, which is one of the jewels of the volume
of Poems of 1858.

Mrs. Alfred Baldwin possesses another work of the

same period, which Morris gave her when a girl in London during that winter. It is a page of illuminated manuscript on vellum. The text, which is in prose, is founded on a fairy tale from Grimm. The writing, which is in the Gothic character, is rather cramped and uncertain. But the design and colouring of the border, and the treatment of a picture in a large initial letter, show a complete grasp of the principles and methods of the art. It is probable that no illumination had been done since the fifteenth century which was so full of the mediæval spirit.

A holiday during this Red Lion Square time was nearly always spent at the Zoological Gardens. For the greater birds Morris had always a special affection. He would imitate an eagle with considerable skill and humour, climbing on to a chair and, after a sullen pause, coming down with a soft heavy flop; and for some time an owl was one of the tenants of Red Lion Square, in spite of a standing feud between it and Rossetti. The evenings were pretty often spent at the theatre, seeing Robson at the Olympic, or Kean's Shakespearean pageants at the Princess's. Among all this series of spectacular plays, "Richard the Second" (March to July, 1857) was Morris's special favourite. For the beautiful fluency and copiousness of the language in this play he had an immense admiration; and in Kean's production there was a dance with mediæval music which gave him great delight. It was his first, or almost his first, introduction to early non-ecclesiastical music. When all the rest of the day's work or amusement was over, there were gatherings at Rossetti's rooms in Chatham Place, beginning about midnight and often lasting far into the morning.

How long Rossetti's daily influence might have kept him labouring at what he could not do, when there was work all round that he could do, on the whole, better

than any man living, it is needless to inquire. But the
first piece of work which took him away from life in a
painter's studio, and began his career as a decorator, was
of Rossetti's own initiation.

In the early part of the Long Vacation of 1857,
Rossetti went down to Oxford to see his friend Benjamin
Woodward, the architect. Morris, always delighted to
take a day at Oxford, went with him. The long battle
between the Palladian and Gothic styles for the new
University Museum had been at last decided by the
Oxford authorities in favour of the latter. Woodward's
plans, in a style of mixed Rhenish and Venetian Gothic,
had been accepted, and the museum was now in progress.
Besides his principal work at the museum, he was engaged in building a debating hall for the Union Society.
That hall, now the principal library, was just roofed in.
In form, the hall was a long building with apsidal ends.
A narrow gallery fitted with bookshelves ran completely
round it, and above the shelves was a broad belt of wall
divided into ten bays, pierced by twenty six-foil circular
windows, and surmounted by an open timber roof.
Rossetti was at once fired with the idea of painting the
space thus given. In his notions of the application of
painting to architectural surfaces, Woodward, an ardent
admirer and a skilled imitator of the Venetian builders,
cordially concurred ; and it was at once settled that the
ten bays and the whole of the ceiling should be covered
with painting in tempera. The Building Committee of
the Union, who had a general discretion as regards the
work to be done during the Long Vacation, were induced
to authorize the work without waiting to refer the matter
to a general meeting of the Society. It was arranged
that the paintings should forthwith be designed and carried
out under Rossetti's superintendence. He himself, and
other artists whom he should invite to join him, were to

be the executants.   The Union was to defray the expense
of scaffolding and materials, and the travelling and lodging expenses of the artists, who, beyond this, were to give
their services for nothing.   No sooner was this settled,
than Rossetti went straight back to London and issued
his orders :   Burne-Jones and Morris were to lay aside
all other work and start on the new scheme at once.   He
had it all planned in his mind.   The ten paintings on
the walls were to be a series of scenes from the " Morte
d'Arthur," and the roof above them was to be covered
with a floriated design.   For the pictures, ten men had
to be found, each of whom should execute one bay, and
the work, in the first enthusiasm, was estimated as a
matter of six weeks or so.   Arthur Hughes, Spencer
Stanhope, Val Prinsep, and Hungerford Pollen, were
drawn into the scheme and agreed to take a picture
each ;   Madox Brown was also asked to execute one, but
declined.   Rossetti undertook to do two, or if possible
three, himself, and Morris and Burne-Jones were each to
do one under his eye and with his guidance : eight or
nine of the ten bays were thus accounted for, and the
remainder of the space was for the moment left to
chance.

The story of these paintings, of which the mouldering
and undecipherable remains still glimmer like faded
ghosts on the walls of the Union Library, is one of
work hastily undertaken, executed under impossible
conditions, and finally abandoned after time and labour
had been spent on it quite disproportionate to the
original design.   A scheme of mural decoration which
was practically new in England, and which involved the
most careful preparation and the most complete fore-
thought, was rushed into with a light heart ; all difficulties
were ignored, and many of the most obvious precautions
neglected.   None of the painters engaged in it had then

any practical knowledge of the art of mural painting, nor do they seem to have thought that any kind of colour could not be applied to any kind of surface. The tradition of the art of fresco painting was then so wholly lost that paintings in distemper on a naked wall were commonly spoken of as frescoes, and were expected to last as a fresco painting would. The walls were newly built, and the mortar still damp. Each of the spaces to be painted over was pierced by two circular windows, and the effect on the design as well as on the lighting of the pictures may be imagined. No ground whatever was laid over the brickwork except a coat of whitewash: and on this the colour was to be laid with a small brush, like water-colour on paper.

Morris set to work with his usual energy. Before either of the others had made a design, he was in Oxford and had begun his painting. Presently Rossetti and Burne-Jones joined him there, and for the rest of the vacation they lived together in lodgings in the High Street, in a house now pulled down to make room for the new Schools. The other four painters came later, and the work, at first carried on with happy diligence through long hours day after day, became more intermittent as winter advanced, and trailed on into the following spring. Morris's was the first picture finished as it had been the first begun. The subject was one for which he felt a singular and almost a morbid attraction, that of the unsuccessful man and despised lover. The motive was the same which he had treated in prose a year before in the Oxford and Cambridge Magazine with many details which were directly taken from his own life. It was entitled " How Sir Palomydes loved La Belle Iseult with exceeding great love out of measure, and how she loved not him again but rather Sir Tristram." All of it that now traceably survives is the faded gleam of sunflowers with which part of the foreground was covered. On the profusion of these sunflowers Rossetti was a little sarcastic, and suggested that he should help another of the painters out of difficulties by filling up the foreground of that bay with scarlet-runners. But no sooner had Morris finished his picture than he set to work with fresh animation and with triumphant success on the decoration of the roof. The design for this was made in a single day, and surprised all the rest of the painters by its singular beauty and fitness. All the rest of the autumn he was working on the roof high over the heads of the others, carrying out the greater part of the decoration with his own hands. But Faulkner, now Fellow and Mathematical Tutor of University, came pretty regularly in the afternoons to help. "Charley comes out tremendously strong on the roof with all kinds of quaint beasts and birds," Burne-Jones wrote home in October. After term began, Price and others were impressed to assist as they came up. "I worked with him," Canon Dixon tells me, "on his picture of the famous sunflowers for several days, and was pleased to hear him say that it was improved." The day's work began at eight o'clock and went on as long as daylight lasted. "If we needed models," Sir Edward Burne-Jones writes, "we sat to each other, and Morris had a head always fit for Lancelot or Tristram. For the purposes of our drawing we often needed armour, and of a date and design so remote that no examples existed for our use. Therefore Morris, whose knowledge of all these things seemed to have been born in him, and who never at any time needed books of reference for anything, set to work to make designs for an ancient kind of helmet called a basinet, and for a great surcoat of ringed mail with a hood of mail and the skirt coming below the knees. These were made for him by a stout little smith who had a forge near the Castle. Morris's visits to the forge were daily, but what scenes happened there we shall never know; the encounters between these two workmen were always stubborn and angry as far as I could see. One afternoon when I was working high up at my picture, I heard a strange bellowing in the building, and turning round to find the cause, saw an unwonted sight. The basinet was being tried on, but the visor, for some reason, would not lift, and I saw Morris embedded in iron, dancing with rage and roaring inside. The mail coat came in due time, and was so satisfactory to its designer that the first day it came he chose to dine in it. It became him well; he looked very splendid. When it lay in coils on the ground, one could lift it with great difficulty, but once put on the body its weight was so evenly ordered that it was less uncomfortable than any top coat I ever wore. I have the basinet still, and the sword that was made by the same smith."

The decoration of the roof was finished early in November. But Morris did not leave Oxford, and for the next year or more lived chiefly there, in the rooms at 17, George Street, which the painters had taken when they had to turn out of their lodgings in High Street at the beginning of the autumn term. Burne-Jones, when he had finished his picture of " The Death of Merlin," returned to Red Lion Square, where he lived practically alone till spring, though his visits to Oxford and Morris's to London were almost weekly.

The decoration of the Union involves so many famous names, and is in itself of such interest as one of the earliest attempts of the sort made in modern times, that a brief digression may be pardonable to set down the rest of the story. From the first, there was a feeling among many members of the Union that the scheme had been rushed on them by Rossetti and Woodward.

The latter, "the stillest creature that ever breathed out
of an oyster shell," as Rossetti called him, had apparently
been talked over by Rossetti into allowing the work to
be begun without obtaining proper sanction. The question was raised at a debate on the 26th of October, 1857,
when the Treasurer, Charles Bowen of Balliol (afterwards
Lord Bowen), admitted that an irregularity had been
committed, and the subject was allowed to drop. A
week later, however, a motion was carried unanimously
"thanking the gentlemen who had kindly and liberally
undertaken to decorate the new building, and expressing
appreciation of the valuable works of art in course of
completion." The names mentioned specially were those
of Rossetti and Hughes, "with some of their friends."
Later in term all the seven painters engaged on the work,
together with Alexander Munro the sculptor, who was
executing a relief in stone, from Rossetti's design, for the
tympanum over the doorway, were elected honorary members, and a loan of £350 was sanctioned to meet the
expense of the work. By the following spring six of
the pictures had been completed: the seventh, Rossetti's
own, "Sir Lancelot's Vision of the Sangrail," had been
broken off when he was called to London by the dangerous illness of Miss Siddal, and was never resumed by him.
Even in its unfinished condition it was by far the finest
and most masterly of the series. "It belonged," says
Sir Edward Burne-Jones, "to the best time and highest
character of his work." In this design, Lancelot lay
asleep against a well on the right hand of the picture:
the Vision of the Grail carried by angels moved along
opposite him; and in the centre, a phantom Guenevere
stood with outstretched arms in front of an apple tree.
The figures are perished quite beyond recognition: but
a drawing made for that of the sleeping Lancelot is one
of the earliest portraits of Burne-Jones. The other two

pictures which Rossetti had designed had for subjects
" Lancelot found in Guenevere's Chamber " and " The
Three Knights of the Sangrail." A pen and ink sketch of
the former, dated 1857, is in the possession of Mr. C. F.
Murray. The small water-colour of the latter, painted
several years afterwards and now in Mr. Heaton's collection, perhaps gives a better idea than anything else of
the method used in the Union paintings, and also of the
extraordinary brilliance of the colouring, nearly all in
radiant greens and reds and blues. But the execution
of these two pictures was never even begun; and after
March, 1858, no more work was done either by Rossetti
or by any other of the artists engaged. A committee then
appointed, after certain communications with Rossetti, of
which no record is preserved, took the matter into their
own hands, and in June, 1859, Mr. William Riviere, the
father of the well-known Academician, who had just left
Cheltenham to become a teacher of painting in Oxford,
was engaged to fill the three vacant bays, and a sum of
£150 voted for his payment.

The impossible conditions under which the work was
performed have already been mentioned. The brickwork
on which the painting was executed was not damp-proof ;
the edges of the bricks caught all the floating dust; the
colour partly sank in and partly flaked off; and to crown
the whole, the hall was lit by naked gas-flames in large
chandeliers, the smoke and heat of which went straight
up on to the painting. William Bell Scott, who went
to see them in June, 1858, when they had not been six
months completed, speaks of them as being even then
much defaced, in Morris's own picture little else appearing
plainly but Tristram's head over a row of sunflowers.
This state of things went on from bad to worse. In
1869, a committee of the Union was appointed " to
enquire into, and report upon, the history, condition,

and treatment of the paintings," which are still obstinately described as frescoes. Inconclusive negotiations
went on with Rossetti for about two years on the
question of completing his unfinished picture; as regards
the rest of the work, though a suggestion to whitewash
it all over was dropped, and another, to replace it by
Morris's then celebrated pomegranate wall-paper, was not
carried, the only point on which the opinion of the
Society was unanimous was that no more money should
be spent. Rossetti took very justifiable offence at a
pamphlet—anonymous, but of well-known authorship—
the effect of which had been to defeat a motion em-
powering expense to be incurred in cleaning and repairing
the paintings; he refused point blank to have anything
further to do with the affair: and the fresco committee
was ultimately dissolved without anything being done.
By the kindness of Mr. J. R. Thursfield, who was chairman of the fresco committee, I am enabled to give a
letter which Morris wrote to him soon after the committee was appointed. It will be noticed that separate
negotiations were going on with Rossetti about his
picture, and that the letter therefore refers only to the
other six of the original seven. The letter is undated,
and written from Queen Square.

        "Dear Sir,
            "I am sorry you are in trouble about the works
at the Union, and hope I shan't increase it by my letter:
I can speak distinctly about two of the pictures in
question, Mr. Hughes', the one at the North end,
and Mr. Burne-Jones' (Nimue and Merlin). Of these
I think the design of Mr. Hughes to be quite among the
best works of that painter, and a very beautiful and remarkable one: I think I have been told it is in a bad
state; but I suppose something might be done to it.

Mr. Burne-Jones' is a beautiful work, and admirably suits its space as to decoration; it would be quite absurd to cover it up. Mr. Pollen's, opposite Mr. Hughes', was never finished; two others, one by Mr. Prinsep, another by Mr. Stanhope, though not very complete in some ways, yet looked very well in their places I think. As for my own, I believe it *has* some merits as to colour, but I must confess I should feel much more comfortable if it had disappeared from the wall, as I'm conscious of its being extremely ludicrous in many ways. In confidence to you I should say that the whole affair was begun and carried out in too piecemeal and unorganized a manner to be a real success—nevertheless it would surely be a pity to destroy some of the pictures, which are really remarkable, and at the worst can do no harm there. I am sorry if this is 'cold comfort'; but I thought you would really like to know what I thought, and so here it is. I must thank you heartily however for the enthusiasm you have shown in the matter; and I wish I could be of more use to you.

" Yours faithfully,

" WILLIAM MORRIS."

The subject of Hughes's picture was " The Death of Arthur." The others were, " Sir Pelleas and the Lady Ettarde," by Prinsep: " How King Arthur received his sword Excalibur from the Lady of the Lake," by Pollen: and " Sir Gawaine and the three Damsels at the Fountain in the Forest of Arroy," by Stanhope.

The re-decoration of the roof, which was carried out by Morris in 1875, left the wall-paintings below untouched; and they still glimmer faintly in their places, blackened, faded, and peeled, the light here and there falling on some still recognizable feature, a long fold of drapery, a patch of ring armour, or the straight line of a

knight's sword.   The only record of their first fugitive
and fairylike beauty is in an article by Mr. Coventry
Patmore in the Saturday Review for the 26th of December, 1857, which speaks of the colour as " sweet, bright,
and pure as a cloud in the sunrise," and " so brilliant as
to make the walls look like the margin of an illuminated
manuscript."

For Morris, the autumn and winter months of 1857-8
were, in spite of the discouragements caused by his slow
progress in the technique of painting, full of hope and
enthusiasm.   Among his old Oxford friends, Price and
Faulkner especially, he regained something of the old
light-heartedness which life in London and the imperious
domination of Rossetti had begun to impair.   A few
extracts from Price's diary during the autumn term give
a picture of the resumed, but altered, life in Oxford.
Term had begun on the 16th of October.

" Oct. 17.   Breakfasted with Top at Johnson's in
George Street.   Rossetti, Hughes, Prinsep, Ted, and
Coventry Patmore there.   To the Union to see the
frescoes.

" Oct. 18. To Rossetti's—R. painting the Marriage
of St. George.   Prinsep there ; six feet one, 15 stone,
not fat, well-built, hair like finest wire, short, curly and
seamless—age only 19.   Stood for Top for two hours
in a dalmatic.

" Oct. 24. Spent afternoon in daubing in black lines
on the Union roof for Topsy.   Whist in the evening
as usual (at Rossetti's).

" Oct. 30. Evening at George Street.   Rossetti, Ted,
Topsy, Hughes, Swan, Faulkner, Bowen of Balliol,
Bennet of Univ., Munro, Hill, Prinsep and Stanhope
there.   Topsy read his grind on Lancelot and Guenevere
—very grand.

" Oct. 31. Stippled and blacklined at Union.   Evening

at George Street: Rossetti and I versus Top and
Faulkner at whist.   Madox Brown turned up.   Rossetti
said that Topsy had the greatest capacity for producing
and annexing dirt of any man he ever met with.

"Nov. 1. To Hill's, where were Topsy, Ted, Swan,
Hatch, Swinburne of Balliol (introduced I think by
Hatch) and Faulkner."

Several of the names mentioned here are new.   Swan,
a friend of Rossetti's and a man of some amount of
genius which verged on eccentricity, had taken a considerable part in executing the decorations on the Union
roof, his name, together with those of Morris, Faulkner,
and St. John Tyrwhitt of Christ Church, being inscribed
on one of the rafters as the artificers.   It is recorded
that up in the dark angles of the roof they sometimes
painted, instead of flowers, little figures of Morris with
his legs straddling out like the portraits of Henry VIII. :
for the slim young man of the previous year was now
not only, in a charming phrase used of him at the
time by Burne-Jones, " unnaturally and unnecessarily
curly," but growing fat.   Bowen, who as Treasurer
of the Union had been primarily responsible for accepting the suggested decoration, gave it afterwards,
as President, his untiring support.   Hill is the well-
known editor of Boswell's " Johnson," who, though a
little junior to the " set," had been closely connected
with it.   Bennet had been Treasurer of the Union just
before Bowen, and succeeded him in the Presidency in
the following year.   Swinburne had come up to Balliol
in January, 1856; the acquaintance now formed with
Morris at Oxford ripened into intimacy in London a few
years later.   He had already written a long poem on
Iseult Blanchemains, and their common enthusiasm for
Malory and the Arthurian legend drew them together.
Swinburne was among the most fervid admirers of

Morris's early poetry, on which he lavished all the habitual generosity of his praise.

The Bohemian life in London had by this time raised Morris's unconventionality, which had always been extreme, to a still more excessive height. To wear long hair, and a soft felt hat, and to smoke a pipe in season and out of season, was still, as in the earlier days of Clive Newcome, the mark of an artist. But Morris exceeded even the customary licence of Gandish's. "Morris went to Jones's on Sunday night," runs a note in Miss Price's diary, " while they were here ; and his hair was so long and he looked so wild that the servant who opened the door would not let him in, thinking he was a burglar." He forswore dress clothes, and there is a ludicrous story of his ineffectual attempt to get into Hughes's evening trousers when he was going to dine at high table in Christ Church. To go into society was torture to him, and he never took pains to conceal it. One of the tribulations of these months was the task, equally hard in either case, of evading or accepting the invitations of Dr. Henry Acland, whose intimacy with Ruskin and appreciation of the Pre-Raphaelite school led him to offer constant hospitality to the young painters. Once, when they were to dine with Dr. Acland, Morris invented an illness and sent his apologies by Burne-Jones. Unfortunately, Burne-Jones arrived with this message when there still wanted a few minutes to dinner-time. Acland, who was all kindness, instantly, to Burne-Jones's infinite dismay, put on his hat and went round to see the sick man in his lodgings : he was found, apparently in the best of health and spirits, sitting at dinner with Faulkner and playing cribbage over the meal. He had to confess recovery, and be led off to dinner. Another story of the same period is equally characteristic. At dinner one evening in George Street, Prinsep said some-

thing, whether intentionally or not, which offended
Morris. Every one expected an outburst of fury. But
by a prodigious effort of self-control Morris swallowed
his anger, and only bit his fork—one of the common
four-pronged fiddle-pattern kind—which was crushed
and twisted about almost beyond recognition. During
these months, too, he was feeling his way in other arts
and handicrafts: carving a block of freestone into a
capital of foliage and birds, done with great spirit and
life, Mr. Arthur Hughes says ; drawing and colouring
designs for stained-glass windows ; and modelling from
the life in clay. Price sat to him for a clay head which
he was modelling; it was never finished, because whenever Morris grew impatient he flew at it and smashed it
up. In carving the stone block he struck a splinter
into his own eye ; and his language to Dr. Acland, who
was called in to look after the injury, was even for him
unequalled in its force and copiousness. About the
same time he was making his first experiments in reviving
the decayed art of embroidery. He had a frame made
from an old pattern, and worsteds specially dyed for
him by an old French dyer. He worked at this till he
had mastered the principles of laying and radiating the
stitches so as to cover the ground closely and smoothly.
A piece of work he began then with a bird and tree pattern
embroidered on it is still in existence. In these months
also were written a number of the finest of the poems
published, early in 1858, in Morris's first volume, "The
Defence of Guenevere and other Poems."

This volume is so well known that any detailed account
or criticism of its contents would be superfluous. It is
one of those books which, without ever reaching a wide
circulation or a large popularity, have acted with great
intensity on a small circle of minds, and, to those on
whom they struck fully home, given a new colour to the

art of poetry and the whole imaginative aspect of things. On its appearance, it met with no acclamations; it did not even gain the distinction of abuse: it simply went unnoticed. Only two or three contemporary notices of it have been traced. One other, which really showed some appreciation of its unusual qualities, somewhat missed its object by not appearing for eight years. A reviewer in the Athenæum treated it as a mere piece of Pre-Raphaelite eccentricity, "a curiosity which shows how far affectation may mislead an earnest man towards the fog-land of Art."

The volume seems to have had, on the whole, all the usual chances at its entrance into the world. Morris, it is true, was then a bad and an impatient corrector of proofs: the punctuation of the poems is deplorable, and there are a good many serious misprints. But such minute points hardly affect a book's fortunes, and in other respects the volume is pleasant-looking, and even handsome. Some two hundred and fifty copies were sold and given away, and the remainder of the edition stayed long on the publishers' shelves. So late as 1871 there were still copies to be had. Even the reprint of 1875, made at the instance of Mr. F. S. Ellis, owed such popularity as it had mainly to its being by the author of "The Earthly Paradise."

But if the value of poetry is to be measured (to use the phrase of the logicians) in intension, few volumes have a more marked place in modern literature. Mr. Swinburne's just and tempered language as to the reception of "The Defence of Guenevere" hardly needs to be supplemented. "Here and there," he wrote of it when Morris had leaped into fame and even popularity with the appearance of "Jason," "it met with eager recognition and earnest applause; nowhere, if I err not, with just praise or blame worth heeding. It seems to have been now lauded and now decried as the result and expression of a school rather than a man, of a theory or tradition rather than a poet or student. Those who so judged were blind guides. Such things as were in this book are taught and learnt in no school but that of instinct. Upon no piece of work in the world was the impress of native character ever more distinctly stamped, more deeply branded. It needed no exceptional acuteness of ear or eye to see or hear that this poet held of none, stole from none, clung to none, as tenant, or as beggar, or as thief. Not yet a master, he was assuredly no longer a pupil."

It is of the four Arthurian poems which stand at the beginning of the volume that Mr. Swinburne more specially speaks, and these to many readers are no doubt the flower of the whole. One can well imagine with what hushed admiration, with what a shock and surprise of emotion, that little gathering at George Street, on the 30th of October, 1857, heard, for the first time, "King Arthur's Tomb." Here again Mr. Swinburne's words are the final ones: "There is scarcely connection here, and scarcely composition. There is hardly a trace of narrative power or mechanical arrangement. There is a perceptible want of tact and practice, which leaves the poem in parts indecorous and chaotic. But where among other and older poets of his time and country is one comparable for perception and experience of tragic truth, of subtle and noble, terrible and piteous things? where a touch of passion at once so broad and so sure?"

Mr. J. W. Hoole, the son of a neighbour of the Morrises in Essex, who was then an undergraduate at Queen's, contributes a curious remark that Morris made with regard to these Arthurian poems. "He took me across to his lodgings opposite Queen's College and read me 'The Defence of Guenevere,' before it was printed. On my enquiring—with not very good taste to an original poet—in whose style the poem was written, he answered 'More like Browning than any one else, I suppose.'" This may at first seem a lightly-uttered fancy; but the more one thinks over it, the more is one struck with its truth. The author of "The Defence of Guenevere" approaches poetry from the same side, one may so put it, as the author of "Men and Women." What both alike aim at and attain is the realization, keen, swift, and minute, of some tragic event or situation, and the expression with absolute sincerity of that exact event or situation precisely as thus realized and no further, disregarding conventions of poetical treatment, and too eager to pause over finesse of workmanship. The affinity is perhaps closer, as it is more evident, in the other group of poems, constituting about half the volume, which are suggested more or less directly by Froissart, as the Arthurian poems are by Malory. They might aptly be headed Dramatic Lyrics and Dramatic Romances of the fourteenth century. The range is much less than Browning's; but the intensity of realization is even greater, and it is free from the slightest trace of parade or pedantry. For to Morris the Middle Ages, out of which he sometimes seemed to have strayed by some accident into the nineteenth century, were his habitual environment: he lived in them as really and as simply as if he had been translated back to them in actual vision. The Little Tower and the Haystack in the Floods are as clearly before his eyes as if the riding of the knights had gone by but a day before: the talk of Sir Peter Harpdon and his man seems transcribed from memory. It is this amazing power of realization, when he is dealing with his own period, that gives to the masterpiece of his later years, "The Dream of John Ball," so vivid a colour and truth; it is the want of it, when he

is off that ground, that leaves him open to the accusation
of being mannered or languid when he deals with a story
which is either not mediæval or not treated in a frankly
mediæval spirit.

Browning himself, it may not be without interest to
know, was one of the earliest and the most enthusiastic
admirers of this volume. " It has been my delight," he
said of it many years afterwards, " ever since I read it."
When the first volume of " The Earthly Paradise " was
published, he wrote to Morris a letter of warm and
finely-appreciative praise. " It is a double delight to
me," he added, " to read such poetry, and know you of
all the world wrote it,—you whose songs I used to sing
while galloping by Fiesole in old days,—' Ho, is there
any will ride with me?' "

Between the charm of the Malory poems and that of
the Froissart poems the choice is one of personal feeling.
But the part of the volume which one gathers to represent
its spirit and form most intimately to many lovers of
poetry, is neither of these. It consists of the poems of
a wholly unbased and fantastic romance, in which any
traceable poetical influence is that of Poe rather than
of Browning. Their very names—such names as " The
Blue Closet," or " The Sailing of the Sword," or " Two
Red Roses across the Moon"—are taken straight out of
dreamland. It is these poems on which the unjust
praise and the blame not worth heeding which the
volume drew on itself were primarily spent. They
lend themselves alike to the purposes of the *précieux*
and the parodist. Never perhaps has poetry come
nearer to what some theorists have laid down as its goal,
the emotional effect of music, than in some of these
remarkable pieces—"The Wind," "Spellbound," "Near
Avalon." Even now, to those to whom they have been
long familiar, their faint beauty comes back, ever and

again, like a fugitive and haunting scent, or the vague trouble of a dream remembered in a dream.

It was part, and a very necessary part, of the Pre-Raphaelite creed to disregard both neglect and criticism: and Morris, of all persons in the world, was one who was only happy in his own content, and over whom the opinions of others slipped without leaving much impression. For professional literary criticism, beyond all, his feeling was something between amusement and contempt. "To think of a beggar making a living by selling his opinion about other people!" he characteristically said: "and fancy any one paying him for it!" he added, in a climax of scorn. Yet an author's first book, and more so if it be a book of poems, is a thing by itself: and it would seem that the little notice the volume met with united with other causes to make him for a time stop writing poetry. In the few months before its publication he had been producing very fast, and with a swift growth in range of manner and power of expression. The turbid quality which weakens, or even disfigures, so many of the earlier poems was daily running clearer. "King Arthur's Tomb," "The Eve of Crecy," "Praise of my Lady," all written in these months, sound a chord of imaginative beauty such as Tennyson himself, at the same age, had not surpassed. The mixed lyric and dramatic method invented by him for "Sir Peter Harpdon's End," with its odd and fascinating use of blank verse, had in it all kinds of possibilities. He had already planned, and begun to write, a cycle of poems in this form on subjects from the War of Troy. There are a few surviving fragments of "The Maying of Guenevere," the opening piece of an Arthurian cycle which would have ended with "King Arthur's Tomb," and in which, it has been thought, he would have found his most real inspiration. Tennyson's "Morte d'Arthur" still stood alone, an inimitable fragment; it was not till 1859 that the first of "The Idyls of the King" were published. After that, the treatment of the story in a different, even if a simpler and sincerer manner, was almost precluded by the imposing brilliance of the Tennysonian version, and its remarkable conquest of both critical approval and popular fame. But now this, and all other poetry, was laid aside; and when Morris laid a thing aside, he did so with the same energy with which he had taken it up. "It is to be regretted," says Canon Dixon, speaking as one who has remained faithful to the earlier aims and ideals of Morris's art, "that he did so. He could have produced more of the same sort then. When he afterwards took up poetry again, he could not do it. His 'Jason' was better than his 'Earthly Paradise,' but the first flavour was gone from them both."

"The Defence of Guenevere" was published in March. About the same time Burne-Jones, left much alone in Red Lion Square since the beginning of the year, had fallen rather dangerously ill, and was carried off by Mrs. Prinsep, the kind friend of all artists, to Little Holland House, to be taken care of and nursed back to health. He stayed there during a great part of the year. There was, therefore, no permanent companion for Morris in Red Lion Square; and though it remained his London lodging, much the greater part of the year was spent by him at Oxford, either in his rooms in the city or at Summertown with the Maclarens. There he went on painting hard, but with continued dissatisfaction. He even sold a picture for the considerable sum of £70 to Mr. Plint of Leeds. The negotiation was conducted by Rossetti, who loved making bargains for his friends as well as for himself. This picture, which has now, after many wanderings, returned to the possession of his family, is believed to be the only finished easel-painting by Morris certainly

known to exist.   It was exhibited in London at the New
Gallery in January, 1898.

There was, however, a further and a stronger reason
for his prolonged stay at Oxford.   Towards the end of
the Long Vacation of 1857, Rossetti and Burne-Jones,
who had gone, after a day's work at the Union, to the
little Oxford theatre, found sitting just behind them two
girls, daughters of Mr. Robert Burden, of Holywell
Street. The elder attracted their attention at once by her
remarkable beauty, of a type not common in England, and
specially admired by Rossetti. They made her acquaintance ; and after some little negotiation she was persuaded
to sit to him and his friends, and continued to do so while
the work at the Union was going on. With Morris the
attraction went deeper, and soon after his volume of poems
appeared they became engaged. Only a few flitting notices
can be gathered of his life, or thoughts, or occupations,
during this summer and the following winter. Sometimes there are traces of him at his mother's new house
at Leyton, sometimes in London at Red Lion Square,
or at Little Holland House, drawing from a tree that
overhung a pond in the garden—pond, tree, and garden
now long vanished; sometimes painting in the Maclarens'
orchard at Summertown, where the holes he dug in the
grass by wriggling his chair about as he sat at his easel,
and the force of his language when a gust of wind blew
the canvas off wet side down, were long remembered;
or reading aloud interminably to the group of friends
assembled there from Froissart and Monstrelet and
Malory's " Morte d'Arthur."   In August he was once
more in Northern France, and rowed down the Seine
from Paris—then an unusual and adventurous thing
to do—with Faulkner and Webb.   An Oxford boat
had been sent over from Bossom's to Paris, where it
arrived with a large hole in its bottom.   The mending

of the boat, and the start from the Quai du Louvre amid the satire of the populace, as the three English-men embarked with three carpet bags and half-a-dozen bottles of wine for their luggage, were the beginnings of an almost epic voyage. During this trip the plan of building himself a house was discussed between him and Webb, and on their return there was much travelling about to look at possible sites for it. In the late autumn there are references to an illness, cheerfully attributed by his friends to his eating and drinking too much, or rather to his being quite careless (as he remained always) of what he ate and drank. In October he was in France again, "to buy old manuscripts and armour and iron-work and enamel." The instability which he found, or thought he found, in his own character became for a time acute. The overstrain of the crowded years through which he had been passing, with all their inward revolu-tions, all their pangs of growth and fevers of imagination, had left him, like some lover in one of his own poems, languid and subject to strange fluctuations of mood. In a curious and illuminating phrase used by one of his friends in writing about him some little time before, " he has lately taken a strong fancy for the human." One thing at all events became more and more certain, that the external impulse under which he had become a painter had exhausted its force. A new kind of life opened out vaguely before him, in which that "small Palace of Art of my own," long ago recognized by him as one of his besetting dreams, was now peopled with the forms of wife and children, and contracted to the limits of some actual home, in which life and its central purposes need not be thwarted by any baseness or ugliness of immediate surroundings: an undertaking for a lifetime, and much more than a lifetime, as it turned out, but then certainly conceived as possible.

On Tuesday the 26th of April, 1859, William Morris and Jane Burden were married in the little ancient parish church of St. Michael's in Oxford; he was then just five and twenty. Dixon, who had by this time taken Orders and was curate of St. Mary's, Lambeth, came down to perform the ceremony; Faulkner was best man; and Burne-Jones and a few more of the old Oxford set were there. It was the last scene in the Oxford life of the Brotherhood.

CHAPTER V

AFTER a six weeks' tour to Paris, Belgium, and the
Rhine, as far as Basle, Mr. and Mrs. Morris returned
to London, to furnished rooms at 41, Great Ormond
Street, where they lived while their own house was being
built. The establishment at Red Lion Square was
finally broken up, Burne-Jones going into lodgings of
his own in Charlotte Street. Webb had just left Street's
office to set up as an architect on his own account, and
the building of the new house was placed in his hands.
The house was to be a proving piece. In it the theories
of its owner and its architect on domestic building and
decoration were to be worked out in practice: and the
scheme and details were the joint invention of the two.
The notion of building a house after his own fancy was
one which had already been in Morris's mind for a considerable time. He wanted it not merely as a place to
live in, but as a fixed centre and background for his
artistic work. He hated designing in the air, without
relation to a definite material and a particular purpose.
While his whole work as a decorative manufacturer
may be not untruly said to have sprung directly out of
the building and furnishing of this house, it would be
almost equally true to say that the house, first in idea
and then in fact, sprung out of his devoting himself to
the practice of decorative art and requiring, as one

might say, a canvas to work upon. When his approaching marriage made a home of some sort, other than London or Oxford lodgings, a necessity, the building of the house followed as a matter of course

It was to be in the country, and by preference not far from London, though as to this he was really indifferent. The great network of suburban railways had then hardly begun to exist, and the spot finally fixed upon, though little more than ten miles from London by road, was about three miles from the nearest station, that at Abbey Wood on the North Kent Line. From the Plumstead marshes, along the inner edge of which this railway runs, a steep ascent leads southward through wooded slopes to a gently undulating country, intersected by the great high road from London to Dover, the ancient Watling Street. On the part of this plateau known as Bexley Heath, close to the little village of Upton, Morris had bought an orchard and meadow, and it was settled to build the house in the orchard so that it should have apple and cherry trees all round it from the first. Three or four labourers' cottages close by were locally known as Hog's Hole; the discovery of this name affording unspeakable and lasting satisfaction to Rossetti. The district, even when less built over than it is now, was not one of any remarkable charm: it had something of the sadness of that common English lowland country of which Morris was so fond; but was fertile, well wooded and watered, and interspersed with pleasant orchards and coppices.

What Morris required in a country was that it should be open and fertile, and have in it some central and distinguishing natural feature of hill or river. In the normal English landscape, " so rich and so limited, no big hill, no wide river to lead one's thoughts or hopes along," and everywhere inclosed, he felt a sense of imprisonment.

The wide arid heaths of Surrey and the close rich Devonshire valleys were alike distasteful to him ; he set his own plain and rather ugly Essex country far before either.   But, till he went to live on the upper Thames, Kent was probably his favourite county ; and he may have pleased himself with the notion of living close to the track of the Canterbury pilgrims, the *vena porta* of mediæval England.   Just below him lay the little valley of the Cray, beaded with its string of villages ; and further off, but within an easy walk, the beautiful valley of the Darenth.   At Abbey Farm were the remains of an Augustinian Priory, one of those suppressed by Wolsey in order to found his great college at Oxford. The particular spot, however, was very much chosen because the orchard seemed to suit his requirements as nearly as possible.   It was one of a number of places advertised for sale which he had looked at in the previous summer.

The reaction from early Victorian stucco had just begun to set in, but had not yet begun to produce any visible effect over the country.   Nowadays, when the red brick of the common modern country house is to be seen on every roadside, this, the first house that Webb built, might be passed without any remark by a casual traveller.   But Mr. Norman Shaw was then a clerk in Street's office ; stucco and slate still reigned supreme in all districts where stone was not the native building material ; and the name of Red House given to the new building was sufficient to describe it without ambiguity to all the neighbourhood.   Its planning was as original as its material.   The type of house which Morris was fond of describing as a square box with a lid was completely abandoned : it was planned as an L-shaped building, two-storied, with a high-pitched roof of red tile.   The beautiful oak staircase filled a bold projection in the angle, and corridors ran from it along both the inner walls, so that the rooms on both limbs of the house faced outward on to the garden.   The two other sides of this half-quadrangle were masked by rose-trellises, inclosing a square inner court, in the middle of which rose the most striking architectural feature of the building, a well-house of brickwork and oak timber, with a steep conical tiled roof.   Externally the house was plain almost to severity, and depended for its effect on its solidity and fine proportion.   The decorative features it possessed were constructional, not of the nature of applied ornament : the frankly emphasized relieving arches over the windows, the deep cornice moulding, the louvre in the high open roof over the staircase, and the two spacious recessed porches.   Inside, its most remark-able feature was the large drawing-room, which filled the external angle of the L on the upper floor.   It looked by its main end window northwards towards the road and the open country ; and a projecting oriel in the western side overlooked the long bowling green, which ran, encircled with apple trees, close under the length of that wing.   The decoration of this room, and of the staircase by which it was reached, was to be the work of several years for Morris and his friends : and he boldly announced that he meant to make it the most beautiful room in England.   But through the whole house, inside and out, the same ideal standard was, so far as possible, to be kept up.

It was at this point that the problem of decoration began.   The bricklaying and carpentering could be exe-cuted directly from the architect's designs.   But when the shell of the house was completed, and stood clean and bare among its apple trees, everything, or nearly every-thing, that was to furnish or decorate it had to be like-wise designed and made.   Only in a few isolated cases

RED HOUSE, UPTON.

—such as Persian carpets, and blue china or delft for vessels of household use—was there anything then to be bought ready-made that Morris could be content with in his own house. Not a chair, or table, or bed; not a cloth or paper hanging for the walls; nor tiles to line fireplaces or passages; nor a curtain or a candlestick; nor a jug to hold wine or a glass to drink it out of, but had to be reinvented, one might almost say, to escape the flat ugliness of the current article. The great painted settle from Red Lion Square was taken and set up in the drawing-room, the top of it being railed in so as to form a small music gallery. Much of the furniture was specially designed by Webb and executed under his eye: the great oak dining-table, other tables, chairs, cupboards, massive copper candlesticks, fire-dogs, and table glass of extreme beauty. The plastered walls and ceilings were treated with simple designs in tempera, and for the hall and main living rooms a richer and more elaborate scheme of decoration was designed and gradually began to be executed. The garden was planned with the same care and originality as the house; in both alike the study of older models never sank into mere antiquarianism or imitation of obsolete forms. Morris's knowledge of architecture was so entirely a part of himself that he never seemed to think about it as anything peculiar. But in his knowledge of gardening he did, and did with reason, pride himself. It is very doubtful whether he was ever seen with a spade in his hands; in later years at Kelmscott his manual work in the garden was almost limited to clipping his yew hedges. But of flowers and vegetables and fruit trees he knew all the ways and capabilities. Red House garden, with its long grass walks, its midsummer lilies and autumn sunflowers, its wattled rose-trellises inclosing richly-flowered square garden plots, was then as unique as the house it surrounded. The building had been planned with such care that hardly a tree in the orchard had to be cut down; apples fell in at the windows as they stood open on hot autumn nights.

Red House was sufficiently advanced for occupation towards the end of the summer of 1860. It was meant to be a permanent home. Circumstances then unforeseen obliged him to leave it after only five years, while it was still growing in beauty. But the five years spent there were probably the happiest and not the least fruitful of his life.

The difficulty of furnishing the house when built was one that demanded some more practical solution than that of getting each article singly and laboriously manufactured, even had it been easier than it was to find manufacturers who would accept such orders. Instances like that of Messrs. Powell, the great glass-makers in Whitefriars, who were receptive of new ideas and really eager to produce beautiful objects, were of the rarest occurrence; the ordinary manufacturer, like the ordinary purchaser, looked at any beautiful design with a feeling compounded of fear, apathy, and contempt. Meanwhile Morris's apprenticeship to the arts of building and painting, with their subsidiary industries, had fully kindled his inborn instinct for handicraft: from the mood of idleness into which he had for a short time fallen he plunged back into the mood of energy, and his brain and fingers tingled to be at work. The eagerness of the maker, the joy of craftsmanship, had come to him, and came to stay. So it was that in half-unconscious adaptation to the conditions of modern life, the monastery of his Oxford dreams rose into being as a workshop, and the Brotherhood became a firm registered under the Companies Acts.

The first notion of the firm of Morris & Company, the name and wares of which have since become so widely spread, sprang up among the friends in talk, and cannot be assigned to any single author. It was in a large measure due to Madox Brown; but perhaps even more to Rossetti, who, poet and idealist as he was, had business qualities of a high order, and the eye of the trained financier for anything that had money in it. To Morris himself, who had not yet been forced by business experience into being a business man, the firm probably meant little more than a definite agreement for co-operation and common work among friends who were also artists. The directions in which it turned its energies were to be determined, primarily, by the things which he wanted to make or to have made for his own private use, and then by the requirements, towards the purposes of their own professional work, of the rest of his associates. Of these associates Burne-Jones and Madox Brown were already regularly employed in making designs for stained glass, mainly, of course, for church windows. Webb was not only an architect, but a designer of the smaller work which is usually separate from that of the architect, or only taken up by him as by-play; a master of proportion and ornament, whether applied to the larger masses of architecture or to such things as tables and chairs and lamps. Faulkner, deeply bitten with the enthusiasms of his friends, and unable to bear the loneliness of Oxford now that all the rest were gone, had resigned the mathematical tutorship which he held together with his Fellowship at University, and had come to London to learn the business of a civil engineer. As a man with a head for figures, who could keep the accounts of the business, he was a valuable associate; and though he had no gift of design, he contributed a good deal of work as a craftsman. He helped in executing mural decorations; he painted pattern-tiles, and figure-tiles on which the design had been drawn by a more skilled hand; and he even, in March, 1862, successfully cut a wood-block, on which Rossetti had drawn the well-known illustration for his sister's poem of "Goblin Market."

Church decoration was at first the main employment of the new firm. It was just at that time rising into the rank of an important industry. Jowett, writing to a friend in 1865, remarks that "Muscular Christianity is gone out," and notices, as a prominent sign of the times, the æsthetico-Catholic revival going on in the London churches. But that movement had sprung up some years earlier, while the school of Kingsley and Maurice was still living and powerful. A large section of the neo-Catholic party, abandoning the exhausted battlefields of theology, had turned from theory to practice and from the fourth to the thirteenth century. Their earlier campaign had been among the clergy; and there they had won a decided, though in itself a barren, victory. Now with fresh ardour and with more practical sagacity, they flung themselves into the task of winning over the laity. Plain men and women, to whom primitive tradition and apostolical succession were tiresome or meaningless sounds, could appreciate the sensible beauty of Anglo-Catholic ritual. In the building of new, and the re-decoration of old, churches, there was a demand for glass, tiles, altar-cloths, and every sort of furnishing, which was but feebly met by the established producers of upholsterer's Gothic. Through the architects Street and Bodley the newly-formed company had at once work of this sort put in their hands. The Rev. A. H. Mackonochie, curate-in-charge of St. Alban's, Holborn, whose name became so notorious a few years later in connexion with questions of the mixed chalice and altar lights, was one of the firm's earliest customers. St. Alban's was being built in 1862, and after its consecration in February, 1863, much remained to be done to it in the way of decoration. But their first commissions, and the principal pieces of their first year's business, were for the decoration of two new churches which were being built by Bodley, those of St. Martin's, Scarborough, and St. Michael's, Brighton. In the latter, the chancel-roof was painted by Morris, Webb, and Faulkner, with their own hands: and the windows were executed from designs by Madox Brown and Burne-Jones.

This typical instance of co-operation shows obvious reasons for the inclusion in the firm of the five members named. As for Rossetti, he contributed a few designs for both glass and tiles; but if asked why he had become a partner in a manufacturing firm, he might have, with some truth, given the reply, *Quia nominor leo*: he was looked up to by the younger men as their master mind, and they would hardly have thought of starting any new scheme without him. The seventh member of the company, Mr. Peter Paul Marshall, was a friend of Madox Brown's, by profession a surveyor and sanitary engineer at Tottenham. He contributed several cartoons for glass, and a few designs for furniture and church decoration, but otherwise took little part in the work of the firm. His inclusion was, even at the moment, rather unaccountable. There had been talk of asking others to join, and the matter seems to have been hurried through at the end owing to Morris's excitement and eagerness to get to work. Mr. Arthur Hughes had actually been included as a member, and his name appears in the first prospectus issued by the new firm, but he withdrew from it before it was formally registered. "I was living far off in the country," Mr. Hughes tells me, "while the others were in town, and attending the meetings was inconvenient for me, and also I rather despaired of its establishment, and I wrote asking to be let go. Curiously,

my letter was crossed by one from Morris asking me to
make a design for a portion of a window, and another
for a piece of jewel work. I did the drawing for the
window, and it remains my only contribution."

With the formation, in April, 1861, of the firm of
Morris, Marshall, Faulkner & Co., the old Oxford
Brotherhood, with its ideas of common life and united
action, finally fell asunder. The outer fringe of that
company had already passed into circles and interests of
their own. Fulford and Dixon had taken Orders; Macdonald had gone to America. Price, the only other
member of the inner circle, had, at the end of 1860,
accepted an appointment in Russia, which took him
away from England for three years. Morris, Burne-
Jones, and Faulkner were actually in a minority on
the new association. The Round Table was dissolved
indeed.

Seldom has a business been begun on a smaller capital.
Each of the members held one share, and on the
11th of April the finance of the company began with a
call of £1 per share. On this, and on an unsecured
loan of £100 from Mrs. Morris of Leyton, the first
year's trading was done. Premises were taken from
Lady Day, 1861, at 8, Red Lion Square, a few doors
off Morris's and Burne-Jones's old rooms. The ground
floor of the house was occupied by a working jeweller:
the firm rented the first floor for an office and show
room, and the third floor, with part of the basement, for
workshops. In the basement a small kiln was built, for
firing glass and tiles. As the work grew on their hands,
about a dozen men and boys came to be regularly employed on the premises. The boys were got from a
Boys' Home in the Euston Road; the men chiefly from
Camden Town. The foreman, Mr. George Campfield,
was a glass-painter who had come under Morris's notice

as a pupil at the evening classes of the Working Men's College in Great Ormond Street. He is still in the employment of the firm at Merton Abbey. There were regular weekly meetings of the firm on Wednesday evenings, but otherwise Morris and Faulkner were the only two partners who partook in the active management of the business.

The following letter from Morris to his old tutor, inclosing a copy of the circular announcing the starting of the business, shows that church decoration was what he chiefly looked to for custom. Among the early purchases entered as house expenses in the books of the firm is a Clergy List, and—divided from it only by an entry for fluoric acid—a Vulgate. Work in Bodley's two new churches at Scarborough and Brighton, and in a third, that of Selsley All Saints, near Stroud, was the main business of this year.

"8, Red Lion Square,
"April 19th, 1861.

"My dear Guy,
"By reading the enclosed you will see that I have started as a decorator which I have long meant to do when I could get men of reputation to join me, and to this end mainly I have built my fine house. You see we are, or consider ourselves to be, the only really artistic firm of the kind, the others being only glass painters in point of fact, (like Clayton & Bell) or else that curious nondescript mixture of clerical tailor and decorator that flourishes in Southampton Street, Strand; whereas we shall do—most things. However, what we are most anxious to get at present is wall-decoration, and I want to know if you could be so kind as to send me (without troubling yourself) a list of clergymen and others, to whom it *might* be any use to send a circular.

In about a month we shall have some things to show in these rooms, painted cabinets, embroidery and all the rest of it, and perhaps you could look us up then : I suppose till the holidays you couldn't come down to Red House : I was very much disappointed that you called when I was out before.

> " With kind regards to Mrs. Guy,
> " Believe me
> " Yours very truly
> " WILLIAM MORRIS."

But household furniture and decoration had also been taken in hand. Some of the table glass designed by Webb and executed by Messrs. Powell was the first thing actually sold : and designs of Webb's for furniture and jewellery were also being carried out, the former by Mr. Curwen, a cabinet-maker in the neighbourhood, the latter by the working jeweller on the ground floor at Red Lion Square. The circular referred to lays no stress on the ecclesiastical side of decoration. It is headed " Morris, Marshall, Faulkner & Co., Fine Art Workmen in Painting, Carving, Furniture, and the Metals "; and the eight names of the members (including, as has been explained, that of Mr. Arthur Hughes) follow in alphabetical order.

" The growth of Decorative Art in this country," it proceeds, " owing to the efforts of English Architects, has now reached a point at which it seems desirable that Artists of reputation should devote their time to it. Although no doubt particular instances of success may be cited, still it must be generally felt that attempts of this kind hitherto have been crude and fragmentary. Up to this time, the want of that artistic supervision, which can alone bring about harmony between the various parts of a successful work, has been increased by the necessarily excessive outlay, consequent on taking one individual artist from his pictorial labours.

" The Artists whose names appear above hope by association to do away with this difficulty. Having among their number men of varied qualifications, they will be able to undertake any species of decoration, mural or otherwise, from pictures, properly so called, down to the consideration of the smallest work susceptible of art beauty. It is anticipated that by such co-operation, the largest amount of what is essentially the artist's work, along with his constant supervision, will be secured at the smallest possible expense, while the work done must necessarily be of a much more complete order, than if any single artist were incidentally employed in the usual manner.

" These Artists having for many years been deeply attached to the study of the Decorative Arts of all times and countries, have felt more than most people the want of some one place, where they could either obtain or get produced work of a genuine and beautiful character. They have therefore now established themselves as a firm, for the production, by themselves and under their supervision, of—

I. Mural Decoration, either in Pictures or in Pattern Work, or merely in the arrangement of Colours, as applied to dwelling-houses, churches, or public buildings.

II. Carving generally, as applied to Architecture.

III. Stained Glass, especially with reference to its harmony with Mural Decoration.

IV. Metal Work in all its branches, including Jewellery.

V. Furniture, either depending for its beauty on its own design, on the application of materials hitherto overlooked, or on its conjunction with Figure and Pattern Painting. Under this head is included Embroidery of all kinds, Stamped Leather, and ornamental work in other such materials, besides every article necessary for domestic use.

"It is only requisite to state further, that work of all the above classes will be estimated for, and executed in a business-like manner; and it is believed that good decoration, involving rather the luxury of taste than the luxury of costliness, will be found to be much less expensive than is generally supposed."

In this interesting document it is not difficult to trace the slashing hand and imperious accent of Rossetti, now as always contemptuous of all difficulties and not over-scrupulous in accuracy of statement. The most generous of men towards brother artists, he at once put all young men in whom he saw the elements of genius on an equal footing with himself, and claimed for them the full status and privilege which he and Madox Brown had earned by long years of work. Burne-Jones and Morris had indeed by now established a claim to this equality. But even Faulkner, as their friend, was swept in with the rest as an artist of reputation and a profound student of the decorative arts.

The circular is said, no doubt with truth, to have set up the backs of the established firms of decorators, and the new firm met with some obloquy. But it throve in spite of their jealousy. By the end of the year the business was in full working order, and began to be put under more formal management. In January, 1862, a further call of £19 a share was made on the partners, raising the paid-up capital to £140, which was never increased till the dissolution of the firm in 1874. A few hundred pounds of further capital was supplied by loans, which bore, or were supposed to bear, interest at five per cent., from Morris himself and from his mother. Work done for the firm by any member was credited to his account at fixed rates, and paid for like any other debt. Morris was to receive a salary of £150 as general manager; and in May Faulkner was formally appointed book-keeper and business manager at the same salary.

The weak point of the whole business was the want of anything like real capital. For each piece of work executed a price could be charged, such as customers were found willing to pay, which covered the cost of its production. But the output was slow, the sales uncertain, and there was no reserve to draw upon; the conduct of the work was therefore necessarily from hand to mouth, and had to be guided by the exigencies of the moment. Any extension of the business, however ultimately remunerative, threw its finances off their very unstable equilibrium. In the course of the first three or four years Morris had, bit by bit, advanced all he could to the concern, and was not yet beginning to receive any appreciable returns. This was an anxious time for him, and perhaps the only time in his life when he was really in trouble about money. Once or twice in these early years the accounts showed an actual loss on the year's working. Fortunately his resources did prove sufficient to tide over this period, and thereafter a capital began to form itself out of accumulated profits. But these were in strict law divisible among the partners equally; and the initial fault of the enterprise very nearly led to disastrous results upon the dissolution of the partnership. Morris had yet to learn by unpleasant experiences of more kinds than one the principles on which sound business can be conducted. That he did so, and that while he was doing so he carried the business almost unaided through so crucial a period, was due to a persistency, a sagacity, an unweariable industry, for which he has seldom received adequate credit.

The designing of the work carried out by the firm was of course mainly done by the firm themselves. But other artists, including Albert Moore, William De Morgan, and Simeon Solomon, made occasional designs for glass and tiles; and, as in the days of the Union paintings, every one who could be got hold of was expected to bear a hand. Faulkner's two sisters joined him in painting tiles and pottery. Mrs. Morris and her sister, Miss Burden, with several women working under them, executed embroidery on cloth and silk. Mrs. Burne-Jones, besides embroidering, painted figured tiles. Mrs. Campfield, the foreman's wife, helped to execute altar-cloths. The works became a small whirlpool of industry that sucked in every one who came near them. Morris's own manual labour at every kind of work which the firm undertook was unremitting. Among the various forms of mural decoration started were serge hangings, with figures and floral designs wrought on them in coloured wools. A coarse serge, in quiet but rather dull colours, was supplied by the Yorkshire manfacturers, and served well enough as a ground for the brightly-coloured embroideries. Even this Morris started with his own hands : " Top has taken to worsted work," was Rossetti's sarcastic comment. The payments for work credited to him in 1862 are more than those to all the other six partners put together; and in later years the disproportion increased still further.

At the Exhibition of 1862 the firm had two stalls, one of stained glass, the other, entered in the catalogue as "decorated furniture, tapestries, etc.," representing the beginnings of decorative work in many directions. The so-called tapestries were, of course, embroideries ; it was not till many years later that Morris took up the art of weaving. Among the furniture designed by Webb during this and the following year were specimens of most articles of common domestic use, some large and highly decorated, but the greater number quite plain, and depending for their quality on their simplicity and elegant proportion. The list includes a chest, a book-case, a wardrobe, a sideboard, a washstand, a dressing-table, a towel-horse, a looking-glass, long and round tables, an iron bedstead, table glass, and metal candle-sticks. There were also painted tiles designed by Rossetti, Burne-Jones, Webb, and Morris himself, and a small amount of jewellery. Some of the tiles which were painted with subjects had also upon them verses by the firm's poet, as it amused Morris to describe himself. The work shown at the Exhibition, though from the jury it received only a colourless and vague approbation, attracted much attention, both favourable and adverse. That it really made some impression on the public is shown by the fact that nearly a hundred and fifty pounds' worth of goods were sold from the stalls.

"I perfectly remember," writes Mrs. Richmond Ritchie of a visit to Red Lion Square early in 1862, "going with Val Prinsep one foggy morning to some square, miles away; we came into an empty ground floor room, and Val Prinsep called 'Topsy' very loud, and some one came from above with hair on end and in a nonchalant way began to show one or two of his curious, and to my uninitiated soul, bewildering treasures. I think Morris said the glasses would stand firm when he put them on the table. I bought two tumblers of which Val Prinsep praised the shape. He and Val wrapped them up in paper, and I came away very much amused and interested, with a general impression of sympathetic shyness and shadows and dim green glass."

Chintzes, paper-hangings, and carpets, afterwards the staple products of the firm, were the successive develop-ments of later years. Paper-hangings came first; and it was with them, owing to mere exigencies of space, that the firm was forced to deviate from its first intention of turning out the manufactured article complete from their own doors. The well-known trellis wall-paper was the first designed, the rose trellis by Morris, and the birds in it by Webb. This design was made in November, 1862, and it was at first attempted to print it in oil colours from etched zinc plates. But the process proved very tedious and not satisfactory. It was soon given up, and the design recut on wooden pear-tree blocks, from which the paper was printed, in the ordinary distemper, by Messrs. Jeffreys of Islington. Meanwhile other papers had been designed and cut on wood-blocks; and so it happened that the Daisy paper, still one of the most widely used, was, though not the first designed, the first published and placed upon the market. Once the blocks were cut, the success of the printing depended almost wholly on the care and fidelity of the colour-mixer; and to this Mr. Metford Warner, the managing partner of Messrs. Jeffreys' works, gave real and constant attention.

This first series of Morris wall-papers, the designing of which went on rapidly for several years, culminates in the favourite and beautiful pattern known as the Pomegranate. Beyond it that manner of decorating a surface could not go. When Morris resumed paper-designing, he abandoned the innocence of those formal early designs, and struck out a larger and more mature scheme of pattern. It is the later wall-papers, with their large masses and masterly composition, that are more admirable to the eye of the artist ; but in those simple early patterns there is a charm of straightforward simplicity that appeals more directly to the first childlike instinct for beauty, the sense of form and colour that is undeveloped, but, so far as it reaches, perfectly true.

Some account of the progress of the business during

its first year is given in a letter written by Faulkner to
Price from Red Lion Square in April, 1862.

"Since Christmas, I have certainly been busy enough,
what between the business of engineering, and our business in Red Lion Square.   Moreover, Rossetti, with
remarkable confidence, gave me a wood-block to engrave,
which I with marvellous boldness, not to say impudence,
undertook to do, and by jingo I have done it, and it is
published, and flattering friends say it is not so bad for
a beginning.   Our business in the stained glass and
general decoration line flourishes so successfully that I
have decided to give up engineering and take part in it :
so henceforth, or rather after a week or two, Topsy will
give himself more to the artistic part of the work while
I shall be the business manager.   I don't know whether
you have heard of our firm before from me or any one else.
If not, I may just as well tell you that it is composed of
Brown, Rossetti, Jones, Webb, Marshall, Morris, Faulkner ; that it commenced with a capital which might be
considered an infinitesimal of the second order, that it
has meetings once or twice a fortnight which have rather
the character of a meeting of the ' Jolly Masons ' or the
jolly something elses than of a meeting to discuss business.   Beginning at 8 for 9 p.m. they open with the
relation of anecdotes which have been culled by members
of the firm since the last meeting—this store being exhausted, Topsy and Brown will perhaps discuss the relative
merits of the art of the thirteenth and fifteenth century,
and then perhaps after a few more anecdotes business
matters will come up about 10 or 11 o'clock and be
furiously discussed till 12, 1, or 2.

"Our firm has arrived at the dignity of exhibition at
the great exhibition, where we have already sent some
stained glass, and shall shortly send some furniture
which will doubtless cause the majority of spectators

to admire. The getting ready of our things first has cost more tribulation and swearing to Topsy than three exhibitions will be worth. I am going down to Topsy's this afternoon and shall try to finish this letter there.

" Dear Crom," the letter goes on, " after a delay of about a fortnight I recommence my letter. You see I did not succeed in completing it when staying down at Topsy's : the day was so beautiful and there was so much to do in the way of playing bowls and smoking pipes that the day passed without leaving time to do anything."

Life at Red House in those years was indeed realized felicity for the group of friends to a greater degree than often falls to the lot of schemes deliberately planned for happiness. The garden, skilfully laid out amid the old orchard, had developed its full beauty, and the adornment of the house kept growing into greater and greater elaboration. A scheme had been designed for the mural decoration of the hall, staircase, and drawing-room, upon various parts of which work went on intermittently for several years. The walls of the spacious and finely-proportioned staircase were to be completely covered with paintings in tempera of scenes from the War of Troy, to be designed and executed by Burne-Jones. Below them, on a large wall-space in the hall, was to be a great ship carrying the Greek heroes. It was designed, as the rest of the Troy-series were also to have been, in a frankly mediæval spirit ; a warship indeed of the fourteenth century, with the shields of the kings hung over the bulwarks. Round the drawing-room, at a height of about five feet from the floor, was to be a continuous belt of pictures, the subjects of which were scenes from the fifteenth-century English romance of " Sir Degrevaunt." Three of them were executed by Burne-Jones,

and remain on the walls now.   Below them the wall was
to have been covered with magnificent embroidered
hangings. The principal bedroom was hung with indigo-
dyed blue serge (then a substance which could only be
procured with great difficulty) with a pattern of flowers
worked on it in bright-coloured wools. For the dining-
room embroidered hangings of a much more elaborate
and splendid nature were designed and partly executed,
in a scheme of design like those of his later tapestries
when he revived the art of tapestry-weaving, of twelve
figures with trees between and above them, and a belt of
flowers running below their feet. Yet another hanging,
executed by Morris with his own hands, was of green
trees with gaily-coloured birds among them, and a
running scroll emblazoned with his motto in English,
" If I can."   The same motto in French reappeared in
the painted glass with which a number of the windows
of the house were gradually filled, and on the tiles (also
executed at the works in Red Lion Square) which lined
the deep porches.   In the hall, a second great cupboard
began to be painted with scenes from the Niebelungenlied. There were no paper-hangings in the house. The
rooms that had not painted walls were hung with flower-
embroidered cloth worked from his designs by Mrs.
Morris and other needlewomen. Even the ceilings were
decorated with bold simple patterns in distemper, the
design being pricked into the plaster so as to admit of
the ceiling being re-whitewashed and the decoration
renewed. " Top thrives though bandy," writes Burne-
Jones in February, 1862, "and is slowly making Red
House the beautifullest place on earth."

    Here, as soon as the Morrises moved into it at the
close of the wet summer of 1860, open house was kept
for all their friends. Burne-Jones and his wife—he had
been married that June—spent their Sundays there

almost regularly. Rossetti, Faulkner and his two sisters, Webb, Swinburne, Madox Brown, Arthur Hughes, were also frequent and welcome visitors. Mr. Hughes remembers once riding down from London, and Morris riding back a good part of the way with him next day. In summer bowls were always played a great deal; and drives were taken about the country in a carriage which Morris had specially built for himself, with leather curtains, and a decided flavour of the Middle Ages about it. The winter festivities were even merrier: it was a home of young people full of the high spirits of youth. "O the joy of those Saturdays to Mondays at Red House!" writes one of the frequent guests of those days, " the getting out at Abbey Wood Station and smelling the sweet air, and then the scrambling, swinging drive of three miles or so to the house; and the beautiful roomy place where we seemed to be coming home just as much as when we returned to our own rooms. No protestations—only certainty of contentment in each other's society. We laughed because we were happy." " It was the most beautiful sight in the world," says another of his old friends of the Red House days, " to see Morris coming up from the cellar before dinner, beaming with joy, with his hands full of bottles of wine and others tucked under his arms."

Here were born his two children. On the 18th of January, 1861, he writes to Madox Brown, with a fine affectation of unconcern.

"My dear Brown,
      "Kid having appeared, Mrs. Brown kindly says she will stay till Monday, when you are to come to fetch her, please. I send a list of trains in evening to Abbey Wood met by bus, viz., from London Bridge, 2.20

p.m., 4.20 p.m., 6.0 p.m., and 7.15 p.m. Janey and
kid (girl) are both very well."

At the christening of the baby, named Jane Alice,
after his wife and his youngest sister, there was a great
gathering of friends. "The day of the christening,"
one of them writes, "was rainy and windy. I remember
the flapping of the cover of the wagonette and a feeling
of hurry-skurry through the weather in the short drive
to Bexley Church. The dinner was at a T-shaped table.
It must have been at it that I remember Gabriel sitting
in a royal manner and munching raisins from a dish in
front of him before dessert time. The Marshalls, the
Browns, Swinburne, were there. Janey and I went
together with a candle to look at the beds strewn about
the drawing room for the men. Swinburne had a sofa;
I think P. P. Marshall's was made on the floor."
On the 25th of March in the following year a second
girl was born, and named Mary, after the Lady of the day.
The life of those years at Red House was for Morris
one of almost complete contentment. "I grieve to say,"
Faulkner writes just before the Christmas of 1863, "he
has only kicked one panel out of a door for this twelve-
month past." The orderly civic element, which was
always one of the strongest threads in his nature, developed till he became what he would himself have
called in later days a typical bourgeois, the sort of father
of a family whose features were being weekly registered
by Leech. Indeed, as he quite realized himself, there
was in him a distinct strain of Mr. Briggs. Like tens of
thousands of his fellow-citizens, he joined a volunteer
corps during the war scare of the winter of 1859-60.
Lady Burne-Jones remembers that he was in camp with
his battalion at Wimbledon in June, 1861, when the
great Tooley Street fire broke out, and how he brought

I.   M

down news of its progress on returning to Red House. "I always did hate fireworks," he wrote afterwards while mentioning a fire at the works in Islington where his wall-papers were printed, "especially since I saw Cotton's wharf ablaze some eighteen years ago." The memory of that terrible sight of the blazing river seems to have been lifelong with all who witnessed it.

With a growing family and a constant hospitality, the expense of living at Red House and continuing its decoration on the same lavish scale became greater year by year. At the same time the copper mine, from which the greater part of his permanent income was still derived, began to yield rapidly diminishing returns. The business in Red Lion Square had not ceased to be a drain on these diminishing revenues, and was not till some years later a trustworthy source of income. Its prospects were indeed improving. The movement towards restoring to Anglican churches and church services some part of their ancient beauty and symbolism was taking definite shape all over the country, and was beginning to be known by the name of Ritualism. Commissions for church decoration in the form of wall-painting, embroideries, or hangings, altar-cloths, stained-glass windows, and floor-tiles, came in more and more steadily. And the movement was just beginning to spread from ecclesiastical into secular life, and become what was afterwards called Æstheticism.

But this very increase in the firm's work had already made the premises in Red Lion Square insufficient for their purpose, while, as Morris had to give more of his time to its management, the expense and fatigue of managing it from Upton both increased likewise. Early in 1864 the question of removing the works to Upton and setting up a manufactory there began to be seriously discussed. A plan was suggested and elaborated for the addition of another wing to Red House so as to make room for Burne-Jones to live there also; and ground for workshops was to be had on moderate terms close by. The scheme was very near being carried out. But before the end of the year, a series of misfortunes happened which altered the whole case for both.

In September, the Morrises had gone to seaside lodgings at Littlehampton with the Burne-Joneses and Faulkners. Scarlet fever broke out there. Miss Faulkner and Burne-Jones's little boy took back the infection with them to London. With them it ran its normal course; but a little later it developed in Mrs. Burne-Jones also, and she had a long and dangerous illness. Just then Morris caught a chill on a wet, cold journey between London and Upton, which brought on a severe attack of rheumatic fever. For some time he was wholly crippled. When he recovered, his health still was such as to make a daily journey to London quite out of the question. Burne-Jones, himself in very delicate health, in deep anxiety about his wife, and dependent for the means of actual livelihood on his daily work, felt that he could not cast himself loose from the resources and conveniences of London. The plan of a joint establishment had to be dropped. Had the business of the firm reached anything like the scale which it attained ten years later, it might have been practicable, and would have had obvious advantages, that Morris should move the works down to Upton, keeping a show-room and office in London under a resident manager. But such an expense was, as yet, out of the question. And when health began to be a serious consideration, Red House had certain disadvantages. Planned and begun in the extraordinarily hot dry summer of 1859, it had been made to face north and was very cold in winter: it was not well situated for medical or other aid on emergencies, and the drive between it and Abbey Wood was over an exposed plateau across which eastern and northerly winds raged unchecked. Reluctantly Morris was forced to the conclusion that short of giving up the business (and with it, the power of guiding his life otherwise as he chose) the only alternative left was to give up the beautiful house into which he had put so much of his best thought and work, in which he had enjoyed five years of almost unclouded happiness, and go back to live in London.

A letter to Burne-Jones, dated " In bed, Red House," and written in a very shaky hand, towards the end of November, when he was beginning to recover from the rheumatic fever, shows how deep the disappointment was at having to give up the plan of a joint home, even before the necessity of leaving Red House himself had been forced on him.

" As to our palace of art, I confess your letter was a blow to me at first, though hardly an unexpected one: in short I cried, but I have got over it now; of course I see it from your point of view but I like the idea of not giving it up for good even if it is delusive.   But now I am only thirty years old; I shan't always have the rheumatism, and we shall have lots of jolly years of invention and lustre plates together I hope.   I have been resting and thinking of what you are to do: I really think you must take some sort of house in London —unless indeed you might think of living a little way out and sharing a studio in town: Stanhope and I might join in this you know.   There is only one other thing I can think of, which is when you come back from Hastings come and stay with me for a month or two, there is plenty of room for everybody and everything: you can do your work quietly and uninterruptedly; I shall have a good horse by then and Georgie and J. will

be able to drive about, meantime you need not be hurried
in taking your new crib. I would give £5 to see you old
chap; wouldn't it be safe for you to come down here one
day before you go to Hastings ? "

At the end of the year the Burne-Joneses removed to
Kensington, where they lived for the next three years.
The giving up of Red House was fast becoming a
settled thing, and it only remained to find a new home
in London. It was finally found in one of the old
houses in Queen Square, Bloomsbury. The house, with
its yard and outbuildings behind, was large enough to
serve for both living place and workshops. It was taken
on lease from Midsummer, 1865, and thither, in the
autumn, the business of Morris & Company was transferred from Red Lion Square, and the Morrises themselves removed from Upton in November. Red House
was sold, together with such portions of its furniture and
decorations as were either unremovable or too cumbrous
to transfer to a house for which they had not been designed. Among the treasures thus abandoned were the
whole of the tempera paintings executed on the walls,
the magnificent sideboard which Webb had designed for
the dining-room, and both the great painted cupboards;
but the painted panels in one of these last were taken
out and replaced by plain panels. There is still enough
of its original decoration left at Red House to make it
unique on that account alone. After he left it that
autumn, Morris never set eyes on it again, confessing
that the sight of it would be more than he could bear.

If emotion recollected in tranquillity were a working
definition of poetry, it is in these five years, so busily
tranquil after as long a period of stormy emotion, that
one might expect to find poetical production the most
copious. But the facts are quite the reverse. The latest

poems printed in " The Defence of Guenevere " show the author in the full current of imaginative growth, reaching from manner to manner and just on the point (so one might fancy) of mastering a mixed lyrical and dramatic method capable of the most radiant and astonishing effects.   For one reason or another, these beginnings were not destined to bear their natural fruit.   The cycle of poems from the Trojan War, which had been planned and begun about that time, was fragmentarily continued at Red House, but remained unfinished and was soon wholly laid aside.   When he began to write again, after he resumed life in London, the dramatic method was abandoned, and he reappeared to the world, not as a writer of lyrical romances, but as the author of long continuous narrative poems, of which the type was set and the fame assured by the single one first published, " The Life and Death of Jason."

Of the twelve poems which were to make up the Trojan cycle, only six were ever completed; there are imperfect drafts of two more, and of the remaining four no trace is extant.   But the full list of the titles is noted down by Morris himself in a manuscript book probably dating from 1857, on a page following a fragment of the unfinished and unpublished " Maying of Guenevere." It is as follows, under the general heading of " Scenes from the Fall of Troy":

1. Helen Arming Paris.
2. The Defiance of the Greeks.
3. Hector's Last Battle.
4. Hector brought Dead to Troy.
5. Helen's Chamber.
6. Achilles' Love-Letter.
7. The Wedding of Polyxena.
8. The last Fight before Troy.

9. The Wooden Horse.
10. The Descent from the Wooden Horse.
11. Helen and Menelaus.
12. Æneas on Shipboard.

The completed scenes run to about 200 lines each in
length, and the whole poem, therefore, would have been
of about the bulk of a five-act play.

The story of the Trojan War is one which has for all
story lovers the greatest and most abiding fascination ;
and its strange ending, the events that happened after
the Iliad, was the part of the story which attracted
Morris the most.   In itself that part of the story is full
of remarkably picturesque and romantic incident, which
breaks out even in the dull records of Greek mythographers, Ælian and Philostratus, or in the arguments
of the lost epics of the Cycle—the Æthiopiad, the Little
Iliad, the Taking of Troy.   It was these events which
excited the imagination of the Middle Ages most; and
it was in the same mediæval and romantic spirit that
Morris saw and felt the whole story.   He did so by
instinct, long before he knew of Caxton's " Historyes
of Troye," or of the vast body of mediæval romances
that may be traced back to Benoît de Sainte-More and
Guido delle Colonne.   But when he came to know these
he found them just what he meant and what he wanted ;
and to the last he pleased himself by fancying some
thread of real tradition which had filtered down alongside
of the regular literary channels of the Greek epic, and
reappeared, after the lapse of many centuries, in Dares
Phrygius and Dictys Cretensis.

" To-day," Sir Edward Burne-Jones writes in a letter
of thirty years afterwards, " to breakfast came Morris,
and we talked hard all morning, mainly of one subject,
why the mediæval world was always on the side of the

Trojans, and of Quintus Smyrnæus, and how Penthesilea came to be tenderly dealt with in ancient tales and tapestries.   He was quite happy."

Troy is to his imagination a town exactly like Bruges or Chartres: spired and gabled, red-roofed, filled (like the city of King Æetes in "The Life and Death of Jason") with towers and swinging bells.   The Trojan princes go out, like knights in Froissart, to tilt at the barriers, and look down from their walls on

> Our great wet ditches, where the carp and tench,
> In spite of arblasts and petrariæ,
> Suck at the floating lilies all day long.

But over the city broods a strange and almost a spectral stillness, an atmosphere like that of a sultry afternoon, darkening to thunder.   None of his poems, earlier or later, are more steeped in sadness.   All the fierce joy of the war has long gone by; it drags wearily on towards its inevitable close.

> Yea, they fought well, and ever, like a man
> That hangs legs off the ground by both his hands
> Over some great height, did they struggle sore,
> Quite sure to slip at last; wherefore, take note
> How almost all men, reading that sad siege,
> Hold for the Trojans; as I did at least,
> Thought Hector the best knight a long way—

So he had already written in his first volume, and the tone in these Troy poems is precisely the same.   But here we only catch a last glimpse of Hector as he goes bravely to meet his fate, and with him all the sunlight seems to fade off Troy.   The struggle becomes cruel and base on both sides.   Paris arms himself again, but like a man in a nightmare.

Yea, like some man am I that lies and dreams
That he is dead, and turning round to wake
Is slain at once without a cry for help.

In what must be the most dolorous arming-song ever
written he bids Helen a weary farewell.   The lyric, in
an altered shape and setting, is well known: recast, and
with its sadness turned into a pensive tenderness, it
occurs in the tale of "Ogier the Dane," as a song
which Ogier hears sung early on a May morning by
two young lovers.   This is its original form:

Love, within the hawthorn brake
Pray you be merry for my sake,
While I last, for who knoweth
How near I may be my death?

Sweet, be long in growing old!
Life and love in age grow cold;
Hold fast to life, for who knoweth
What thing cometh after death?

Trouble must be kept afar,
Therefore go I to the war:
Less trouble is there among spears
Than with hard words about your ears.

Love me then, my sweet and fair,
And curse the folk that drive me there.
Kiss me, sweet, for who knoweth
What thing cometh after death?

Even in the Greek camp there is the same weariness
and bitter languor.   The homes they have left grow dim
and strange:

Within the cedar presses the gold fades
Upon the garments they were wont to wear;

Red poppies grow now where their apple trees
Began to redden in late summer days.
Wheat grows upon their water-meadows now,
And wains pass over where the water ran.

This feeling culminates in a weird lyric sung by Hecuba,
while still Queen in Troy, and plotting with Paris the
murder of Achilles in the temple to which he is to be
lured by the forged letter of Polyxena. "Ah, times
are changed, the merry days are gone," has been the re-
current burden of her long speech to Paris; and then all
at once she breaks into strange ballad music:

Yea, in the merry days of old
The sailors all grew overbold.
Whereof should days remembered be
That brought bitter ill to me?
  Days agone I wore but gold,
Like a light town across the wold
Seen by the stars, I shone out bright;
Many a slave was mine of right.
  Ah, but in the days of old
The sea-kings were waxen bold;
The yellow sands ran red with blood,
The towns burned up, both brick and wood;
In their long ship they carried me
And set me down by a strange sea;
None of the gods remembered me.
  Ah, in the merry days of old
My garments were all made of gold:
Now have I but one poor gown,
Woven of black wool and brown.
I draw water from the well;
I bind wood that the men fell;
Whoso willeth smiteth me,
An old woman by the sea.

In the scenes of the last night of Troy, as they are given in " The Descent from the Wooden Horse " and " Helen and Menelaus," this effect of weird breathlessness rises to a height that is almost overwhelming. That the Greek captains in the wooden horse should be wrought up to the highest pitch of nervous tension is indeed no modernism; it was clearly before the minds of the Greek ballad-singers three thousand years ago. But the strange story, preserved in the Odyssey, of Helen singing round the horse, is used here with extraordinary effect. As they lie crowded in the darkness a voice is heard singing from without—

> O my merchants, whence come ye
> Landing laden from the sea?
> —Behold, we come from Sicily:
> Corn and wine and oil have we,
> Blue cloths and cloths of red.
> —Merry merchants, when you are dead
> We shall gain that you have lorn:
> Out-merchants from the sea,
> Your graves are not in Sicily.
> The corn for me, the wine for thee,
> The blue and the red for our ladies free.

So singing, the voice passes away. The night is dark, rainy, and windless, as they slip out of the horse and take their plotted ways. Menelaus leaves the rest, and, all alone, goes straight to the house of Deiphobus.

There, in a dimly lighted chamber, Helen cannot sleep. Deiphobus, her new husband, lies sunk in the first undisturbed repose that the Trojan princes had taken since the ten years' war began, his sword hung above the bed. But she wanders through the room restlessly, wondering if she is growing old.

Three hours after midnight, I should think,
And I hear nothing but the quiet rain.
The Greeks are gone, think now, the Greeks are gone.
Henceforward a new life of quiet days
In this old town of Troy is now for me,
And I shall note it as it goeth past
Quietly as the rain does, day by day,
Eld creeping on me.   Shall I live sometimes
In these old days whereof this is the last?
Yea shall I live sometimes with sweet Paris
In that old happiness twixt mirth and tears?
The fitting on of arms and going forth,
The dreadful quiet sitting while they fought,
The kissing when he came back to my arms,
And all that I remember like a tale!

Thus musing to herself, she opens the window and thrusts out her bare arm into the cool wet darkness.   There is a rustle in the room behind her.   Before she can turn she is in the grasp of a mail-clad man, and hears the fierce whisper of her first husband.   All her strength collapses in a moment.   As in a trance, she dumbly obeys his order to lean over the bed and reach down Deiphobus's sword, and to hold down his feet while Menelaus thrusts him through.   Menelaus drags the bloody corpse out on to the floor and takes its place himself.

I am the Menelaus that you knew
Come back to fetch a thing I left behind.
You think me changed : it is ten years ago,
And many weary things have happened since.
Behold me lying in my own place now :
Abed, Helen, before the night goes by !

But on the horror of this moment there breaks a great

and mingled clamour from without, the roar of the taken
city.   A struggling mob of Greeks and Trojans sweep
by.   Menelaus and Helen go to the window; a Trojan
sees the hated beautiful face in the glimmer of flaming
houses, and shoots at her ; the arrow just misses, and
sings through the window-hole. Pyrrhus, still dripping
with the blood of Priam, and after him Teucer, fresh
from the outrage of Ajax on Cassandra, successively appear. In the middle of their story a cry is raised that the
Trojans are making a fresh stand: and all hurry off amid
a growing tumult of shouting as dawn begins to glimmer,
ending in a long shrill cry of the rallied Trojans,

" Æneas and Antenor to the ships! "

Between this vivid and startling dramatic method, and
the equable sweetness of the later manner as it appears
in its first perfection in " The Life and Death of Jason,"
the interval is great indeed; nor can it be matter of
wonder that the transition took place through a period
of silence.   But there is more in it than that.   Hitherto
the poetry has been, alike in its beauties and in its defects,
immature.   When it is resumed, it is in a manner, and
of a substance, deliberately chosen ; we hear in it what
we may like or dislike, may regard with admiration or
with indifference, what appeals to various minds variously;
but it is the serious voice of the grown man.

CHAPTER VI

THE EARTHLY PARADISE
1865-1870

QUEEN SQUARE, in which Morris himself and the firm of Morris & Company took up house together in the autumn of 1865, is a backwater of older Bloomsbury, which then retained some traces of its original dignity as a suburb of the London of Queen Anne. Put out of fashion half a century before by the more modern splendours of Russell Square, it had lingered on as a residential neighbourhood; and the famous girls' school established in it about the middle of last century, and commonly known as "the ladies' Eton," had only been finally closed during the Crimean War. The residential was now becoming mingled with an industrial element. The house on the east side, No. 26, taken by Morris, and the headquarters of his work for the next seventeen years, has disappeared to make room for an extension of the National Hospital for the Paralysed and Epileptic. The ground floor was turned into an office and show-room. A large ball-room which had been built at the end of the yard, and connected with the dwelling-house by a wooden gallery, was turned into a principal work-shop. There was room for other workshops in the small court at the back, and further accommodation was found when needed in Ormond Yard close by.

With Morris now continuously on the spot, the company became little more than a name as far as regarded the direction and management of the business. Rossetti had never taken much concern in the work. After his wife's death he had been for a long time almost a recluse: now he was living in Chelsea, at the other end of London, and was wholly absorbed in his painting. Faulkner, who had no productive gift, and whose great mathematical ability was somewhat thrown away on keeping the books of the firm, had returned to work in Oxford the year before; but in his vacations he stayed much with his mother and sisters, who had a house in Queen Square a few doors off, and at these times his intercourse with Morris was constant and his share in the conduct of the business not inconsiderable. Marshall had resumed his own line of work. Burne-Jones and Madox Brown continued to supply designs for stained glass, and Webb for furniture. But the whole of the production, and, except in glass and furniture, practically the whole of the design was now in Morris's sole hands. All the kinds of work begun at Red Lion Square went on here: and gradually there began to be added other industries which afterwards became the staple production of the firm—weaving, dyeing, and printing on cloth. No long time after Red House was given up, it became possible to have supplied it from the works at Queen Square with almost everything necessary to complete its decoration and furnishing. Such is the irony of human affairs.

But the management of the rapidly extending business had been just at this time put into capable and energetic hands. To Mr. George Warrington Taylor, business manager of Morris & Company from 1865 until his illness and death at the beginning of 1870, it was mainly due that the business became organized and prosperous. Mr. Taylor was a Catholic, of good family, who had been educated at Eton and was afterwards for some time in the Army; but he had been unfortunate in his affairs and was then almost penniless.   He was full of enthusiasms in art, more especially in music; he was an ardent admirer of Wagner, whose name then was little known in England, and was also an enthusiastic follower of Rossetti and the Pre-Raphaelites in painting.   He had introduced himself to Morris at Red House, and common tastes, to which Taylor added really great knowledge, confirmed the acquaintance.   In 1865 he was earning a scanty livelihood as a check-taker at the Opera House in the Haymarket, and gladly accepted a post under the firm.   He was a man of great ability and sweetness of character, incapable of taking care of his own affairs, but shrewd and careful in his management of other people's business.   The intermittent supervision which was all that Faulkner had been able to give to the accounts of the firm since the Easter of 1864 was now replaced by the continuous care of a man who was not only a master of figures, but an expert in business methods. Morris was able to give to designing and manual work the greater part of the time that had been occupied before by employment less congenial to him. But no part of the business came amiss to him.   There is a record of visits made to Queen Square in its first days by purchasers who had accidently seen some of his wall-papers; one in 1865, when Morris himself, in a dark blue linen blouse, showed the patterns and made out the bill, and a second in the following year, when he was found at work on the design for the Pomegranate paper.   In 1867 the firm obtained what was their first really important commission in non-ecclesiastical decorative work, the decoration of the Green Dining Room at the South Kensington Museum.   This piece of work, seen as it is yearly by many thousands of persons, was of great value at the time in making known the name of

the firm and the specific character of their work. It
remains intact now. The original cost was heavy, and
the heads of the Department had some scruples about
passing the estimate. But their decision was, even on
grounds of economy, fully justified. The excellence of
the work, apart from its singular decorative merit, has
more than repaid its cost. In the long run it has proved
(so I am allowed to state on the authority of the
Directors of the Museum) the cheapest piece of work
in the buildings; for, except that the ceiling had to be
repainted where it was blackened by the smoke from the
gaslights, the work has never required any repair in any
portion.

While the business thus went on increasing, his leisure
also grew on his hands. The saving of time caused by
his return to London was, of course, immense. From
three to four hours were added to his working day; in
spite of all depressions caused by his loss of the country,
and by the crowded squalor of the district immediately
adjoining this end of Bloomsbury, he felt "as if he
could kiss the London pavement" when he got quit of
the daily journey. It was in this increased leisure that
he resumed, in new forms, the writing of poetry.

The instinct for story-telling, in its simpler forms an
almost universal faculty, in its full meaning one of the
rarest and most valuable of literary qualities, was strong in
Morris from the first. It appears in the schoolboy tales
of romantic adventure for which he was noted at Marlborough, and in the prose romances of the Oxford and
Cambridge Magazine; but now he recognized that it
was his special and unique gift, and that it might be combined with lyrical qualities into a form of poetry where
he could put out all his strength. Strangely enough,
English poetry, so rich in nearly every form, has seldom
reached its highest perfection in this one. After Chaucer,

its first and greatest master, narrative poetry remained, with the great exceptions of Dryden and Keats, mostly in the hands of poets of the second rank. The rhetorical and dramatic turn of the Elizabethans stood in the way of their telling a story simply and lucidly. The seventeenth and eighteenth centuries were entangled in the traditions of a conventional epic. Of more modern poets, Shelley (who " had no eyes," Morris used to say) always flounders in narration; Byron, with all his admirable directness and vividness in detached passages, has not the art of carrying on a continuous story; and Scott, whose narrative instinct, whether in prose or verse, is unsurpassed, did not claim to be a master in the distinguishing qualities of poetry, and cheerfully abandoned verse for prose. It was to Chaucer, therefore, that, even apart from his delight in and kinship with the age of Chaucer, Morris might naturally turn for his model : and the plan of a cycle of romantic stories connected by some common purpose or occasion was directly suggested by the Canterbury Tales.

Some such design had already been talked over at Red House, but no beginning was made till after the removal to London. For the stories, all sources, classical and romantic alike, were to be drawn from; the world's stock of stories, in fact, which was still much the same as it had been in Chaucer's time, was to be reviewed and selected from anew. The earliest poems written were from the mythology and heroic legends of Greece : and to these were gradually added others from Eastern, Western, and Northern sources. The next idea which occurred was to make half of the stories be taken from the Greek, and half from non-Greek, or what might be broadly described as romantic literature. To create a possible or plausible common setting for both groups, he fell back on his favourite fancy of a continued thread of living Greek tradition coming down almost to the end of the Middle Ages among Greek-speaking people, and overlapping the full development of romanticism in Western Europe. It was but a fancy, yet one which had real analogies in history. The Greek epic, it is true, ends in the fifth century; but Greek poetry went on being written certainly till the eleventh; and the collection of minor poetry known as the Anthology owes its final form to a Byzantine scholar who was ambassador to Venice at the time of Edward III.'s accession to the crown of England, and was probably still alive when Chaucer was born. Byzantine Greeks of the fourteenth century inherited a continuous literary tradition regarding the incidents and characters of the ancient Greek epic, which can be traced upwards to compilers of the second and third centuries, and again through these to mythographers who may have been the contemporaries of Herodotus. Given, then, this living tradition of early Greece, inherited by some outlying fragment of the Greek speech and blood such as actually existed for some hundreds of years in Central Asia, for some hundreds more in Southern Russia, and might conceivably have existed in some remote ocean fastness much longer: given a sufficient reason for the inheritors of this tradition being joined, in their forgotten island, by a group of mixed Western blood, Germanic, Norse, and Celtic, bearing with them the mass of stories current in their own time throughout Western Europe; and a setting is provided in which may be rationally included any story in the world. Make this reason a combination of the Norse explorations of the Atlantic and the earliest discoveries of America with the flight out of a land stricken with the Black Death, and there results the whole idea and structure of " The Earthly Paradise."

It is worth while calling attention to this simple yet

elaborate artifice of structure on more than one ground; partly because of the care with which Morris worked it out in detail, as a piece, one might say, of architectural construction; partly because, unless it be kept in mind, much of the meaning of "The Earthly Paradise," and of the special fitness of the stories in it as regards both substance and manner, is of necessity lost. It is, for instance, one of the commonest criticisms made on the Greek stories in "The Earthly Paradise," that the atmosphere and treatment are not Greek but mediæval; that the feelings, incidents, and decoration are neither those of classical poetry, nor yet of the stories of ancient Greece as interpreted and modernized by the taste of the present day. This is precisely true, and precisely what Morris meant. Ancient Greek poetry he admired for its own qualities, and appreciated more than is generally known—a criticism which he once made on Pindar showed insight much greater than that of the average classical scholar—but its way was not his way; and still less his way was the sort of modernization, beautiful and touching as that is, which other poets of this age have applied to the Greek legends—the method of Tennyson in "Oenone" or "Tiresias," the method of Matthew Arnold in "Empedocles," the method of Mr. Swinburne in "Atalanta in Calydon." To Morris the mediæval method—using the term to cover the whole period of four or five centuries from the age of the *chansons de geste* and the Icelandic epic to the close of the Middle Ages in Chaucer—was beyond all question or comparison the best; was so much the best that it was practically the only one. To adopt this method, however naturally it came to him, without warning, and, as it were, in the air, would put a needless strain on the intelligence of his public. It was prepared for, nay more, it was rendered both natural and appropriate, by this device of laying the scene of the stories themselves at the end of the fourteenth century, and telling them as they would have been told then : as they were in fact told then in Western Europe, but with the greater sweetness of tone and purity of line, the less mystic or fantastic turn, which might be expected from a purely Greek tradition ; and with something also of that stately Greek melancholy which seems inherent in the Hellenic blood, and clings, the shadow of its brightness, to the whole of ancient Greek poetry from Homer to Theocritus.

Nor was this the only advantage gained by placing the scene of the poems in the age of Chaucer. Any earlier time would have cut him off from some of the great tales of the world; from that, for instance, of "The Hill of Venus," which is of late mediæval origin, and cannot be traced further back than the fourteenth century: and any later time would have made the Chaucerian manner inappropriate and unhistorical. The next step that poetry took in Europe, after the close of the Middle Ages, was to entangle itself in rhetoric on the one hand, in classicalism on the other; and classicalism and rhetoric, admirable as are some of the results they have produced, were just the two things that Morris could not bear. In the scheme of "The Earthly Paradise" as it stands, the two corner stones are the Greek and the northern epic cycles, the two greatest bodies of imaginative narration which the world has produced. The stories which he chose out of both are told by Greeks and by Norsemen of the later Middle Ages, in the form in which they would then have been imagined and in the manner which, to his mind, was the best of all manners. But alongside of these great fountainheads were other sources, European and Oriental ; and for these also, subject to the same conditions, a place is found by simple and probable devices. Among the adventurers who had started on the search for eternal youth are Laurence the Swabian, who knows the mediæval chronicles, and Nicholas the Breton, who is familiar with the French epics. Rolf himself, the Norseman who heads the expedition, had spent his youth at Byzantium, where his father was an officer of the Varangian Guard, and in that meeting-place of East and West has heard the stories which became familiar to Europe later through the Arabian Nights. The field of story thus laid open was in fact almost too large, was at all events too large to be fully utilized. Oriental sources were but little drawn upon. The Persian heroic cycle, which Morris placed next in interest after the epics of Greece and Scandinavia, is left wholly untouched; and a single story, that of "The Man who never Laughed again," was taken with much hesitation from the Arabic. Even in dealing with purely European sources much was set aside, including the whole immense mass of the Arthurian cycle. The Breton who sails in search of the Earthly Paradise dies on the voyage; and the story of "Ogier the Dane," coming from him at second hand, is the only one in the whole work which is derived from Celtic sources. The mythology of Ireland (with which Morris was less in sympathy) never appears at all.

This architectural design of a great body of poetry, an immense variety of subject brought by certain dominating conceptions within a single method and common scope, grew up gradually in his mind : but meanwhile the poems themselves were being produced with extraordinary speed. Among the earliest written were three from Greek sources, which had strangely different fortunes, but were alike in this, that none of them finally appeared in "The Earthly Paradise." The subjects were Orpheus and Eurydice, the Quest of the Golden Fleece, and the life of the half mythical Dorian chief, Aristomenes of Messene. These were written in 1866.

For the first, which was completed, but still remains unpublished, Burne-Jones made an elaborate series of designs. The "Aristomenes" was never finished. Morris had been attracted to the story by the obviously and indeed startlingly romantic features which it bears as briefly told by Pausanias. Greece proper had had its own period of an early romanticism. For the most part it was crushed out, partly by the literary supremacy of Athens, and partly by the contempt for literature of all kinds which was natural to Greeks of the pure Dorian blood: and this is one of a few instances in which it has survived through, and reappeared after, the classical period. But in spite of this, and of the further pleasure that it gave him to think of the Spartans being outfought and outwitted, the story was too unsubstantial for history, and at the same time too historical to allow free play for invention. He felt that it did not accommodate itself to vaguely romantic treatment, and that to deal with it properly he should first have to visit Greece. It was dropped at the time; was afterwards taken up again more than once some eight or ten years later, but was finally abandoned. The only part of it which has ever been printed is a fragment of about a hundred and fifty lines which he published, or allowed to be published, in the Athenæum for the 13th of May, 1876.

The fortunes of the Quest of the Golden Fleece were very different. The story, in itself one of the richest and most splendid out of the whole Greek mythology, and capable of almost indefinite expansion in detail, grew on his hands till it became obvious that it had outgrown its destined place. Its length, which is between that of the Æneid and the Odyssey, reached the scale of the regular epic. It was separately published in June, 1867, under the title of "The Life and Death of Jason."

The success of "Jason" was immediate and great. In

those years Tennyson reigned almost without a rival; but people had grown weary of his imitators, and his own inspiration no longer, in the opinion of many admirers, kept pace with the elaborate beauty of his execution. It was time for new poetry. The appearance, two years before, of "Atalanta in Calydon" had roused a tempest of excitement and applause. It was felt that a new generation had arisen. This new poem of "The Life and Death of Jason," in which the refinement and charm of mature art were combined with the reawakened sense of romanticism, with extraordinary fertility of movement and incident, and with a largeness, straightforwardness, and sweetness that were all its own, found an audience ready for it. It had just enough of archaism or mannerism to interest critics without rousing their ridicule. When the Pall Mall Gazette, then the great arbiter of cultured opinion, could find little in "Jason" to condemn beyond an "indifference to manners" shown in the passage where "Medea obtains her first interview with Jason by knocking unexpectedly at his chamber door" (instead, we must infer, of sending him a note by the footman), its fortunes with the critics were secured. Morris's name began to be mentioned with respect. People were even led to assume a knowledge of his earlier work of which they were wholly innocent. "No one," observed one of the leading daily newspapers in a eulogistic notice of "The Life and Death of Jason," "acquainted with Mr. Morris's previous volume will be surprised to find that he has again chosen a classical subject." No testimony could be more eloquent than this to the feebleness of the impression made on the public by "The Defence of Guenevere." It may be true that, as another review of "Jason" states, the earlier volume had gradually gained for itself an increasing audience; but that audience even now might be counted by scores or dozens, and the first

edition was still not nearly exhausted. With " The Life
and Death of Jason" Morris reached real popularity. A
second edition (in which numerous corrections were made)
was called for almost immediately; and thereafter a steady
sale led to successive reprints. The poem received a
final revision from the author in the eighth edition, published fifteen years after its original appearance.

Indifferent as Morris habitually was to criticism, the
reception which " The Life and Death of Jason" met
with was a source of no little encouragement and pleasure, as that of " The Defence of Guenevere" had undoubtedly been chilling, and had even joined with other
reasons to make him for a time lay aside poetry. The
fortunes of the " Jason" were an index to the public
reception of the longer work, with which he had already
made large progress, and in the course of which, as in
the course of all long labours, there were periods when
he grew discouraged.

" Naturally I am in good spirits after the puffs," he
writes on the 20th of June, " but I reserve any huge
delight till I see what the ' Pall Mall' and 'Saturday'
say, one of which is pretty sure to act Advocatus
Diaboli. However I fancy I shall do pretty well now;
last week I had made up my mind that I shouldn't be
able to publish ' The Earthly Paradise' and was very
low: I am as anxious as you are to get on with that
work, and am going to set to work hard now. I hope
you won't let any rubbish pass without collaring it. I am
too old now for that kind of game."

The seriousness of mind which had been so remarkable in him from the first comes out here again. No
great artist was ever less self-conscious about his own
work, more absolutely free from either vanity or fatuity.
But it was matter of simple duty with him, in a poem as
in a design for decoration, to do everything he did as

well as he could. It was not with him a matter of in-spiration—he never used either the word or the idea—but of sheer honesty and seriousness of workmanship. "That's jolly!" he would say of a piece of his own work, with the same simplicity as if it were anything else that he admired: yet on the other hand he never spoke, or apparently thought, of poetry as involving more than the craftsman's qualities: singleness of eye, trained apti-tude of hand, and such integrity of mind as would not consciously produce "rubbish," or slip it in unnoticed among really honest work. "That talk of inspiration is sheer nonsense, I may tell you that flat," he once said in later years when poetry, not his own, was being discussed: "there is no such thing: it is a mere matter of craftsmanship." The idea that poetry could, or should, be cultivated as an isolated and specific artistic product, or that towards its production it was desirable to isolate one's self from common interests and occupations, and stand a little apart from all the turmoils or trivialities of common life, was one which he found not so much un-true as unintelligible. "If a chap can't compose an epic poem while he's weaving tapestry," he once said, "he had better shut up, he'll never do any good at all."

In the fresh satisfaction of seeing "The Life and Death of Jason" in print, and finding that it had given him a recognized position among the English poets, he resumed work on "The Earthly Paradise" with renewed heart, and the speed and sustained excellence of his pro-duction for the rest of the year were even for him phenomenal. The verse flowed off his pen. Seven hundred lines were once composed in a single day. During part of the Long Vacation Mr. and Mrs. Burne-Jones and their children were living at Oxford, where Faulkner stayed up and had his mother and sister with

him. The Morrises were also there, in lodgings in
Beaumont Street, he going up to London now and then
for the day to look after the business. Every evening
he would read aloud what he had written that day.
There were excursions on the river in golden summer
weather, long remembered as the happiest in more lives
than one. Two of them are recorded in the lovely introductory verses to June and August in " The Earthly
Paradise." The first of these recalls a day on the lonely
and beautiful upper river, where issuing from the sad
marshland, it takes the steel-blue Windrush by the
Gothic arches of New Bridge, passes all in loops and
links to Eynsham, and curves round the Wytham hills
through the meadows of the Evenlode. His later home
by these upper waters was then unknown ; it was with
a strange premonition of it that he wrote now—

> What better place than this then could we find
> By this sweet stream that knows not of the sea,
> That guesses not the city's misery,
> This little stream whose hamlets scarce have names,
> This far-off, lonely mother of the Thames?

The other excursion was down the river to Dorchester,
on a day of burning splendour in late August. The
long Abbey Church, the weir by Day's Lock, and the
huge prehistoric fortifications on Sinodun Hill and across
the meadow-land girt by the arc of the river, are there
now unchanged, though havoc has been made among
the willow beds, and the kingfisher is seldom seen by
the weir.

> Across the gap made by our English hinds,
> Amidst the Roman's handiwork, behold
> Far off the long-roofed church ; the shepherd binds
> The withy round the hurdles of his fold,

Down in the foss the river fed of old,
That through long lapse of time has grown to be
The little grassy valley that you see.

Rest here awhile, not yet the eve is still,
The bees are wandering yet, and you may hear
The barley mowers on the trenched hill,
The sheep-bells, and the restless changing weir,
All little sounds made musical and clear
Beneath the sky that burning August gives,
While yet the thought of glorious summer lives.

Even when Morris had to go up to his business at
Queen Square he always returned with sheet on sheet of
fresh manuscript : and it was for this river party that he
brought down with him, and read aloud by the river-
side, " The Story of the Wanderers," the prologue of
" The Earthly Paradise " in its second or published
form. There could be no more striking instance of his
seriousness of workmanship, and his determination not
to " let any rubbish pass," than his resolution to rewrite
this story wholly and its completely successful result.
The earlier and unpublished version is still extant. It
had been composed nearly two years before, and still
laboured under the defects of his earlier poetry; un-
evenness in transitions, a lumbering structure, awkward
and often needlessly violent rhythm and diction. What
pains Morris took to form a style, as people would say
—to get his work right, as he would himself have rather
termed it—can be judged from comparison of the two :
this crude and laboured poem, and the later version with
its quiet refinement, its grace of diction, the melodious
music of its verse.

Summer ended ; and still the flow of rhyme continued
as powerful and as sweet. By the spring of 1868 at
least seventeen of the twenty-four tales which were pro-

posed for the complete design had been written : The
Son of Crœsus, Cupid and Psyche, Pygmalion and the
Image, The Man Born to be King, Atalanta's Race,
The Story of Perseus, The Watching of the Falcon,
The Lady of the Land, The Writing on the Image, The
Proud King, The Love of Alcestis, Ogier the Dane,
The King's Treasure House, Orpheus and Eurydice,
The Fortunes of Gyges, The Dolphins and the Lovers,
and The Story of St. Dorothea.   The method of publication had been much discussed.   The first idea was to
produce the complete work in one folio volume, with
woodcuts from designs by Burne-Jones.   Of these there
were to be no less than five hundred.   The greatest
achievements of the Kelmscott Press were more than
anticipated in this project ; but it was a generation too
soon.   The art of producing books had sunk to a
deplorable condition, and it became evident that the
proposed work was impossible without the organized
labour of years.   The poet and the designer were prepared with their part ; but the type-founder, the com-
positor, the printer, the wood-engraver, had all to be
educated.   Upwards of a hundred designs for pictures,
including a complete set for the story of Cupid and
Psyche, were made by Burne-Jones ; and many of them
were cut by Morris himself and the professional or
amateur workers for the firm, who were still employed,
with the old simple audacity, to do their best without
any regular training.   Morris himself worked hard at
wood-cutting, and, according to the opinion of experts,
improved rapidly, and at last did it very well.   One of
these woodcuts, representing the scene of Psyche borne
off by Zephyrus, has recently been published as a fron-
tispiece to Mr. S. C. Cockerell's history of the Kelmscott
Press.   As to the wood-cutting, Mr. George Wardle
writes to me :

" Mr. Morris asked me soon after this to put on wood some drawings Burne-Jones was then making for illustration of the Cupid and Psyche. I was very glad to do so; and here began an experience often repeated when I came to know more of the ways of the firm. It was practically impossible to get the drawings properly cut. Perhaps if Mr. Morris could have given the price which a first-rate cutter would have charged for doing the work with his own hand, they might have come out as they were drawn, but in the ordinary course of the trade it was impossible: I think also that same ' course' would have prevented the arrangement, had there been no other difficulty.

" Mr. Morris asked me then if I would try to cut these blocks. This I did, and after a few experiments, he was well enough pleased to give me one and then another; but after that I got no more, and wondered for a while why, as I thought the second was certainly better than the first. The reason was, Mr. Morris became possessed by the idea of cutting the blocks himself: and he took them all in hand and carried them through, not without some lively scenes in Queen Square. He cut with great ardour and with much knowledge, but the work did not always go to his mind. It was necessarily slow and he was constitutionally quick : there were then quarrels between them."

But when two trial sheets of the folio " Earthly Paradise " were set up at the Chiswick Press, the effect was very discouraging. The page, while not without a certain quality of distinction, suffers from technical defects, in both typography and woodcuts, which are all the more emphasized by the high mark aimed at. Two etchings made by Burne-Jones for the story of "The Ring given to Venus" were not considered more satisfactory in their result as decoration for a page. Gradually, with labour and patience, these difficulties might have been remedied; but only at immense cost and after years of delay. The scheme was therefore laid aside, though not abandoned. " The Earthly Paradise" appeared in the ordinary form: but the great edition of it was on the verge of being realized at the author's death. " To the very last," Sir Edward Burne-Jones writes, "we held to our first idea, and hoped yet to see the book published in the Kelmscott Press in all the fulness of its first design."

Notwithstanding the high pressure of his poetry, the records of the firm show that his work as a decorator was pursued with unremitting diligence. The following letter is addressed to Mr. Guy with reference to the projected decoration of the Chapel in the Forest School at Walthamstow.

" 26, Queen Square,
" Nov. 25th, 1867.

" My dear Guy,
" The plan I think perfectly applicable to mosaic, but of course the designs want making out—avoid anything *spiky* in mosaic, it is too easy, and looks so. I don't think it is worth while using the material unless the work is very elaborate ; and there ought to be a great deal of gold in it ; the part between the bands ought also to be at least of marble or alabaster. I don't want to discourage any reasonable plan, but I should think panelling the proper thing for your east end, picked out with colour and gold if you please ; the next best I should think would be hangings. I scarcely fancy mosaics on such a small scale, and they are the proper decorations of curved surfaces, domes, and are the concomitants of a round-arched style and great magnificence of decoration in general. But on the whole

panelling is the thing; couldn't your friend paint some figures and things on the panels? Anyhow, I will help if you wish it, with the designs, whatever you settle on.

"I have to thank you very much for your friendliness with reference to Jason—it makes me laugh to be in the position of nuisance to schoolboys.

"Yours very truly,

"W. MORRIS."

This same November Burne-Jones had left Kensington for the house in which he lived for the rest of his life, The Grange, in North End Lane, Fulham, then a pleasant quiet place with great elms in the road and surrounded by fields and market-gardens. "As this removed us further from him," he writes, "I wrote and proposed that he and Webb should come every Sunday to bind us together. A letter he wrote in answer was more full of warm response than he often permitted himself. This was the beginning of our Sundays. There were times of discontinuance, at first, for one reason or another. But for all the later years it was his weekly custom that he should come to breakfast and spend the morning: then we planned our work and talked of our schemes; and so it continued till the end. The last three Sundays of his life I went to him."

At the beginning of 1868, the plan of a single-volume "Earthly Paradise" in a costly form having been given up, arrangements were made for printing the first half of the work and issuing it separately. It was then meant that the whole work should be in two volumes. But the second half turned out to be so much longer than the first that it had to be broken up and separately issued in two portions, as Part III. and Part IV. : the volume of 1868 comprising Parts I. and II. The reissue in four volumes, each containing one of the four seasons, was only made some years later. The agreement for publication, which is dated the 6th of February, 1868, specifies the whole work as extending to about 34,000 lines. It actually exceeded 42,000.

"To-day," writes Morris on the 3rd of February, "I took first piece of copy to printer. Yesterday I wrote 33 stanzas of Pygmalion. If you want my company (usually considered of no use to anybody but the owner) please say so. I believe I shall get on so fast with my work that I shall be able to idle." The book went through the press without delay, and was published at the end of April. The only decoration was the well-known woodcut on the title-page of the three women playing on instruments. It was cut by Morris himself from Burne-Jones's drawing; it does not, however, represent the best of what he could do in wood-cutting.

"The Earthly Paradise" was published by Mr. F. S. Ellis, whose recent acquaintance with Morris had already become a warm friendship. Their relations as author and publisher were ended in 1885 by Mr. Ellis's retirement from business, but they remained attached friends through the rest of Morris's life; Mr. Ellis was much with him in his last illness and was one of his executors. The acquaintance had begun about the year 1864. Mr. Ellis was then in business in King Street, Covent Garden, principally as a dealer in manuscripts and rare printed books. Morris was first brought there by Swinburne, and afterwards often looked in on his way from Red Lion Square to London Bridge Station when he was going down to Upton in the evening. When he came to live in London his visits grew more frequent and less hurried. His knowledge of and admiration for fifteenth-century printing, generally thought of as a new development of his later years, was then already fully grown.

"The first dealing of any importance," Mr. Ellis

writes, "that we had, was over a very fine copy of the 1473 Ulm edition of Boccaccio's ' De Claris Mulieribus' with the famous woodcuts. I had bought it at a sale in Paris for £23—considered in those days to be quite an extravagant price." (The volume would now fetch at least three times as much.) "It was a very fine clean crisp copy bound in sixteenth-century vellum stained yellow. This took his fancy hugely, but the price which I asked, £26 or thereabouts, was a matter for consideration, and he asked me to keep the book till he could bring a friend to advise with him. In a day or two he called in company with his friend, a pale and fragile-looking young man. This was Burne-Jones. ' Buy the book by all means,' was the advice of the counsellor; ' how much better worth it is than any number of books of less value.' Years afterwards this volume was sacrificed at the altar of Socialism, and passed into the hands of a wealthy collector, who stripped off its yellow cover and put it into a gorgeous modern binding."

When the first edition of " Jason " was published in 1867, Morris gave a copy to Ellis, remarking that it was hard luck to have to publish a poem at one's own expense. Bell and Daldy, the publishers of the Oxford and Cambridge Magazine and of " The Defence of Guenevere," had brought " Jason " out, and in view of their experiences with the earlier volume it was not surprising that they should decline to undertake any risk. But when the first edition was exhausted, as it was within a few months, Mr. Ellis had become his adviser, and the publishers paid a substantial sum for the right to print a second. After this second edition, " Jason " was transferred to Ellis, who had already, entered into an agreement to publish " The Earthly Paradise." It may be added, that the sale of the first volume of " The Earthly Paradise " proved so satisfactory that this first agreement was cancelled, and replaced by another which gave to the author a larger share in the profits.

"How much," Mr. Ellis writes to me, "I owe of the bright side of life to him I cannot reckon. He was the very soul of honour, truthfulness, and justice. Not only would he never deviate from the truth, but in thinking carefully over the matter I do not remember him ever to have made plausible excuses for doing or not doing a thing—he would always say straightforwardly exactly what he meant." The relation of author and publisher, so often one of jealousy and discontent, was in this case without a shadow. Mr. Ellis is even willing to generalize from his own experience : "any publisher," he adds, "unless he be dishonest, can get on with an author, whose books sell, with perfect ease. Difficulties and heartburnings usually arise with authors whose books will not sell." Publishers, as a body, have a bad name with the general vague opinion of the public. That this is so, seems mainly due to a fault for which they are indeed responsible, but responsible only in the second degree—their readiness, for the sake of small but secured gains, to abet incompetent authors in forcing essentially unsaleable books upon the market.

At the end of the first volume of "The Earthly Paradise" was an announcement of the contents of the second, or concluding, volume. The twelve new tales there promised were as follows : six from Greek sources ; The Story of Theseus, Orpheus and Eurydice, The Story of Rhodope, The Dolphins and the Lovers, The Fortunes of Gyges, and The Story of Bellerophon : other six from mediæval sources, Eastern or Western ; The Hill of Venus, The Man who never Laughed again, The Palace East of the Sun, Dorothea, The Ring given to Venus, and Amis and Amillion. But after the publication of the first volume the scheme underwent large changes, partly from his replacing a number of the stories already written or planned by others, and partly from the introduction into his life, where it soon took a place second to no other interest, of the heroic literature of Iceland. The first-fruits of this new field appeared in the next portion of "The Earthly Paradise" published. Of the six stories it contained, only three belonged to the original scheme: The Story of Rhodope; The Palace East of the Sun, with its title altered to "The Land East of the Sun and West of the Moon"; and the single story drawn from Oriental sources, The Man who never Laughed again. To fill the remaining three places, two short Greek stories, "Acontius and Cydippe," and "The Death of Paris," were brought up from his reserve stores, and replaced the long and elaborate tales of Orpheus and Theseus, for which there was not room; and ending the volume, on a scale more than double that of any of the tales hitherto printed, came the noble version of the Laxdaela Saga, entitled "The Lovers of Gudrun."

In the eighteen months which passed between the appearance of this and of the earlier volume a silent revolution had been effected in the poet. It was not at once realized, even by himself. Yet here and there a critic observed that the Chaucerian manner which had been so unqualified in "Jason" and so powerful in the earlier stories of "The Earthly Paradise" was wearing off, and a new manner replacing it. Some deepening of the poetry they felt there was. What it really meant was a development of capital importance, the transformation of romance into epic. There will be occasion to mark the further progress of this change in the final volume of "The Earthly Paradise" and in "Sigurd the Volsung." But "The Lovers of Gudrun," his first essay in epic poetry, is in its way as complete and as satisfying

as any of his later achievements. Between this poem
and the story of " The Man Born to be King," a perfect
example of the pure romance, there is in truth no comparison possible. They cannot be weighed in the same
scales.

Criticism may reasonably point out this distinction,
than which none in literature is really more fundamental. But Morris himself, who was an artist and not
a critic, never took pains to emphasize the difference of
the two methods. What he cared for was the work
done; and with all his intolerance for bad work, or
work that he conceived to be bad, he had the largest
catholicity of admiration for work that he conceived to
be good; for the Chanson de Roland or the Roman de la
Rose, for the Heimskringla or the Arabian Nights, for
Beowulf, or Froissart, or the Shah Nameh. This catholicity, and this carelessness to distinguish among forms
of art which from his central and unentangled outlook
he perceived to be threaded from one centre though
they might lie on widely-severed arcs, are alike well
shown in a letter which he wrote many years later. A
German student had written to him from Marburg asking whether it were true, as the text-books said, that
Chaucer had been his model, and expressing his own
doubt on the matter.

"I quite agree," Morris answered, "as to the resemblance of my work to Chaucer; it only comes of our
both using the narrative method : and even then my
turn is decidedly more to Romance than was Chaucer's.
I admit that I have been a great admirer of Chaucer,
and that his work has had, especially in early years,
much influence on me; but I think not much on my
style. In fact I cannot think that I ever consciously
aimed at any particular style. I by nature turn to
Romance rather than classicalism, and naturally, with-

out effort, shrink from rhetoric. I may say that I am
fairly steeped in mediævalism generally; but the Icelandic Sagas, our own Border Ballads, and Froissart
(through Berners' translation of about 1520) have had
as much influence over me as (or more than) anything
else. I have translated a great deal from the Icelandic,
a little from old French; and of late have translated
Beowulf, for which I have a very great admiration."

It is obvious that the term "mediævalism" is used
here in a very largely extended meaning. It includes
Beowulf and the Elder Edda on the one hand, and
Chaucer and the Border Ballads on the other. As
regards Morris's special relation to Chaucer, nothing
need be added to his own published utterances. They
are three in number. One is the famous apostrophe to
Chaucer in the seventeenth book of "The Life and Death
of Jason":

——Would that I
Had but some portion of that mastery
That from the rose-hung lanes of woody Kent
Through these five hundred years such songs have sent
To us, who, meshed within this smoky net
Of unrejoicing labour, love them yet.
And thou, O Master! Yea, my Master still,
Whatever feet have scaled Parnassus' hill,
Since like thy measures, clear and sweet and strong,
Thames' stream scarce fettered drave the dace along
Unto the bastioned bridge, his only chain—
O Master, pardon me if yet in vain
Thou art my Master, and I fail to bring
Before men's eyes the image of the thing
My heart is filled with: thou whose dreamy eyes
Beheld the flush to Cressid's cheeks arise,
When Troilus rode up the praising street,

As clearly as they saw thy townsmen meet
Those who in vineyards of Poiƈtou withstood
The glittering horror of the steel-topped wood.

The second is in the less known, but more intimately
beautiful *Envoi* to " The Earthly Paradise ":

That land's name, say'st thou? and the road thereto?
Nay, Book, thou mockest, saying thou know'st it not;
Surely no book of verse I ever knew
But ever was the heart within him hot
To gain the Land of Matters Unforgot—
There, now we both laugh—as the whole world may,
At us poor singers of an empty day.

Nay, let it pass, and hearken! Hast thou heard
That therein I believe I have a friend,
Of whom for love I may not be afeard?
It is to him indeed I bid thee wend ;
Yea, he perchance may meet thee ere thou end,
Dying so far off from the hedge of bay,
Thou idle singer of an empty day !

Well, think of him, I bid thee, on the road,
And if it hap that midst of thy defeat,
Fainting beneath thy follies' heavy load,
My Master, Geoffry Chaucer, thou do meet,
Then shalt thou win a space of rest full sweet;
Then be thou bold, and speak the words I say,
The idle singer of an empty day !

" O Master, O thou great of heart and tongue,
Thou well mayst ask me why I wander here,
In raiment rent of stories oft besung !
But of thy gentleness draw thou anear,
And then the heart of one who held thee dear

Mayst thou behold! So near as that I lay
Unto the singer of an empty day.

" O Master, if thine heart could love us yet,
Spite of things left undone, and wrongly done,
Some place in loving hearts then should we get,
For thou, sweet-souled, didst never stand alone,
But knew'st the joy and woe of many an one—
By lovers dead, who live through thee, we pray,
Help thou us singers of an empty day!"

The last and the most emphatic of the three tributes of devotion paid by Morris to his master is the Kelmscott edition of Chaucer's works, the occupation and delight of his latest years, and the final masterpiece of his multiform production.

Soon after the publication of the first part of " The Earthly Paradise," Charles Cowden Clarke wrote to him a letter of warm and sympathetic praise. " Your intimacy with Chaucer especially," he said, " riveted me the moment I felt your appeal; and I am sure that you would not have had a more devoted admirer, and Brother in the faith of Love and Beauty, than in my beloved friend and schoolfellow, John Keats, whom I all but taught his letters." In his reply, Morris speaks of " Keats, for whom I have such boundless admiration, and whom I venture to call one of my masters." It will be easily recognized that while the world which he elected to make his own was largely that of Chaucer, his poetical affinities were with Keats more than with any other poet.

The beginning of Morris's Icelandic studies can be definitely fixed in this year. It coincides with what might be called the final extinction of Rossetti's influence over him as an artist, and the gradual loosening which followed of the closer intimacy between them, though for several years more they still saw much of each other, and for three years, from 1871 to 1874, had a country house in common. The autumn holiday of 1868 was spent by the Morrises at Southwold—a memory of it is in the lovely introductory stanzas for October in "The Earthly Paradise"—and on his return to London he plunged into the study of Icelandic under the guidance of Mr. Magnússon. Till then he had known little of the subject at first hand; Dasent's "Burnt Njal" and "Gisli" were familiar to him, and of the other Sagas he had some general knowledge. Now he began their systematic study. The first Icelandic book he read with Magnússon was the Eyrbyggja Saga. Within a few months he had gone through the bulk of the heroic literature. In the introduction to the translation of the Grettis Saga, published in April, 1869, there is a brief critical analysis of the literature showing that it had been essentially mastered. So early as January, 1869, Morris and Magnússon's translation of the Saga of Gunnlaug Worm-tongue had been published in the Fortnightly Review. And all the while the output of new poems for the remaining part of "The Earthly Paradise" was going on almost unchecked. "Bellerophon" was written in March: "Gudrun's Lovers," begun immediately after the publication of the "Grettis Saga," was finished by June. The treatment of the Bellerophon legend clearly shows the epic manner rising beside and partially overmastering the romantic.

In the autumn, Mrs. Morris's delicate health led to their spending nearly two months at Bad-Ems. From there he wrote to Ellis on the 11th of August:

"Many thanks for your kind letter which was very welcome. If you are not joking I hope indeed you will come to Ems; I think you might even fish there; at any rate I have seen with my own eyes Germans catching small bream in the Lahn, and as they never strike when they have a bite, it is probable that the fish are very hungry. We have had pike and perch to eat withal, so I suppose those monsters inhabit the rather muddy waters of the Lahn : just at Ems it is all widened out into a kind of pond with nearly no stream, but from Ems to Nassau, about six miles (English), there is no lock, and the water runs in rapids. I am sorry for your disappointment at Lechlade, but at all events it is a jolly place. The country about here is very beautiful, there is no doubt of that, and the place itself I shall consider bearable if it does my wife any good, as I hope it will. I have been pretty hard at work, have finished one tale, and begun another since I left, so the book goes on."

" Many thanks for your letter again," he writes a week later, " and the Temple Bar, which did not excoriate my thin hide in spite of a tender contempt with which Mr. Austin seemed to regard me. Commercially I suppose I ought to be grateful to him and am so ; from the critical point of view I think there is so much truth as this in his article, as that we poets of to-day have been a good deal made by those of the Byron and Shelley time—however, in another sixty years or so, when it won't matter three skips of a louse to us (as it don't matter much more now), I suppose we shall quietly fall into our places. I get about three hours' walk (with a pocket-book, Mr. Publisher) every morning, and am in roaring and offensive health, keeping country hours, woke by the band (with a hymn-tune) at seven every morning and going to bed at ten every night. I shall want about a fortnight after I come home before I begin to feed the free burgher of Berwick-upon-Tweed with my immortal MS., and after that I hope there will be no hitch. Believe me, the longest and heaviest of sticks is buzzing about my ears, as you would find out

if you had passed a week at this skin-'em-alive place;
I'm not quite sure now if I shan't have to be sold to the
Prussian government to sweep up horse-dung in Ems
streets (they are very particular about it)—my God,
what a bad bargain I should be!

"I have not got any good wine at Ems, and perhaps
they don't charge for such as they sell you! but the
Grunhauser at Cologne and Coblentz was jolly that hot
weather. Did you ever speculate as to what they fed
German sheep on? deep thought at breakfast time has
led me to suppose india-rubber to be their pabulum—
this is not very encouraging to your journey to Ems,
but you see my wife is not strong enough to get to the
restaurants here; I daresay we could get a tolerable
dinner there.

"Fishing I have not tried yet; I am too lazy to look
up proper baits. The inside of a roll would be about as
far as I should care to go. They don't seem to understand gentles at Ems; nor have I seen anybody trying
either worms or minnow, though there must be perch
here somewhere; I have seen some big chubs about."

The Ems landscape a little later in his stay is described by him in the introductory lines to "The Death
of Paris" in "The Earthly Paradise":

The level ground along the river-side
Was merry through the day with sounds of those
Who gathered apples; o'er the stream arose
The northward-looking slopes where the swine ranged
Over the fields that hook and scythe had changed
Since the last month; but 'twixt the tree-boles grey
Above them did they see the terraced way,
And over that the vine-stocks, row on row,
Whose dusty leaves, well thinned and yellowing now,
But little hid the bright-bloomed vine-bunches.

During this visit Rossetti made a facetious drawing of Morris reading aloud to his wife, entitling it " The Ms at Ems ": the drawing and the title both gave great satisfaction to the circle.

After his return in September, Part III. of " The Earthly Paradise " began to go to press, and was published in December. By that time the whole cycle was practically complete, and for Part IV., though it was not issued till a year later, little remained to be done beyond revision and selection of poems already written. As it finally appeared, that volume contained the "Bellerophon," written early in 1869, and now divided on the ground of its great length into two parts, "Bellerophon in Argos " and " Bellerophon in Lycia "; " The Golden Apples," a brief and rather vague rendering of the story of the eleventh labour of Hercules : two mediæval subjects of the earlier semi-mystical manner, " The Ring given to Venus " and " The Hill of Venus ": and another northern poem, " The Fostering of Aslaug," in which the old and new manners are combined with exceptional skill and unique fascination.

Thus " The Earthly Paradise " stood complete. It may not be inappropriate to add a brief account of the sources from which the stories are derived. For the Greek stories little use was made by Morris of recondite authors ; and indeed the whole body of Græco-Roman mythology has long been so fully explored, and so systematically set forth in dictionaries, that it is accessible to all the world alike. The only one of the twelve tales which is not generally familiar is " The Story of Rhodope." It is founded on a romantic story related by Strabo and Ælian of the beautiful Thracian slave, Rhodôpis of Naucratis, who received imperishable fame from the sisterly jealousy of Sappho, and who became strangely identified in legend with Queen Netaqerti of Egypt, the traditional builder of the Third Pyramid nearly three thousand years before.   Morris turned the name Rhodôpis into Rhodope by pure inadvertence, and was a good deal vexed when he found out the mistake.   But the poem was then published, and there was no help for it.

For the non-classical stories the originals are at once more various and less matter of common knowledge. "The Land East of the Sun and West of the Moon" was suggested to Morris by Thorpe's "Yuletide Stories," a book already mentioned as having been one of his particular favourites at Oxford.   It occurs there under the title of "The Beautiful Palace East of the Sun," with references given to original sources (principally the Volunda Saga), and to variant versions.   The latter part of the story in "The Earthly Paradise," however, diverges entirely from the story in Thorpe, and is founded partly on a French romance and partly on the Arabian Nights; and the remarkable framework of the story, an involution of dream within dream through shadowy transmigrations of personality, is wholly the poet's own.   The two stories of "The Lady of the Land" and "The Watching of the Falcon" are both from Mandeville's "Voiage and Travell," chapters iv. and xiii.   The name of the former story Morris took without change; the latter comes in Mandeville under the title of "The Castle of the Sperhauk."   "The Proud King" is from the "Gesta Romanorum," c. 57 of the French, and c. 23 of the English version: and "The Man Born to be King" mainly from the same (c. 20 of the French, and c. 48 of the English), supplemented from the more elaborate version of the same story in the thirteenth-century French romance of the Emperor Coustans (Nouvelles Françoises en prose du XIIIme Siècle, 1856), and with some further details from the story of

St. Pelagius in Caxton's " Golden Legend." The edition
of the French version of the " Gesta " used by Morris
was Brunet's of 1858, and that of the English, Madden's
of 1838. The stories of " The Writing on the Image "
and " The Ring given to Venus " are both from William
of Malmesbury, in the second book of the " De Gestis
Regum Anglorum": the former is there related of the
celebrated scholar, theologian, and mathematician, Ger-
bert of Aurillac, afterwards Pope Silvester II., known to
the mediæval imagination as a great magician like Michael
Scott. The story of " Ogier the Dane " follows pretty
closely the fourteenth-century French romance of "Ogier
le Danois." " The Hill of Venus " was suggested by
the version of this very widely diffused legend given in
Tieck's "Romances." The story of "The Man who
never Laughed again " is substantially that of the fifth
Wezeer in the story of " The King and his Son and the
Damsel and the Seven Wezeers," as given in the twenty-
first chapter of Lane's Arabian Nights. " The Fostering of Aslaug " follows closely the story as epitomized
from the older sources in Thorpe's " Northern Mythology." " The Lovers of Gudrun " was taken directly
from the original Icelandic of the Laxdaela Saga.

It must be understood that the stories as they re-
shaped themselves in Morris's mind often became quite
different from the form in which they are given in the
older sources, and that, except in the case of the great
legends where no material change is possible, he gave his
imagination free play in re-shaping and combining them.
It might happen that, as in the stories of Aslaug and
of Cupid and Psyche, the traditional form and detail of
the story was quite satisfying to him ; in these the original
sources are followed with great fidelity. But in telling
the story of " The Writing on the Image," he makes
the magician shut up in the death-trap from which he

escapes in the mediæval story; and in " The Land East
of the Sun " the story takes an entirely new course after
the first waking, and goes wandering through new and
strange realms.   This last poem represents the culmina-
tion of the romantic-mediæval method in the strongest
antithesis to the epic treatment of a given story.   The
mediæval mysticism in matters of religion is a familiar
and accepted fact.   Yet the modern divorce between
religion and life is so profound that this religious mysticism is oddly regarded as something apart and by itself,
not as the application by men to religion of their ordinary
way of thinking about anything which moved them at
all deeply.   " Mr. Morris," said a brilliant critic of this
very story, " dreams of certain old mariners of Norway
who dream of Gregory, who dreams of some one else,
whom he also dreams to be himself : and this two-faced
Janus of a dreamer dreams of another dreamer still, who
lives on the edge of two worlds, and like the old monk who
sat before the Cenacolo, can hardly discriminate between
the shadow and the substance."   This description is admirably exact ; and the attitude of mind so described
is the essence of that romantic mysticism from which
Morris was recalled by the great imperious voice of the
Icelandic epic, yet to which he kept perpetually reverting.   It reappears in unqualified dominance in the prose
romances of his latest years.   In this larger view the influence on him of the epic, were it the Odyssey or the
Æneid, the Laxdaela Saga or the Volsunga Saga, was in
its nature a perturbing influence, that drew him for a
time out of the orbit into which finally he swung back.

Besides the abandoned " Aristomenes," several other
stories were written for " The Earthly Paradise " which
remain unpublished.   Three at least of these are complete : two of them, " Orpheus and Eurydice " and " St.
Dorothea," belonging to the plan of contents at first

drawn out. The third, "The Wooing of Swanhild," though written on the whole in the earlier or romantic manner, may be inferred from its subject, which is one taken from the last chapters of the Volsunga Saga, to belong to the later period of distinct Icelandic influence. A number of others were destroyed by their author. Of "The Fortunes of Gyges" only two pages have been preserved by some accident. The tales of "The King's Treasure House" (the famous Herodotean story of Rhampsinitus) and of "The Dolphins and the Lovers," a strangely romantic story given in bare outline by Plutarch in the work entitled "The Banquet of the Seven Sages," have wholly disappeared; nor can any trace be discovered of the poem founded on the beautiful thirteenth-century French romance of "Amis and Amile." It is a rather curious fact that Morris was dissatisfied with "The Death of Paris," and meant to rewrite it. Tennyson's "Oenone" was a poem for which he had a boundless admiration; and in "The Death of Paris" he seems to have had an uneasy feeling that the subject was one on which the last word had been already said.

Meanwhile his unresting activity was striking into fresh channel. The "Grettis Saga" of 1869 was followed by the "Volsunga Saga" of 1870. This translation also was executed in collaboration with Mr. Magnússon, and was published in May. In the previous month he had been sitting to Watts for the well-known portrait which represents him in the full prime of his life and vigour. But even before then he had found that "The Earthly Paradise" was practically off his hands, and had turned to the relaxation of changed employment. He thought of taking up painting again, and drew from the model for a while in Mr. C. F. Murray's studio. From painting he soon diverged to illumination. In February the beautiful illuminated book of his own poems, given by him to Mrs. Burne-Jones, had been begun. It was the first of a series of illuminated manuscripts on which he was much occupied for several years.

"I have been hard at work," he writes to Mrs. Morris on the 14th of March, "but have not done much except the translations, as they are rather pressing now, and I want to get all my Volsung work done this week: then I shall set to work about Gabriel's review, which I must say rather terrifies me. Ned came to see me on Sunday; I read him my stanzas for the Volsunga and he thought them good. I did hope to be able to give you the news of my hair being cut this morning, but I had to stay in fair-copying for Strangeways."

The article on Rossetti's "Poems" here alluded to appeared in the Academy, a journal then just founded, on the 14th of May. Rossetti's strange fancy of a literary conspiracy against him, and his elaborate attempts to inspire favourable notices of the volume, are matter of common knowledge. Morris, with other friends, had been dragged into the business; and his article bears all the traces of a task, for once, executed against his will. It is stiff and laboured, and as nearly colourless as anything of his writing well could be.

His translation and illumination were not enough to fill his thoughts; and he wavered for a while between an instinct to break new ground in poetry and a reaction from the immense production of the last three years. The Arthurian legend once more attracted him, not now filling his mind, but making in it something of a counterpoise to the Northern Sagas. But on its mystical and religious side the cycle of the Sangreal was a subject from which, like Tennyson, though for different reasons, he instinctively shrank: and the long narrative poem on the story of Tristram, and the other on that of Balin and Balan, which were much in his mind this summer, never came to birth. In this year, too, the suggestion was made to him that he should translate the Odyssey; but neither had the time come for that.

Before the end of 1870, the last sheets of "The Earthly Paradise" had left his hands. "I feel rather lost at having done my book," he writes on the 25th of November; "I find now I liked working at it better than I thought. I must try to get something serious to do as soon as may be." And again a few days later: "I confess I am dull now my book is done; one doesn't know sometimes how much service a thing has done us till it is gone: however one has time yet; and perhaps something else of importance will turn up soon."

The pity with which he clung to it, and the forlornness in which it left him when the two had to sever company, he has written down with absolute truth and sweetness in the words of the Epilogue. Shy and reserved in life, as to many matters that lay near his heart, he had all the instinct of the born man of letters for laying himself open in his books, and having no concealments from the widest circle of all. In the verses that frame the stories of "The Earthly Paradise" there is an autobiography so delicate and so outspoken that it must needs be left to speak for itself: and the final words which he puts in the mouth of his book, when he sends it forth to seek a place with Chaucer, are the plain truth about his own life so far as he understood it, as well as his deepest thought on the mystery of things.

> "For this he ever said, who sent me forth
> To seek a place amid thy company;
> That howsoever little was my worth,
> Yet was he worth e'en just so much as I;
> He said that rhyme hath little skill to lie;

Nor feigned to cast his worser part away
In idle singing for an empty day.

"I have beheld him tremble oft enough
At things he could not choose but trust to me,
Although he knew the world was wise and rough:
And never did he fail to let me see
His love,—his folly and faithlessness, maybe;
And still in turn I gave him voice to pray
Such prayers as cling about an empty day.

"Thou, keen-eyed, reading me, mayst read him through,
For surely little is there left behind;
No power great deeds unnameable to do;
No knowledge for which words he may not find,
No love of things as vague as autumn wind—
Earth of the earth lies hidden by my clay,
The idle singer of an empty day!

"Children we twain are, saith he, late made wise,
In love, but in all else most childish still,
And seeking still the pleasure of our eyes,
And what our ears with sweetest sounds may fill;
Not fearing Love, lest these things he should kill;
Howe'er his pain by pleasure doth he lay,
Making a strange tale of an empty day.

"Death have we hated, knowing not what it meant;
Life have we loved, through green leaf and through sere,
Though still the less we knew of its intent:
The Earth and Heaven through countless year on year,
Slow changing, were to us but curtains fair,
Hung round about a little room, where play
Weeping and laughter of man's empty day."

"I don't think," he writes within a few days of the date of these verses, "people really want to die because of mental pain, that is, if they are imaginative people; they want to live to see the play played out fairly." Such at all events was his own feeling. People who have not this imaginative instinct often wonder how a poet can bear to lay open his inmost feelings, and uncover the weaknesses of which man is made: still oftener the self-revelation passes clean over the heads of his audience, and so far are they from wondering that they do not even notice. It is the knowledge, no doubt, that all of his innermost heart, his love and hope and sorrow, which he pours into his verses is to the unsympathetic reader simply meaningless, which allows a poet to write fearlessly what, being a poet, he must write in any case. *Sorge nie dass ich verrathe!* so true still are Heine's bitter words: *sorge nie! diese Welt glaubt nicht an Flammen, und sie nimmt's für Poesie.*

THE MANOR HOUSE, KELMSCOTT, FROM THE FARM.

CHAPTER VII

MORRIS AND KELMSCOTT

AT the age of thirty-six, in the full prime of vigour and in the rising light of fame which had not yet drawn after it its inevitable shadows of imitation and detraction, Morris occupied a position in some ways as enviable as could have been devised for him by his own imaginings. Watts's great portrait is the memorial which represents him at this stage of his life most fully if not most intimately. From it looks out the " powerful and beautiful face " which impressed itself unforgettably even on those who saw it but once. The massive head with its thickly clustering dark curls ; the vague inexpressive eyes ; the sensitive mouth, a little overweighted by the broad frank brows, are recorded in it with the felicity of genius. One sees in it the dreamer of dreams, as he described himself in a much quoted phrase, who is at the same time the man of action, overflowing with practical energy, and as eager as he had been in the days of his earliest enthusiasm, not only "to do and say and see so many things," but to carry out "things I have thought of for the bettering of the world as far as lies in me."

Of Morris as a poet and as an artist, the truest record is to be found in his actual work. In both cases alike he gave his best to the world quite simply, without ostentation, and without concealment ; and with the world, as a still living influence, what was permanent in it remains. But of the personality behind it, that work, without the actual living speech and gesture and movement of the man, gives only partial glimpses : nor does it bear any trace at all of what made his personality most unique, that "rum and indescribable deportment" which was a perpetual fascination to all his acquaintance.

By some indefinable mixture of blood, the romantic element which was so powerful in his nature, and which made one side of his inner life one long dream, was united with that natural piety, that steady and almost stolid dutifulness, which has been the saving strength of his nation. Nor upon that side of his nature was he merely a typical Englishman; he was also a typical Londoner of the middle class, though the force of his genius transformed all the habits and thoughts and acts of his class into something quite individual. In this there was a striking resemblance between him and his great master. Among all his townsmen who have before our own day been eminent as men of letters or artists, it is to Chaucer that one would turn by the first instinct for a parallel. The resemblance even extended to physical features : the corpulent person, the demure smile, the "close silent eye." In his devotion to angling beyond all other pastimes, and his delight in all the simplest rural pleasures—the joy of the townsman taking a day in the country—he had something in common with Izaak Walton, the scholar and man of letters who sold chintzes and brocades in Fleet Street. With the most famous of all later Londoners there was in certain aspects even a closer analogy, which became more marked in the later years of Morris's life. None of his friends could fail to notice how his potent and imperious personality recalled that of Samuel Johnson. The delight in contradiction and paradox under which there lay a fundamental integrity of intellect; the sanity and strong practical sense; the haunting fear of death, to a degree which would be called morbid in any less imaginative nature; even the slovenliness in dress and the inveterate habit of tea drinking, were as marked in the one as in the other.

The combination of the dreaminess which habitually lives in a world of its own creation with a hot and passionate temper is one which is perhaps not rare, but which seldom exists in so intense a form as it did in Morris. When "The Earthly Paradise" was being published "the men at the shop thought a great deal of it": but if they had been inclined to think meanly of him as a poet, they would in any case have respected and admired the employer whose language was so forcible and copious when things were not going to his mind. In one of his tempers he was capable of almost anything. Once at Red Lion Square he hurled a fifteenth-century folio, which in ordinary circumstances he would hardly have allowed any one but himself to touch, at the head of an offending workman. It missed the workman and drove a panel out of the workshop door. His "tempestuous and exacting company," in the phrase of one of his most intimate friends, had something of the quality of an overwhelming natural force; like the north wind, it braced and buffeted in almost equal measure. He had the incessant restlessness of a wild creature. One of his friends describes him, on the occasion of their first meeting in 1871, as pacing up and down the room like a caged lion. Even at work or at meals he could not sit still for long, but must be continually shifting and fidgeting, getting up to cross the room or look out of the window and then sitting down again. This restless movement was a necessity to him as a means of working off his great bodily strength and superabundant vitality. In his gusts of temper he seemed insensible to pain and almost superhuman in his strength : he has been known to drive his head against a wall so as to make a deep dent in the plaster, and bite almost through the woodwork of a window frame.   He could lift the heaviest weight in his teeth with apparent ease.   Once when describing how he had seen passengers staggering off a Channel steamer loaded with luggage, he illustrated his point to the amusement and horror of his audience by getting a chair under each arm and then stooping and lifting the coal-scuttle in his teeth.   His eyes, the most quick-sighted among all his acquaintance, had the filmed unobservant look of an eagle's.   " When he was young," Sir Edward Burne-Jones says, " he was very handsome, and yet even then his eyes were the most inexpressive I ever saw. They say nothing to you, nor much look at you, but are so swift, they have taken in everything there is to be seen while you are wondering when they will open. If you saw him, he wouldn't look at you, but would know everything you had on, and all your expression, without being seen to look."   The only expressive feature of the face was his firm, mobile, and delicately modelled mouth.

The familiar figure of more recent years had altered but little, except for the inevitable changes of age, from that of his prime.   His dress always seemed full of his individuality.   Certain youthful indiscretions in the way of purple trousers are remembered as having belonged to the time of the Oxford Brotherhood.   But his ordinary dress had no special quality except great simplicity and untidiness.   In 1871 he accepted a place on the directorate of the mining company from which a large portion of the income of his mother and sisters as well as his own was derived.   For the purpose of attending directors' meetings he kept a tall hat, which he hardly wore on any other occasion, and which caused him untold discomfort. His daughter May remembers, when a little child, finding this strange object in the house, and asking her mother first what it was, and then whether Papa wore it. Morris himself once said with perfect simplicity to a friend, "You see, one can't go about London in a top hat, it looks so devilish odd." And this was the mere truth in his case; for it was only in conventional dress that he looked really peculiar. When he resigned his directorship four years afterwards he came home from the last meeting he had attended and solemnly sat down upon his tall hat, which was never replaced. In his suit of blue serge and soft felt hat, he had something of the look of a working engineer and something of that of a sailor. He was walking down Kensington High Street one morning when a fireman from the brigade station stopped him and said, "Beg pardon, sir, but were you ever captain of the Sea Swallow?" Indeed a stranger might very well, not only from his clothing, but from his rocking walk and ruddy complexion, have taken him for a Baltic sea-captain. In those days he had not yet adopted the blue cotton shirts which, in later years, became his invariable dress and almost of the essence of his appearance. The capacity for producing and annexing dirt, noted by Rossetti, remained strong in him; and when he began to add dyeing to the other handicrafts which he practised, appearances were completely given up. After he ceased to live at Queen Square in 1872, he very often went to lunch at the Faulkners' house a few doors off. He went along, if the day were fine, without a hat and in his French workman's blouse; and a new housemaid of the Faulkners' when she let him in thus dressed for the first time, went down to the kitchen in some perplexity, describing him to the cook as the butcher. Mr. Ellis, in the days of their first acquaintance, was privately warned by his confidential clerk "not to let that Mr. Morris run up a long account." How he looked to other people was a matter that never entered his head, and he never looked at himself. He had a curious dislike of mirrors. One of the most obvious peculiarities of his house at all times was the absence of mirrors or looking-glasses; there were none at all in any of the living rooms, and none in his bedroom.

With his great physical strength went the gift of profound and almost dreamless sleep, taken, to use his own phrase, in solid bars. From this he awoke at the full height of his energy. Within ten minutes of waking in the morning he had dressed and begun the business of the day. He was often at work at his writing, or his designing, or his loom, by the summer sunrise; and in those undisturbed hours lay a great part of the secret of the immense copiousness of his production both as a poet and as a decorative artist.

For one who made his whole work into a fascinating and absorbing recreation, and who could turn from one kind of work to another with such ease and swiftness, what is ordinarily called recreation was a thing of less importance than to most men. The only form of sport to which he was thoroughly devoted was angling. When he had a house of his own on the upper Thames, it was his delight at all times of the year, and in all weathers, to escape from London for a day's fishing. He was often accompanied on these expeditions by Ellis, who was an equal enthusiast; and before that, they had fished over most of the river between Windsor and Richmond. But he never shot, and seldom rode when he could drive. His only other outdoor amusement was playing bowls. The bowling green had been one of the features of Red House, and he played the game a great deal when he had a garden of his own again at Hammersmith. His chief indoor games were backgammon, draughts, and cribbage; and at one time he played whist pretty regularly. The need of games to pass the time—the reason why nine persons out of ten after they are grown up play games at all—was a thing that he probably never felt. His mind was always working, and his hands never long idle. Nor, in spite of his exceptional swiftness in reading and the immense detailed knowledge which he acquired from books, was he what is called a great reader. His power of rapid reading did not degenerate into the mere physical craving to read. He always knew whether he wanted to read a book or not, and when he did not, nothing could induce him to read it. His library, until he began to collect early printed books, was not large, nor was it either selected or kept with any special care. He lost books which were not precious in themselves almost as fast as he read them; and his shelves were half filled with a strange collection of the yellow-backed novels which he had bought on railway journeys. His knowledge of mediæval English poetry and ballads was both large and accurate, but the Elizabethan and later authors he knew very imperfectly and read but little. Some of the great names of English poetry were his special aversions. Milton he always abused, though he sometimes betrayed more knowledge of him than he would have been willing to admit; Wordsworth he disliked; he had little admiration for the later works of Browning, once so great a master to him, nor did he care much for anything of Tennyson's after " Maud." Keats he held the first of modern English poets.

Among the great prose authors under whose influence he had fallen at Oxford, Carlyle and Ruskin were the two who continued to hold him most strongly. For the latter, whose influence over him was indeed much the more profound and far-reaching, his admiration was sometimes crossed by that defiance which had been observed in his Oxford days to mingle with his enthusiasm for Tennyson. The earlier volumes of "Modern Painters" had been received by him with an admiration akin to worship; he was heard to describe the fifth volume, when it appeared in 1860, in a phrase characteristic of a swallower of formulas, as "mostly gammon." But this was the caprice of a momentary impatience; and all his serious references to Ruskin showed that he retained towards him the attitude of a scholar to a great teacher and master, not only in matters of art, but throughout the whole sphere of human life.

In a very different spirit he was devoted to George Borrow and read him perpetually; and no less devoted to the more obscured fame of William Cobbett, with whom he had many tastes and prejudices in common, and whose "Rural Rides" he knew almost by heart. Peacock was another of his favourite authors. But volumes which he read perhaps more than any of these, and which he imposed on his friends unflinchingly, were those describing the sayings and doings of the celebrated Mr. Jorrocks. With a feeling that was not all love of paradox, though that had its share, he placed Surtees in the same rank with Dickens as a master of life. In a man who never hunted, who seldom even rode, and to whom the life of a country house in the hunting season was not merely alien but odious, this preference must remain something of an unexplained mystery. Of Dickens himself his knowledge and appreciation were both complete. It is not without value as an illustration of his curiously compounded personality that in the moods when he was not dreaming of himself as Tristram or Sigurd, he identified himself very closely with two creations of a quite different mould, Joe Gargery and Mr.

Boffin. Both of those amiable characters he more or less consciously copied, if it be not truer to say more or less naturally resembled, and knew that he resembled. The " Morning, morning!" of the latter, and the " Wot larks!" of the former he adopted as his own favourite methods of salutation. And one of the phrases that were most constantly on his lips, which he used indiscriminately to indicate his disapproval of anything from Parliamentary institutions to the architecture of St. Paul's Cathedral, was, as all his friends will remember, the last recorded saying of Mr. F.'s Aunt, " Bring him forard, and I'll chuck him out o' winder."

The recollection of these middle years, by those who shared in them as children and are now themselves in the midway path of life, is one of strenuous work mingled with much talk and laughter, and broken by many little feasts and holidays. Nothing was more amazing in Morris than the way in which he always seemed at leisure, and always was ready for enjoyment. Neither in work nor in play was he wasteful ; he had learned, in a way that few can, the great secret of not doing, whether it took the guise of work or of amusement, what he did not want to do. The so-called claims of society, so far as they did not represent anything for which he really cared, he quite simply and unaffectedly ignored. He never throughout his life belonged to a club. The drudgery of business he could not wholly escape, but he never allowed it either to absorb his time or to master his intelligence. That neglect of detail which is one of the secrets of success came to him naturally. For the intricacies of business he had no taste and little patience. "I keep fifteen clerks doing my accounts," he once observed, when inveighing against the artificial complexity of modern commerce, "and yet I cannot find out how much money I have got." If he had insisted on finding out, he might perhaps have known, but at the cost of this striking quality of detachment from routine. And for one so simple in his pleasures as he was, the routine of pleasure was as little worth its price to him as the routine of business. But with his chief friends the daily intercourse of pleasure was constant. For years a week day hardly ever passed, when he was in London, without his looking in on the Faulkners in Queen Square. At a later period the supper in the Strand on Thursday evenings, with Webb and one or two others, after the meetings of the Society for Protection of Ancient Buildings, was equally constant. His Sunday mornings at Burne-Jones's house, which only ceased with his last illness, have already been mentioned. For many years he also dined there regularly on Wednesdays: "there was no music on those evenings," is a child's recollection, "and he would read aloud."

"Once when I had been upstairs in the nursery at Kensington Square," a friend writes of a visit to Burne-Jones's house in the winter of 1866-7, "I came down and found Morris in the parlour. He was nibbing a pen, and he said after a few words of chat, 'Now you see, I'm going to write poetry, so you'll have to cut. I'm sorry, but it can't be helped.' So I cut; and I have a notion that I know what he wrote that evening, as next Saturday when I turned up as I always did, he read us a lot of the story of Psyche. I recollect his remarking that it was very hard work writing that sort of thing. I took it he was speaking of the thrashing Psyche gets at the hands of Venus. He really felt for her, and was evidently glad it was over."

But even when writing poetry he was by no means intolerant of interruption. Some years later Miss Mary De Morgan, when staying at Kelmscott Manor, came one day into the tapestry room, and found him alone

there, busy writing at a side table.   Seeing his occupation by the look of the manuscript, she was turning to
leave the room again, when he called out to her, " Where
are you going, Mary?"   " I thought you were busy
writing poetry," she said.   " What the devil has that
got to do with it?" he cheerfully replied.   " Sit down
and tell me a tale."

But while he found perpetual amusement in his work,
his amusements had always a strong element of seriousness.   " At my first visit," Mr. William De Morgan
notes—this was at Red Lion Square in 1864—" I chiefly
recollect his dressing himself in vestments and playing
on a regal, to illustrate points in connection with stained
glass.   As I went home it suddenly crossed my mind as
a strange thing that he should, while doing what was so
trivial and almost grotesque, continue to leave on my
memory so strong an impression of his power—he certainly did, somehow."   And this was true of all his
diversions.   Another friend of his who had been staying
a few days with him was asked, after he came away, what
they had talked about.   He confessed that he could not
remember that they had talked of anything but eating:
" and yet," he added, " I came away feeling myself enlarged and liberalized."   For to Morris cookery had an
important place among the arts of human life, and he
knew a great deal about it in theory, and something also
in practice.   His wonderful memory served him here as
in other things.   Once he astonished a friend by giving
off-hand the recipe for some rather unusual dish, and
when she asked how he came to know it, told her that
he had once had to stay a night at an inn where there
was nothing to read but a cookery book, and had as-
similated it in the course of the evening.   His happiness
in a day's fishing was much enhanced by cooking the
fish he had caught.   A few years later than this, talk

had happened to turn on the problems of domestic service. " I wouldn't at all mind being a cook," Morris said, "for I understand cooking." " Now and again," he went on, " I would give you all a good feast, but feasts are spoiled if you have them every day, and I promise you I should keep up good strict discipline. I should say to you, ' Now this is tripe and onion day,' and on another day, ' Now this is porridge day,' and you should not have any choice." " I wouldn't be a parlour maid," he said in the course of the same discussion. " I wouldn't answer bells after a certain time, and if you rang the bells I should shy my boots at them." In the matter of food, as also of wine (in which he had a fine judgment), his taste was more French than modern English. " I always bless God," he once said, " for making anything so strong as an onion." One of his favourite illustrations of the decadence of England from its mediæval state was the barbarism of modern English cookery and in especial the abuse or disuse of vegetables. " There are two things," he said in one of his perverse moods, " about which women know absolutely nothing, dress and cookery: their twist isn't that way. They have no sense of colour or grace in drapery, and they never invented a new dish or failed to half spoil an old one." A passage in the fifth book of Lucretius will occur to the classical reader as a parallel: and, indeed, all of that wonderful description of the origins of civilization, alike in its swift insight and in a certain childlike interest in details, is not unlike the talk which Morris would often pour out to his friends.

Above all, beyond even his delight in great buildings, in history, in the masterpieces of human invention, lay in him that intense passion for Nature, "my love of the earth and worship of it," which, soon after the completion of " The Earthly Paradise," obtained a centre in the Manor House at Kelmscott. For the twenty-five years during which this beautiful old house was his country home, he found in it a peace and joy that no other place gave him, and his attachment to it became more and more deep—one may boldly say, more and more passionate : for with him the love of things had all the romance and passion that is generally associated with the love of persons only. " It has come to be to me," he wrote in 1882, " the type of the pleasant places of the earth, and of the homes of harmless simple people not overburdened with the intricacies of life; and as others love the race of man through their lovers or their children, so I love the earth through that small space of it."

Kelmscott was found out by accident. Five years in Bloomsbury had not reconciled Morris or his family to the prospect of unmitigated London, and they had been looking out vaguely for some little country place which they might make more or less permanently their own, and which would release them from that incubus of middle class London life, the recurring choice of a place for summer quarters, and the discomforts of a holiday in lodgings. An advertisement of Kelmscott Manor House in a London house-agent's list in the early spring of 1871 seemed to offer a place that would just suit them, and when he went down to see it, the reality exceeded his best expectations.

On the 17th of May he writes to Faulkner : " I have been looking about for a house for the wife and kids, and whither do you guess my eye is turned now? Kelmscott, a little village about two miles above Radcott Bridge—a heaven on earth; an old stone Elizabethan house like Water Eaton, and such a garden! close down on the river, a boat house and all things handy. I am going there again on Saturday with Ros-

setti and my wife : Rossetti because he thinks of sharing
it with us if the thing looks likely."

The house stands on the upper Thames, thirty miles
by water from Oxford. It is approached by lanes from
the little town of Lechlade, three miles off, to which
there is now a railway. At that time, however, that
line did not go beyond Witney, and Kelmscott had to
be reached from Faringdon, by a long drive through the
Berkshire hills. Both may be called back ways of approaching it; the grand entry, up the lovely lonely
waterway, was described by Morris himself thus, nearly
twenty years later:

" On we went, turning a sharp angle and going north
a little. Presently we saw before us a bank of elm-trees,
which told us of a house amidst them. In a few minutes
we had passed through a deep eddying pool into the
sharp stream that ran from the ford, and beached our
craft on a tiny strand of limestone gravel, and stepped
ashore.

" Mounting on the cart-road that ran along the river
some feet above the water, I looked round about me.
The river came down through a wide meadow on my
left, which was grey now with the ripened seeding
grasses; the gleaming water was lost presently by a
turn of the bank, but over the meadow I could see the
gables of a building where I knew the lock must be. A
low wooded ridge bounded the river-plain to the south
and south-east whence we had come, and a few low
houses lay about its feet and up its slope. I turned a
little to my right and through the hawthorn sprays and
long shoots of the wild roses could see the flat country
spreading out far away under the sun of the calm evening, till something that might be called hills with a look
of sheep-pastures about them bounded it with a soft blue
line. Before one, the elm boughs still hid most of what

houses there might be in this river-side dwelling of men;
but to the right of the cart-road a few grey buildings of
the simplest kind showed here and there.

"My feet moved on along the road they knew. The
raised way led us into a little field bounded by a backwater of the river on one side; on the right hand we
could see a cluster of small houses and barns, and before
us a grey stone barn and a wall partly overgrown with
ivy, over which a few grey gables showed. The village
road ended in the shallow of the backwater. We crossed
the road, and my hand raised the latch of a door in the
wall, and we stood presently on a stone path which led
up to the old house. The garden between the wall and
the house was redolent of the June flowers, and the
roses were rolling over one another with that delicious
superabundance of small well-tended gardens which at
first sight takes away all thought save that of beauty.
The blackbirds were singing their loudest, the doves
were cooing on the roof-ridge, the rooks in the high
elm-trees beyond were garrulous among the young leaves,
and the swifts wheeled whining about the gables. And
the house itself was a fit guardian for all the beauty of
this heart of summer.

"O me! O me! How I love the earth, and the
seasons, and weather and all things that deal with it, and
all that grows out of it—as this has done! The earth
and the growth of it and the life of it! If I could but
say or show how I love it!"

Such, in the romance of a new Arcadia into which the
social revolution might at last lead mankind, is the account Morris gives of his return to the loved place
which he could not wish or fancy but unchanged upon
a changed and happier earth. The pictures of the house
and its surroundings which follow are taken from a more
unimpassioned description, which is nevertheless no less

lovingly and characteristically worded, in an account of Kelmscott which he wrote in the last year of his life for a magazine conducted by members of the Birmingham Guild of Handicraft.

" The village of Kelmscott lies close to the Thames on the Oxfordshire side of it, some five miles (by water) from the present end of the navigation at Inglesham. To the north-east of the village lies the nearly treeless piece of ground formerly Grafton Common, and beyond it is a string of pretty inland villages. On the Berkshire side a range of heights, low but well designed, rise up from the flat meadows.

" The church, at the north-west end of the village, is small but interesting; the mass of it, a nave with a tiny aisle, transept and chancel, being early English of date, though the arches of the aisle are round-headed. There are remains of painting all over the church, the north transept having been painted with figure subjects of the life of Christ in trefoil head panels. The east window has a painted glass image of St. George (in whose honour the church is dedicated) of the time of Edward IV. Most of the windows (which are insertions of the early 14th century) have their inner arches elegantly cusped, a characteristic feature of these Oxfordshire churches. A very beautiful bell-cot formed by two trefoil arches crowns the eastern gable of the nave, and composes pleasantly with the low-pitched roofs over a clerestory, which in the 15th century took the place of the once high-pitched ones. The church is plastered almost all over the walls, as no doubt it was in the earliest days: it is fortunate in having escaped the process of stripping and pointing which so many of our village churches have undergone at the hands of the restoring wiseacres.

" When you turn down from the church towards the Thames you come at a corner of the road on the base of the village cross (probably of the 15th century), and then, turning to the left and bearing round to the right, all of which transaction takes place in about two hundred yards, you come face to face with a mass of grey walls and pearly grey roofs which makes the house, called by courtesy the Manor House, though it seems to have no manorial rights attached to it, which I have held for twenty-three years. It lies at the very end of the village on a road which, brought up shortly by a back-water of the Thames, becomes a mere cart-track leading into the meadows along the river.

" Through a door in the high unpointed stone wall you go up a flagged path through the front garden to the porch. The house from this side is a lowish three storied one with mullioned windows, and at right angles to this another block whose bigger lower windows and pedimented gable-lights indicate a later date. The house is built of well-laid rubble stone of the district, the wall of the latter part being buttered over, so to say, with thin plaster which has now weathered to the same colour as the stone of the walls; the roofs are covered with the beautiful stone slates of the district, the most lovely covering which a roof can have, especially when, as here and in all the traditional old houses of the country-side, they are ' sized down'; the smaller ones to the top and the bigger towards the eaves, which gives one the same sort of pleasure in their orderly beauty as a fish's scales or a bird's feathers.

" The farm buildings stand to the south of the house : a very handsome barn of quite beautiful proportions, and several other sheds, including a good dove-cot, all built in the same way as the house, and grouping delightfully with it.

" The garden, divided by old clipped yew hedges, is quite unaffected and very pleasant, and looks in fact as if it were, if not a part of the house, yet at least the clothes of it: which I think ought to be the aim of the layer out of a garden.

"Going under an arched opening in the yew hedge which makes a little garth about a low door in the middle of the north wall, one comes into a curious passage or lobby, a part of which is screened into a kind of pantry by wooden mullions which have once been glazed. The said lobby leads into what was once the great parlour (the house is not great at all remember) and is now panelled with pleasing George I. panelling painted white: the chimney-piece is no doubt of the date of the building, and is of rude but rather amusing country work; the windows in this room are large and transomed, and it is as pleasant as possible; and I have many a memory of hot summer mornings passed in its coolness amidst the green reflections of the garden.

"The tapestry room is over the big panelled parlour. The walls of it are hung with tapestry of about 1600, representing the story of Samson; they were never great works of art, and now when all the bright colours are faded out, and nothing is left but the indigo blues, the greys and the warm yellowy browns, they look better, I think, than they were meant to look: at any rate they make the walls a very pleasant background for the living people who haunt the room; and, in spite of the designer, they give an air of romance to the room which nothing else would quite do.

"Another charm this room has, that through its south window you not only catch a glimpse of the Thames clover meadows and the pretty little elm-crowned hill over in Berkshire, but if you sit in the proper place, you can see not only the barn aforesaid with its beautiful sharp gable, the grey stone sheds, and the dove-cot, but also the flank of the earlier house and its little gables

THE MANOR HOUSE, KELMSCOTT, FROM THE ORCHARD.

and grey scaled roofs, and this is a beautiful outlook indeed.

" A house that I love ; with a reasonable love I think : for though my words may give you no idea of any special charm about it, yet I assure you that the charm is there ; so much has the old house grown up out of the soil and the lives of those that lived on it : some thin thread of tradition, a half-anxious sense of the delight of meadow and acre and wood and river ; a certain amount (not too much let us hope) of common sense, a liking for making materials serve one's turn, and perhaps at bottom some little grain of sentiment :—this I think was what went to the making of the old house."

To this account of Kelmscott may be added a few observations made by Mr. Webb from his further knowledge as a professional architect :

" From my earliest recollections this general kind of house was familiar to me, where the coarse oolite stone of Thames valley gave the peculiar character to the old buildings in and around Oxford. There are still remaining, in more or less perfect state, many houses of the same quality, though some are more architecturally marked than at Kelmscott.

" It is a known fact that in outlying places, where stone mason's work is the chief part of the building, and there are many quarries giving the same formation of stone, the prevailing traditions of building lasted longer in one place than another. This makes it often difficult in such places to be sure of dates from the style of the masonry, and more particularly in the last centuries, as the masons worked so much in the older way, when in busier places, or districts, changes of fashion told more quickly.

" W. M. often spoke of what was recorded here and there, and of what he had gathered from the natives, as to dates of the Kelmscott house building: I came to no conclusion—save, that the work was really later than it looked to be.

" For so late a time of genuine native building, and from the modesty of the house altogether, it was singular how the regular *plan* of the old English form, of all degrees of importance, was inclosed in the earlier part of it. There was the entrance doorway in the front wall leading through to the opposite doorway in the back wall, with the hall on the right hand, cut off from the passage by the screen, with the kitchen and other offices on the left: the parlour (or ' solar ') at the other end of the hall, by the side of the stairs, with cellar under; all of which was of the smallest and least pretentious work. Then, a comparatively few years later, the large square parlour was built with the tapestry room over, in loftier range, and in a style clearly showing the Renaissance influence, chiefly marked by the two large fire-places, and the small classically shaped windows in the gables of attics in the roofs.

" No unprejudiced person could read the last chapter of ' News from Nowhere ' without being obliged to allow that W. M. had read the influences of the beautiful place in its entirety clearly, and without transformation by imagination; the real wanting no fanciful improvement. The price he paid for this joy in the house and all lying about it was the shadow of the coming change which overhung it: no efforts on his part—and they were many—could stay the piecemeal fungus-growth of disease in building which had begun to eat into the fringe of the surroundings: for each inevitable new element of change had tenfold brutal force in its vulgarization from the collected purity and simplicity on which it was settling down."

The country in which Kelmscott lies is among the

sleepiest and loneliest of southern England. With little
bold or striking beauty, it has a charm of unequalled
subtlety and lastingness. The young Thames winds
through level pastures, among low surrounding hills, in a
landscape that seems as if little change had passed over it
since the English settlement. Beyond the level and often
flooded river-meadows the ground rises imperceptibly
northwards towards the spurs of the Cotswolds, out of
which half-a-dozen small rivers break to mingle with the
Thames. Bibury, one of these little-known Cotswold
villages, "lying down in the winding valley beside the
clear Colne," was described by Morris as "surely the
most beautiful village in England." Churches, houses,
barns, the dry walls of the fields, are all alike built of
the golden-grey limestone underlying the soil. Hardly
a village is without a beautiful church, generally dating
back to the thirteenth century. Broadwell, the parish
next but one to Kelmscott, has a tower and spire built
by the same masons as those who built the tower and
spire of Oxford Cathedral, and on their smaller scale
equal in beauty. At Langford, a mile off, part of the
church dates from before the Norman Conquest. The
parish church of Burford on the Windrush, a sumptu-
ously decorated building of less ancient date, is an epi-
tome of the whole civic life and art of the later Middle
Ages. Much of the domestic building of this region
is little inferior to the churches either in age or architectural beauty. The most splendid example is the tithe
barn at Great Coxwell, a noble structure of the middle
of the thirteenth century, " unapproachable in its dignity,
as beautiful as a cathedral, yet with no ostentation of the
builder's art," its hundred and fifty feet of grey roof
raised on a forest of orderly set oak timbers. It was
always upheld by Morris as one of the finest buildings
in England or in the world. The grey pointed arches

over the Thames, on the solitary highway leading south
out of the Royal Forest of Wychwood, are as beautiful
now as when, six hundred and fifty years ago, they received their still surviving name of the New Bridge.   A
little further off, under the feet of the Cotswolds, is
Chastleton, the finest and most complete of all surviving
Jacobean houses.   In a land remote from commerce, full
of beautiful building, and with perfect building material
everywhere close at hand, it is not strange that the tradition of beauty should have survived longer than elsewhere.

This upper Thames valley, well-wooded and abund-
antly watered, is a land of birds.   The blackbirds sing
at Kelmscott after they have fallen silent elsewhere.
The little island formed by the backwater close to the
house was always filled with song from a hundred throats.
In Morris's letters from Kelmscott there are constant
allusions to the bird-life about it.   The two following
passages belong to the season of late summer:

"The birds were very delightful about us; I have
been of late so steeped in London that it was a quite
fresh pleasure to see the rooks about, who have been
very busy in this showery weather.   There was no lack
of herons in these upper waters, and in the twilight the
stint or summer snipe was crying about us and flitting
from under the bank and across the stream: such a
clean-made, neat-feathered, light grey little chap he is,
with a wild musical little note like all the moor-haunting
birds."

"We have had all the birds here again.   The herons
have been stalking about the field in the gravest manner;
and I have seen the kingfishers very busy.   One ducked
down into the water before me and came out again with
a little fish.   I saw an owl last night come sailing along,
and suddenly turn head over heels and down in the

grass; after a mouse I suppose: such a queer action I never saw."

Another letter in a few brief vivid touches gives a picture of the birds in October:

" The western sky is getting leaden grey and the wind is rain-cold. I heard a heron 'squark' just now, and saw two of them sailing overhead. I have seen the kingfishers twice : one sat three yards from me for two or three minutes and talked to himself before he saw me : he was a beauty."

And again soon after Christmas :

"Bossom told me that the hard winter had killed a huge number of the moor-hens. He said that when the frost was on they would come down to the open water by his barge and drink a drop or two and then die, poor things."

The creek, with its wooden bridge and boat-house, has now been cut off from the house by an earthwork and deep ditch formed to keep out the winter floods from the village, and the weir and gate-house across the meadow have been rebuilt; otherwise there is scarcely a change from thirty years ago in the manor-house and its immediate surroundings.

" The house was then kept," Mr. Ellis says, " by an old couple, Philip Comely and his wife, who were the ideal English villagers, capable, careful, frugal, and industrious. But Morris was much embarrassed by the apparently mechanical arrangement, 'as though it were a trick of machinery,' by which Philip's hand rose to the brim of his hat, or lacking that to his forelock, with every word he uttered. Philip's cottage served as a sort of lodge to the manor-house, rented for a shilling a week, with a good-sized and fruitful garden."

Kelmscott was at first taken by Morris in joint-tenancy with Rossetti. The breakdown in Rossetti's health, which had begun two or three years earlier, was now very

marked, and it was hoped that quiet life in a remote
country house might do much to restore him to bodily
health and relieve his morbid imaginations. For a while
he was much more there than Morris, who could not
easily be away from London and his work for a long
time together. He was there through the summer and
autumn of 1871. In 1872 the dangerous illness of which
details are given in his biography was followed by a long
visit to Scotland, but he was at Kelmscott again from
September all through the winter of 1872-3, and for
the greater part of the following twelve months. In the
summer of 1874 he finally left it; not a little to Morris's
relief for many reasons. The manor-house soon resumed
its quietness and simplicity. The expense of keeping
up a country house in permanence was as yet rather a
severe strain on Morris's unaided means; and the joint-
tenancy was for some years resumed with Mr. Ellis as
the partner. From this time forth it was the haven of
rest to which he always returned with a fresh and deep
delight. All seasons there were alike sweet to him.
The following extracts are taken almost at random from
familiar letters of different years.

February. "The waters are out a little, owing to
the melting snow. It is a cold rather windy day, but
not unpleasant; brilliantly sunny at first, now cloudy
with gleams of sun at times. It froze last night; but
took to a sharp shower in the morning. As to the
garden, they are late here; there are two or three
crocuses out, but most of them are not above ground
even; the winter aconite is not fully in blossom, and the
yellow jasmine is over. Snowdrops are everywhere, but
mostly double, however they give one a delightful idea
of spring about: there are a few violets out and here
and there a coloured primrose; and some of the hepatica
roots have flowered, but show no leaves. But how

pretty it looks to see the promise of things pushing up through the clean un-sooty soil. I think we shall have a beautiful garden this year."

April. " I never yet till now understood how green the grass could be in spring; it is so green that it brings all the distance near and flattens the landscape into a mediæval picture. It is most beautiful; and when we were here in the middle of March the grass was all as grey as grey. You see just now there are not many daisies out, and the bents have not begun to grow, so that the grass is all grass and deep green. It has just been raining May butter, as Izaak Walton says: looked for an hour as if it would never stop raining again; then it got a little lighter, and then of a sudden was the bright sun and a rainbow. Item, I have eaten asparagus and heard the cuckoo: the blackbirds wake me about 4 o'clock a.m.: as for the rooks they never stop all day long. I saw a leash of plovers yesterday squawking away, and making believe that they had no nest close at hand. The garden is full of bullfinches, which are fat pretty dears, and sing a little short song very sweetly."

May. " The fields are all butter-cuppy. The elms are mostly green up to their tops: the hawthorn not out, but the crabs beautiful, and also that white-beam (I think they call it) with the umbelliferous flowers. In the garden we have lots of tulips out looking beautiful; the white bluebells and some blue ones: some of the anemones are in blossom and they all soon will be: they are very lovely. Apple-blossom for the most part only in bud, but that cherry-tree near the arbour opposite my window is a mass of bloom. The heartseases are beautiful; a few of the Iceland poppies are out: the raspberries are showing for blossom."

August. " The fishing is pretty much as it was; the

river higher and the weeds uncut, though not very
visible at the first glance because the water is high.
Altogether a very pleasant river to travel on, the bank
being still very beautiful with flowers; the long purples,
and willow-herb, and that strong-coloured yellow flower
very close and buttony, are the great show : but there is
a very pretty dark blue flower, I think mug-wort,
mixed with all that, besides the purple blossom of the
house-mint and mouse-ear and here and there a bit of
meadow-sweet belated. As to the garden it seems to me
its chief fruit is—blackbirds. However they have left us
some gooseberries, and I shall set to work this morning
to get some before their next sit-down meal. As for
flowers, the July glory has departed as needs must, but
the garden looks pleasant though not very flowery.
Those sweet sultans are run very much to leaf, but the
beds in which they and the scabious are look very pretty,
the latter having very delicate foliage. There are two
tall hollyhocks (O so tall) by the strawberries, one
white, one a very pretty red : there are still a good many
poppies in blossom. Few apples, few plums, plenty of
vegetables else. Weather doubtful; I woke up this
morning to a most splendid but very stormy sunrise.
The nights have been fine, and the moon rises her old
way from behind the great barn."

October. " The garden is nearly over now till spring
comes again, except that there are a good many roses,
and amongst them, a pale sweet-briar blossom among
the scarlet hips, that I am sure I never saw before.
The weather has been wild, stormy and rough, with
the bar of flood-water lying between us and our little
outings. It is bright enough just now, though the wind
is still talking threateningly. Tuesday and Wednesday
nights cost us four more of the elms on the island, which
is now sadly thin."

Such was the rich and perpetually varying background on which life unrolled itself here.   His love for the place grew with the years, and his joy in it was only troubled by a sense of stolen sweetness which sometimes came over him when he thought of work and duty in London.   " I rather want to be in London again," he writes once on a golden day of early September, " for I feel as if my time were passing with too little done in the country : altogether I fear I am a London bird; its soot has been rubbed into me, and even these autumn mornings can't wash me clean of restlessness."

But in the summer of 1871 the visit to Iceland, which he had planned since "The Earthly Paradise" was off his hands, was occupying all his thoughts, and he saw little of Kelmscott till afterwards.   At Whitsuntide Webb went down with him to look over it, and Faulkner joined them from Oxford.   The house was reported to be in sound condition, and was taken from midsummer.   At the beginning of July Morris took his wife and children down, returning himself at once to make the last preparations for his northern voyage.

CHAPTER VIII

JOURNEY TO ICELAND
1871

THE journey through Iceland in the summer of 1871 had, both before and after its occurrence, an importance in Morris's life which can hardly be over-estimated, and which, even to those who knew him well, was not wholly intelligible. To enter into his feelings one must imagine a strange combination of Johnson in the Hebrides and Byron in Greece. The heroic stories of Iceland stood in his mind at the head of the world's literature; the deeds which they chronicled were the summit in their tragic force of all human achievement. And the Icelandic Republic represented, more nearly than any other state of things recorded in history, the political and social framework of life which satisfied his mind and imagination. On the Law-Mound of Thingvalla, by the steads of Herdholt or Lithend, he stood with deeper-kindled emotions than would have been roused in him in the Roman Forum or on the Athenian Acropolis, or where grass grows over the fallen towers of Troy. With such depth of awe and prostration of spirit a pilgrim might approach the desolate and holy places of a land where gods had once walked in the likeness of men. In his poem of "Iceland First Seen" he gave this feeling its fullest utterance. "What went ye into the wilderness for to see?"—this phrase kept perpetually reverting to him as he thought of Iceland: a land waste, black, desolate, grey-grassed, "dreadful with grinding of ice and record of scarce-hidden fire," and yet made by undying tales a treasure-house and queen of lands.

And to this was added the excitement of new and strange adventure. The voyage to Iceland had not become so common an amusement of a summer holiday as it is now : though one reached the island by a mail steamer and could map out the route accurately beforehand, there was enough of strangeness about the whole proceedings to make the planning of the journey quite exciting. The journey itself was one that had to be taken in adventurous explorers' fashion, with guides and a string of packhorses, carrying tents and food and all the means of life : once inland, the traveller was beyond all reach of news : it was a prolonged picnic spiced by hard living and rough riding. "Don't forget to practise riding," he wrote to Faulkner in May. "I began this morning. By Gum the great we shall have plenty of it there according to our program."

The party were four in number. Mr. Magnússon, who was taking this opportunity of paying a visit to his native place and kinsfolk, was the organizer and guide-in-chief. Faulkner was the third of the party ; and the fourth was Mr. W. H. Evans of Forde Abbey in Dorset, a recent acquaintance, who had been planning an Iceland voyage on his own account and was ready to fall in with the wishes of the others as regards all the details of travelling. Morris entered into the preparations for the journey with the delight of a schoolboy. Money had to be sent out to Reykjavik to buy riding and pack horses for the party; tents, blankets, food, and appliances of all kinds were to be bought, and details of travel in the desert were rehearsed in anticipation. The Burne-Jones children long remembered vividly how Morris came one day and built a little hearth in their garden with loose bricks, over which he cooked a stew in the manner of some pirate or backwoodsman in a story-book. As the time drew near he was as excited and fidgety as a boy preparing for the holidays. The importance of the occasion was such that he resolved, for the first time in his life, to keep a diary. This was almost necessary in any case if he wished to bring home any ordered account of his adventures, for from the day the travellers struck inland from Reykjavik until they regained it again there was little chance of sending, any more than of receiving, letters. This diary, scribbled from day to day on the spot, was carefully written out by him when he came home, and afterwards revised and written out again with some idea of publishing it. This idea, however, considered and deferred more than once, was finally rejected by him towards the end of his life. The extracts given here are from the revised manuscript given by him to Mrs. Burne-Jones in 1873.

On the 6th of July, the party (except Mr. Evans, who had gone on to Leith by sea) started from London to take the fortnightly Danish mail boat from Granton. "That morning," says the diarist, " my heart had failed me, and I felt as if I should have been glad of any accident that had kept me at home; yet now it would have seemed unbearable to sleep in London another night." All night in the train he was too excited to sleep; but with the next day's dawn he recovered himself and began to observe things: sunrise among the forges of Darlington, a beautiful sky-landscape strangely confused with the still-glowing furnace fires: the clean Northumberland country, and the poetical-looking bay in which Holy Island lies, with the little town running all up the hill near the end of its long northern horn: Berwick-on-Tweed with its land-locked harbour and the long bridge of many pointed arches: the lovely glens that break down seaward from the skirts of the Lammermuirs, "like one's imagination of what the backgrounds of the Border Ballads ought to be": and finally the imposing masses and doleful detail of Edinburgh. It was his first sight of Scotland, a country which, like Dr. Johnson, he never loved and was always ready to find fault with. The next day the "Diana," one of the two steamers which alternated for the Iceland mail service, came in to Granton harbour, and they sailed the following morning. She was a wooden screw steamer which once had been a Danish gunboat, of about 240 tons, roomy for her size, but with an extraordinary capacity for rolling. The diary sets down a description of her somewhat as though she were a mediæval building :

"The little vessel looked quite clean and tidy now: she is as aforesaid an old gunboat, long and low, rising somewhat forward, and with bulkheads across the deck just forward of the deck-cabin, that seemed to us to forebode plenty of water on board : she has three masts, the forward one has two square sails and a fore and aft sail, the middle one a fore and aft sail, and the after one no sail at all bent on it : round about the rudder is a little raised platform where we lay about a good deal on the voyage out, then comes the deck-cabin with a narrow covered passage leading forward on each side of it, and with a hurricane deck on the top : then there is a small open space broken by the sky-lights of the engine room between the deck-cabin and the galley : there is good space for a walk forward of this, but when there is the least sea on, unless the wind is right astern it is too wet to be pleasant : over the galley, I forgot to say, is the bridge where the captain or mate stands to steer the ship : also our sleeping cabin is reached by stairs from the deck-cabin, and there is a ladies' cabin on the other side of ours—ours is a very small place, and almost pitch dark when the lamps are not lighted; as small as it is we were surprised to find that it really was not very stuffy, for they have managed to ventilate it well."

They had left Granton soon after sunrise on Sunday morning; and on Tuesday at daybreak the Faroes were sighted.

"I have often noticed," says the diary, "in one's expeditions, how hard it is to explain to one's friends afterwards why such and such a day was particularly delightful, or give them any impression of one's pleasure, and such a trouble besets me now about the past day.

"I woke up later than usual, about half-past six, and went on deck in a hurry, because I remembered the mate had promised that we should be at Thorshaven in the Faroes by then, and that we should have sighted the south islands of them long before: and now there we were sure enough, steaming up the smooth water of a narrow firth with the shore close on either board: I confess I shuddered at my first sight of a really northern land in the grey of a coldish morning. (The Faroes seemed to me such a gentle sweet place when we saw them again after Iceland.) The hills were not high, especially on one side, as they slope beachless into the clear but grey water; the grass was grey between greyer ledges of stone that divided the hills in regular steps; it was not savage, but mournfully empty and barren, the grey clouds, dragging over the hill-tops or lying in the hollows, being the only thing that varied the grass, stone, and sea: yet as we went on, the firth opened out on one side and showed wild strange hills and narrow sounds between the islands, that had something, I don't know what, of poetic and attractive about them; and on one side was sign of population in the patches of bright green that showed the home-fields of farms on the hillsides, and at last at the bight's end we saw the pleasant-looking little town of Thorshaven, with its green-roofed little houses clustering round a little bay and up a green hillside: thereby we presently cast anchor, the only other craft in the harbour being three fishing smacks, cutters, who in answer to the hoisting of our flag ran up English colours, and were, we afterwards found out, from Grimsby for Iceland. The shore soon became excited at our arrival, and boats put off to us, the friends of our three passengers for the Faroes, and others, and there was a great deal of kissing on deck presently: then came a smart-looking boat carrying the governor, and having eight oars aside, manned by the queerest old carles, who by way of salute as the boat touched our side, shuffled off their Faroish caps in a very undignified manner. These old fellows, like most (or all) of the men, wore an odd sort of Phrygian cap, stockings and knee-breeches, loose at the knee, and a coat like a knight's *just-au-corps*, only buttoning in front, and generally open. The boats are built high stem and stern, with the keel-rib running up into an ornament at each end, and cannot have changed in the least since the times of the Sagas."

After breakfast the passengers went on shore for the day. "Magnússon took us to the store of a friend of his, a sort of place like a ship's hold, and where they sold everything a Faroese would buy from a tin-tack to a cask of brandy; we found nothing to buy there but Danish cherry-brandy, which was good and cheap; then we went into the private house of the merchant, and were kindly welcomed by his wife into a pretty wooden house very like a ship's cabin, and, to me, still unquiet: it was very clean, painted white, and with roses and ivy planted in great pots growing all over the drawing-room wall (inside). Thence we went out into the town, which pleased me very much: certainly there was a smell of fish, and these creatures, or parts of them, from guts to gutted bodies, hung and lay about in many places; but there was no other dirt apparent; the houses were all of wood, high-roofed with little white casements, the rest of the walls being mostly done over with Stockholm tar; every roof was of turf, and fine crops of flowery grass grew on some of them. The houses were pitched down with little order enough, and in fact the whole town was like a toy Dutch town of my childhood's days. The people we met were very polite, good-tempered, and contented-looking: the women not pretty, but not horrible either, and the men often quite handsome, and always carrying themselves well in their neat dresses; which include, by the bye, skin shoes tied about the ankle with neat thongs: the men were often quite swarthy, and had a curious cast of melancholy on their faces, natural I should think to the dwellers in small remote islands."

After seeing the town they set off to walk across the island of Straumey. "Presently, having gone through the town, we met on a road that ran through little fields of very sweet flowery grass nearly ready for the scythe: it affected me strangely to see all the familiar flowers growing in a place so different to anything one had ever imagined, and withal (it had grown a very bright fresh day by now) there was real beauty about the place of a kind I can't describe. We were soon off these cultivated meadows, however, and in a long deep valley of the open fells, peaty and grass-clad, with a small stream running through it, and not unlike to many Cumberland valleys I have been in: up the hillside on the left we struck, and clomb the hill, whence turning round, we could see the sound we had come up this morning, the little 'Diana' lying in the harbour with boats clustered round her, the little toylike-looking town so small, so small, and be-yond it the mountains, jagged and peaked, of another

island, with the added interest of knowing that there
was a deep sound between us and them : sea and sky
were deep blue now, but the white clouds yet clung to
the mountains here and there.

"We turned away and went along the ridge of the
mountain-neck, and looking all up the valley, could see
it turning off towards the right, and a higher range
above its bounding hill; and again it was exciting to be
told that this higher range was in another island; we
saw it soon, as we turned a corner of the stony stepped
grey hills, and below us lay a deep calm sound, say two
miles broad, a hog-backed steep mountain-island forming
the other side of it, next to which lay a steeper islet,
a mere rock ; and then other islands, the end of which
we could not see, entangled the sound and swallowed it
up; I was most deeply impressed with it all, yet can
scarcely tell you why ; it was like nothing I had ever
seen, but strangely like my old imaginations of places
for sea-wanderers to come to: the day was quite a hot
summer day now, and there was no cloud in the sky,
and the atmosphere was very, very clear, but a little
pillowy cloud kept dragging and always changing yet
always there, over the top of the little rocky islet.   All
the islands, whether sloping or sheer rocks, went right
into the sea without a hand's breadth of beach anywhere;
and, little thing as that seems, I suppose it is this which
gives the air of romanticism to these strange islands.
Close by the sea lay the many gables (black wood with
green turf-roofs) of the farm of Kirkjubae (Kirby), a
little white-washed church being the nearest to the sea,
while close under the basalt cliff was the ruin of a stone
mediæval church: a most beautiful and poetical place it
looked to me, but more remote and melancholy than I
can say, in spite of the flowers and grass and bright sun :
it looked as if you might live for a hundred years before

you would ever see ship sailing into the bay there; as if the old life of the saga-time had gone, and the modern life never reached the place.

"We hastened down, along the high mowing-grass of the home-field, full of buttercups and marsh-marigolds, and so among the buildings: the long-nosed cadaverous parson who guided us took us first to the ruin, which he said had never been finished, as the Reformation had stopped the building of it: in spite of which story, it is visibly not later than 1340 in date, which fact I, with some qualms, stoutly asserted, to the parson's disgust, though 'tis quite a new fault to me to find local antiquaries post-date their antiquities: anyhow it was, or had been, a rich and beautiful Decorated chapel without aisles, and for all I know had never been finished: thence we went into the more modern church (such a flower-bed as its roof was!) which was nevertheless interesting from its having a complete set of bench-ends richly carved (in deal) of the fifteenth century, but quite northern in character, the interlacing work mingling with regular fifteenth-century heraldic work and very well carved figures that yet retained, in costume and style, a strong tinge of the thirteenth century: the ornament of the bishop's throne, a chair with a trefoiled canopy, though I am pretty sure of the same date as the bench-ends, was entirely of the northern interlacing work.

"From the church we went into the bonder's house, which was very clean, and all of unpainted deal, walls, floor and ceiling, with queer painted old presses and chests about it: he turned up with his two children presently, and welcomed us in that queer northern manner I got used to after a little, as if he was thinking of anything else than us, nay, rather as if he were not quite sure if we were there or not."

The "Diana" weighed anchor after dinner. "The evening was very fine still, the sea quite smooth and the tide in our favour; so the captain told us we were going to thread the islands by the sound called the Westmanna-firth, instead of going round about them; so, as it turned out, we had the best of our sight of the Faroes yet to see. Going down the sound we had come up in the morning, we turned round into the sound we had looked down into from Kirby that noon, passing close by the stead itself, and so into the Westmanna-firth, that grew narrower and narrower as we went on, though here and there between breaks of the islands we could see the open ocean: at last we were in the narrowest of it; it was quite smooth, clear and green, and not a furlong across; the coasts were most wonderful on either side; pierced rocks running out from the cliffs under which a brig might have sailed: caves that the water ran up into, how far we could not tell; smooth walls of rock with streams flowing over them right into the sea; or these would sink down into green slopes with farms on them; or be cleft into deep valleys over which would show crater-like or pyramidal mountains: or they would be splintered into jagged spires; one of which, single and huge, just at the point of the last ness before we entered this narrow sound, is named the Trolls-finger; and all this always without one inch of beach to be seen; and always when the cliffs sank you could see little white clouds lying about on the hillsides: at last we could see on ahead a narrow opening, so narrow that you could not imagine that we could sail out of it, and then soon the cliffs on our right gave back and showed a great land-locked bay almost like a lake, with green slopes all round it, and a great mountain towering above them at its end, where lay the houses of a little town, Westmanna-haven; they tell us that the water is ten fathom deep close up to the very shore in here, and that it is, as it looks, a most magnificent harbour. After that, on we went toward the gates that led out into the Atlantic; narrow enough they look even now we are quite near; as the ship's nose was almost in them, I saw close beside us a stead with its home-field sloping down to the sea, the people running out to look at us, and the black cattle grazing all about; then I turned to look ahead as the ship met the first of the swell in the open sea, and when I looked astern a very few minutes after I could see nothing at all of the gates we had come out by, no slopes of grass, or valleys opening out from the shore; nothing but a terrible wall of rent and furrowed rocks, the little clouds still entangled here and there about the tops of them: here the wall would be rent from top to bottom and its two sides would yawn as if they would have fallen asunder, here it was buttressed with great masses of stone that had slipped from its top; there it ran up into all manner of causeless-looking spikes: there was no beach below the wall, no foam breaking at its feet; it was midnight now and everything was grey, and colourless, and shadowless, yet there was light enough in the clear air to see every cranny and nook of the rocks, and in the north-east now the grey sky began to get a little lighter with dawn. I stood near the stern and looked backward a long time, till the coast, which had seemed a great crescent when we came out of the sound, was now a long flat line, and so then I went to bed with the sky brightening quickly."

"I have seen nothing out of a dream," he wrote from Iceland to Mrs. Morris, "so strange as our coming out of the last narrow sound into the Atlantic, and leaving the huge wall of rocks astern in the shadowless midnight twilight: nothing I have ever seen has impressed me so much."

Two days afterwards, early on a grey morning, they sighted the south-eastern coast of Iceland at Berufirth, where the "Diana" had to touch on her way to Reykjavik.

"The sun had not yet shone over the mountains on the east into the firth at whose mouth we were, yet patches of it lay upon the high peaks south-west of where we were: on our left was a dark brown ragged rocky island, Pápey, and many small skerries about it, and beyond that we saw the mainland, a terrible shore indeed: a great mass of dark grey mountains worked into pyramids and shelves, looking as if they had been built and half ruined; they were striped with snow high up, and wreaths of cloud dragged across them here and there, and above them were two peaks and a jagged ridge of pure white snow: we were far enough presently to look into Berufirth, and to see the great pyramid of Buland's Tindr, which stands a little way down the west side of the firth close by the sea; the sea was perfectly calm, and was clear of mist right up to the shore, and then dense clouds hid the low shore, but rose no higher than the mountain's feet: and as I looked the sun overtopped the east hills and the great pyramid grew red halfway down. The east side of the firth showed the regular Icelandic hillside: a great slip of black shale and sand striped with the green of the pastures, that gradually sloped into a wide grass-grown flat, between hill and sea, on which we could see the home-meads of several steads. On the west side we could see a line of rocks and skerries cut out from the shore, low green slopes behind them, and then the mountain feet; looking up the firth, which was all sunlighted now, the great peaks lowered till they seemed to run into the same black, green-striped hillsides as on the east."

Such was the landscape which he afterwards described

through the less precise yet even more vivid medium of verse in the poem of "Iceland First Seen":

Lo, from our loitering ship
   a new land at last to be seen;
Toothed rocks down the side of the firth
   on the east guard a weary wide lea,
And black slope the hillsides above,
   striped adown with their desolate green:
And a peak rises up on the west
   from the meeting of cloud and of sea,
Foursquare from base unto point
   like the buildings of Gods that have been,
The last of that waste of the mountains
   all cloud-wreathed and snow-flecked and grey,
And bright with the dawn that began
   just now at the ending of day.

Running along the southern coast of Iceland with its awful mountain wall, the "Diana" reached Reykjavik on the afternoon of the 14th of July. Zoega, the guide, "a big fellow, red-headed, blue-eyed, and long-chinned, like a Scotch gardener," met them with the news that the horses had been got. Of these they started with twenty, being a double relay for six riders (the four tourists and two guides) and eight packhorses. On the journey, the number was increased for various reasons to twenty-eight. One of the two that Morris himself rode, Mouse, was brought back by him to England, and lived many years at Kelmscott. Then with some difficulty, for the transaction almost exhausted the metallic currency of the capital, the money for the journey, 1,000 silver dollars in canvas bags, was procured. Two days passed at Reykjavik in the various preparations, and in visits to the notable people of the town: "the most noteworthy of them was Jón Sigurdson, the President of

the Althing, whose editions of Sagas I know very well:
he seemed a shy, kind, scholarlike man, and I talked
Icelandic all I might to him."

On Monday, the 17th of July, the preparations were
completed, and the caravan started on its journey. The
route taken had been planned out with the principal object of visiting the scenes of the greater Sagas: first
Lithend and Bergthorsknoll on the southern coast;
then across the wilderness to the fiords on the northern
sea, and over the mountain passes into Laxdale; round
the peninsula of Snaefellsness, the land of the Ere-
dwellers; and so back to Reykjavik by Thingvalla, the
great central place of assembly for Iceland from the
heroic age down to the beginning of the present century.
The Geysirs, the main object of most Icelandic tourists,
which Morris, however, regarded with undisguised contempt, were to be taken on the northward journey.

When they got to camp at the end of the first day's
travel, " we came into a soft grassy meadow bordered
by a little clear stream, and jumped off our horses after
a ride of six hours and a half: it was a cold night,
though clear and fine, and we fell hard to unpack the
tents and pitch them while the guides unburdened the
horses, who were soon rolling about in every direction,
and then set to work diligently to feed: the tents being
pitched, Magnússon and Faulkner set to work to light
the fire, while Evans and I went about looking for game,
about the hill spurs and the borders of a little tarn between the lava and our camp: it was light enough to
see to read; wonderfully clear, but not like daylight,
for there were no shadows at all: I turned back often
from the slopes to look down on the little camp, and the
grey smoke that now began to rise up, and felt an excitement and pleasure not easy to express: till I had to
get to my shooting, which I didn't like at all: however,

I shot two golden plovers and came back to camp with them."

Mr. Evans did most of the shooting that was done on the journey; Morris took no pleasure in it.   "I had to see to my gun," he complains later, "which was rather a heavy charge all through the journey, wanting as much attention as a baby with croup."

From this camping-place they proceeded eastward to the Njala country by Eyrarbakki and Oddi, where they were entertained by Dean Asmundr, "a little hard-bitten apple-cheeked old man, extremely hospitable." "It was a beautiful evening still, and even the eastern sky we saw behind the great mountains of the Eyjafell range was quite red.   Oddi lies on a marked knoll or slope, above a great stretch of boggy land through which Eastern Rangriver winds; the hills under Three-corner, and the long stretch of Fleetlithe gradually leading into the terrible gorges of the ice-mountains, girdle in these grey-green flats: it is a noteworthy place historically, for in fact the men who died here or hereabout still live in people's minds as the writers of most of the great stories and both the Eddas: I don't know if they actually wrote them; it was a mere guess (or tradition perhaps) of the seventeenth century that Saemund the Learned collected the poetic Edda: but at any rate these three men, who all lived here at one time or another of their lives, Saemund, Ari, and Snorri Sturluson, must certainly have been the great guardians of the body of Icelandic lore."   Thence the next day they reached Bergthorsknoll, the home of Njal.   Here Morris made one of his few and unsuccessful attempts to sketch.   It was a thing he could not do.   The sketch-book was soon put up again and the scene photographed in words instead.

" Pastures thick with a bright blue gentian, and other flowers (principally white clover) more familiar to me:

I turned back once or twice to fix the place in my
memory; and here I will recapitulate and tell what Bergthorsknoll looks like to-day, so as to have the matter off
my conscience :

" Three mounds something the shape of limpets rising
from a bright green home-mead with a smooth turf wall
all round it, but divided by a lane river-ward of the
stead, which is pitched on the middle mound ; a wide
shallow ' white ' river with black sands sweeping in a
curve by the last of the mounds, with a strip of smooth
and flowery turf running along its banks : marshy land
all round about, for the rest, all channelled with innumerable ruts, getting greyer and greyer in the distance, till on the south side it meets the sea, from which
rise the castle-like rocks of the Westman Isles, and on
the north is stopped by the long line of the Lithe, above
which the mass of Three-corner shows : westward the
great plain seems limitless, but eastward it is soon stopped
by the great wall which is the outwork of Eyjafell, dark
grey rocks rising without intermediate slopes straight
out of the plain, and with the ice-mountains at last rising
above them."

From Bergthorsknoll they crossed to Lithend, where
the site of Gunnar's hall is shown on a space flattened
out of the hillside near the present house ; and went up
the terrible valley down which the Markfleet comes roaring from the glaciers.

" Past this the cliffs were much higher, and most un-
imaginably strange : they overhung in some places much
more than seemed possible ; they had caves in them
just like the hell-mouths in thirteenth-century illuminations ; or great straight pillars were rent from them
with quite flat tops of grass and a sheep or two feeding
on it, however the devil they got there : two or three
tail-ends of glacier too dribbled over them hereabouts,

and we turned out of our way to go up to one: it seemed to fill up a kind of cleft in the rock wall, which indeed I suppose it had broken down; one could see its spiky white waves against the blue sky as we came up to it. We dismounted and scrambled about it: its great blocks cleft into dismal caves, half blocked up with the sand and dirt it had ground up, and dribbling wretched white streams into the plain below: a cold wind blew over it in the midst of the hot day, and (apart from my having nearly broken my neck on it) I was right glad to be in the saddle again. The great mountain-wall which closes up the valley with its jagged outlying teeth was right before us: often the wall would be cleft, and you would see a horrible winding street, with stupendous straight rocks for houses on either side: the bottom of the cleft quite level, but with a white glacier stream running out of it, and the whole blocked up at the end by the straight line of the master-mountain. Jón told us how he had gone down this valley in the winter with the snow covering either hillside, and the moon at its brightest; of sheep-gatherings he had been at, where every individual sheep has to be carried on horseback over the fords; of expeditions he had made for the fun of the thing up into the pathless wastes about here; and finally, as we crossed one of the streams that run into Markfleet, he told us the timely and cheerful story of how, riding in the autumn-tide with a party down this valley, they coming to this stream concluded it to be fordless, but nevertheless one of the rashest cried out that he would not be stopped, dashed into the water, where his horse was immediately swept off his legs down stream, and the last they saw of the man was him clutching with both arms round the horse's neck, in which position the bodies of both horse and man were found thrown ashore lower down."

On the way back to Lithend they passed a stead where " the bonder, who was very deep in old lore, was flatteringly anxious to see me. He was a grave, black-bearded, intelligent-looking carle of about fifty, and soon he got discussing with Magnússon and Jón minute probabilities of time and place in the Njala, pretty much as if the thing had happened twenty years ago: from that he got to lamenting the wasteful cutting of the woods in that country-side: as we departed I made a bad shot at the saddle trying to mount, *more Icelandico*, on the wrong side, and measured my length on the turf: the bonder, without the ghost of a smile on his face, hoped I wasn't hurt, and only expressed his feelings by saying to Magnússon, ' The Skald is not quite used to riding then.'"

From Lithend the party made northward to the Geysirs, " the place," Morris writes indignantly, " which has made Iceland famous to Mangnall's Questions and the rest, who have never heard the names of Sigurd and Brynhild, of Njal, or Gunnar, or Grettir, or Gisli, or Gudrun: not mentioned in any Icelandic writing before the eighteenth century." He did not regain his temper till they were left behind. " The turf is the only nasty bit of camping-ground we have had yet," he notes: " all bestrewn too with feathers and wings of birds, polished mutton-bones, and above all, pieces of paper. And— must I say it?—the place seemed all too near to that possible column of scalding water I had heard so much of: understand, I was quite ready to break my neck in my quality of pilgrim to the holy places of Iceland: to be drowned in Markfleet, or squelched in climbing up Drangey, seemed to come quite in the day's work: but to wake up boiled while one was acting the part of accomplice to Mangnall's Questions was too disgusting." To these comments, however, Mr. Evans adds another, giving a feeling inspired by this strange place which

Morris was loth to confess, though he admits to the terror suggested by the boiling mud and quivering earth.

"Near our camp," he tells me, "there were several deep holes of beautiful still, blue, boiling water: it was in these holes we boiled our fish and fetched our hot water: but after we had each been several times, Morris on returning from one of these expeditions said it was so uncanny he could not go again."

They had to stay four days there, however, partly from stress of weather and partly because Faulkner was very unwell. On the 29th of July, on a bright cold morning, they started again northward through the wilderness towards Waterdale and the firths of the North Sea. Six cold days of rain and bitter wind among the "horrible black mountains of the waste," including an exploration of the great cave of Surts-hellir, impressed Morris's imagination with a sense of the terror of the land which never quite left him, and which reappears vividly in his descriptions of the mountain journeys in " The Glittering Plain " and " The Well at the World's End." Their route led over the Erne-water-heath, a dismal highland of bogs and pools on the watershed between the northern and western seas, where Grettir lived so long an outlaw; past Erne-water, where he slew Thorir Red-Beard, "a most mournful desolate-looking place with no signs of life as we rode up but for a swan that rose trumpeting from the lakeside"; and so down at last into Waterdale. The original plan had been to get further north and see Drángey, where Grettir lived strangely for the last three years of his life, and where he died at last in the great fight of the two against the eighteen. But time was running short, and this part of the journey had to be given up; they turned westwards, and crossed the ridges into Midfirthdale, where Bjarg, Grettir's birthplace, stands by its castellated rocks; then on to Thorodstead in Hrútafirth, and so round the end of the long sea-inlet and over the pass into Laxdale. On Sunday afternoon, the 6th of August, they rode into Herdholt.

" The little house that stands over so many stories of the old days is rather new and trim, but picturesque enough ; three long gabled aisles, the turf sides of which are laid herring-bone fashion, and there are elaborate dogvanes on the gables. From the door of it one looks down on to the flats about the river, rising gradually into the slopes of the great bounding hill, where among long straight lines of the grey stone banks that old ice-waves have striped the hillside with, parallel to the main lines of the valley, and sad dull yellow-green bogs, lie two emerald green patches, the túns of two steads ; one of them Hauskuld-stead, the parent house of Herdholt. The hill above all this gradually slopes down to Hwamm-firth, and above its lower end show two strange-shaped mountains, like a church roof with a turret at the end of it : the spurs of these again run down into the firth, leaving a space of low hills and boggy plain by the water-side : but beyond, and bounding all to the south-west, lies that sea of peaked mountains that are all about Holyfell. The actual waters of Hwammfirth are hidden from sight here because of the shoulder of the spur on which we are, the higher part of which also hides the mountains to the north. Evans and Faulkner went off to pitch the tent, while I spent my time alone in trying to regain my spirits, which had suddenly fallen very low almost ever since we came into Laxdale. Just think, though, what a mournful place this is—Iceland, I mean—setting aside the pleasure of one's animal life there, the fresh air, the riding and rough life, and feeling of adventure;—how every place and name marks the

death of its short-lived eagerness and glory: and withal so
little is the life changed in some ways: Olaf Peacock went
about summer and winter after his live-stock, and saw
to his hay-making and fishing, just as this little peak-
nosed parson does; setting aside the coffee and brandy,
his victuals under his hall 'marked with famous stories'
were just the same the little parson in his ten foot square
parlour eats: I don't doubt the house stands on the old
ground.—But Lord! what littleness and helplessness has
taken the place of the old passion and violence that had
place here once—and all is unforgotten; so that one has
no power to pass it by unnoticed: yet that must be
something of a reward for the old life of the land, and
I don't think their life now is more unworthy than most
people's elsewhere, and they are happy enough by
seeming—yet it is an awful place: set aside the hope
that the unseen sea gives you here, and the strange
threatening change of the blue spiky mountains beyond
the firth, and the rest seems emptiness and nothing else:
a piece of turf under your feet, and the sky overhead,
that's all: whatever solace your life is to have here must
come out of yourself or these old stories, not over hopeful
themselves.   Something of all this I thought; and
besides our heads were now fairly turned homeward, and
now and again a few times I felt homesick—I hope I may
be forgiven.   Also there was that ceaseless wind all day:
but now towards night it was grown calmer, and was
still very bright, and the day ended with a beautiful and
strange sunset; not violent red in the west, but the
whole sky suffused with it over light green and grey,
with a few bars of bright white clouds dragging over it,
and some big dusky rain-clouds low down among the
Broadfirth mountains: I stood and watched it changing,
till that and rest from the wind, I suppose, made me
contented again."

Here the travellers stayed three days, Evans fishing
in the Laxá and Morris saturating himself with the traditions in which this region is so rich; Herdholt and
Bathstead; Hwamm, the home, in the days of the early
settlers, of Queen Aud the Deep-minded, and in after
times the birthplace of Snorri Sturluson; and the "dreadful lonely dale" where Kiartan was beset by Gudrun's
brothers, and Bolli struck the dolorous stroke.

This was the furthest point of the journey; and hence
the party skirted round the peninsula of Snaefellsness to
get back into the Southland without again traversing the
wilderness. At Stykkisholm, on Broadfirth, they found
a Danish brigantine, the "Holger," in the bay, on her
way from Icefirth to Liverpool. The captain offered
to take letters, and Morris had time to send a hasty note
home.

"There has been but little roughing it," he wrote,
"and I find sleeping in a tent very comfortable even when
the weather is very cold. The weather has been cold,
and rather broken till the last few days; last Thursday
week we had a very bad day riding over the wilderness
in the teeth of a tremendous storm of snow, rain, and
wind. You've no idea what a good stew I can make,
or how well I can fry bacon under difficulties. I have
seen many marvels and some terrible pieces of country;
slept in the home-field of Njal's house, and Gunnar's,
and at Herdholt: I have seen Bjarg, and Bathstead, and
the place where Bolli was killed, and am now a half-
hour's ride from where Gudrun died. I was there yesterday, and from its door you see a great sea of terrible
inky mountains tossing about; there has been a most
wonderful sunset this evening that turned them golden
though. The firth we look on here is full of little
islands that breed innumerable eider-ducks, and a firth
we crossed yesterday was full of swans. Give dear love

to the little ones, and tell them I am going to try to bring them my pretty grey pony home; but if I don't they must not be disappointed, for there may be difficulties, or he may not turn out well. His name is Falcon, and when he is in good condition he ambles beautifully, fast and deliciously soft; he is about thirteen hands high. I wish you could see us to understand how jolly it is when we have got a good piece of road and the whole train of twenty-eight horses is going a good round trot, the tin cups tinkling, and the boxes rattling. Good-bye, my dear, I have so often thought of the sweet fresh garden at Kelmscott, and you and the little ones in it, and wished you happy."

Poor Falcon's hoofs went wrong after this; he came lame into Reykjavik, and had to be sold there instead of being brought back to England. The fleet of swans on Hwammfirth was one of the most strikingly beautiful sights that the travellers saw. Mr. Evans gives an interesting reminiscence of the occasion. "Every little tarn we passed," he says, "was occupied by a pair of wild swans, where they scatter to breed; but the first fiord we reached on the north coast was filled with hundreds, and they looked such splendid marks shining in the sun that I said how I wished I had a rifle, which brought down on me the most severe reproof from Morris: he called me a British officer,"—Mr. Evans held a commission in the Dorset Yeomanry—"which was his most severe term of contempt."

The journey round the peninsula is a long one, lying now along the shore and now over necks of land from firth to firth. On one of the long peninsulas thus formed, but now out of practicable reach in the time at their disposal, is Ere, the centre of the story of the Eyrbyggja Saga, which had been the first book translated by Morris from the Icelandic. In the beautiful manuscript of his translation, which he had executed in the previous April, he had written some verses which express with great simplicity and sincerity the effect on him of the Icelandic literature, and the feeling of his own kinship as a tale-teller with the authors of the Sagas. Perhaps he never elsewhere set forth so fully what the meaning of poetry was to him; a help in the darkness until the new day should come, not for one person or another, but for all the world.

> Lo here an ancient chronicle
> Recording matters that befell
> A folk, whose life and death and pain
> Might touch the great world's loss and gain
> Full little: yet such might had they
> They could not wholly pass away:
> From mouth to mouth they sent a tale,
> That yet for something may avail;
> For midst them all a man they wrought,
> Who all these words together brought,
> Made shadows breathe, quickened the dead,
> And knew what silent mouths once said,
> Till with the life his life might give
> These lived again, and yet shall live.
>
> Where art thou, O thou nameless one?
> And dost thou laugh to look upon
> My eagerness thy tale to read
> Midst such changed hope and fear and need?
> Or somewhere near me dost thou stand,
> And through the dark reach out thine hand?
> Yea, are we friends? Draw nigher then,
> Thou tale-teller of vanished men,
> For we are of one company
> To link the dull years straggling by,

Their lonely hopes and griefs grown cold,
Into a chain of tear-washed gold
That yet shall cling about the Earth
In dawning of her second birth.

Tale-teller, who 'twixt fire and snow
Had heart to turn about and show
With faint half-smile things great and small
That in thy fearful land did fall,
Thou and thy brethren sure did gain
That thing for which I long in vain,
The spell, whereby the mist of fear
Was melted, and your ears might hear
Earth's voices as they are indeed.
Well ye have helped me at my need.

It was not till a week later that the travellers reached
Grettir's lair on the Fairwood-fells, " such a savage and
dreadful place that it gave quite a new turn in my mind
to the whole story, and transfigured Grettir into an
awful and monstrous being, like one of the early giants
of the world." On the 22nd of August they crossed
White-water, and after a day's rest at Reykholt, where
Snorri Sturluson lived and died, set forth for Thingvalla, the last goal of their pilgrimage.

" The wind dropped and a long strip of blue-green
opened in the south-west, and widened and turned bluer
and let the sun out. It is exciting to us to see the in-
digo-coloured peaks whose shapes we know rising up
one after another over the dull heath : and soon we
note the ragged screen of rocks before Ball-Jokul, and
that other range that runs south from Skjaldbreid, and
the whole tumbled sea of peaks that rise between us and
the plain of Thingvellir.

" The heath bettered as we rode on, and we got to

riding into little valleys now, boggy or sandy at bottom
(oftenest the latter), but with the banks about them
grown over with heath-berries, sweet grass and flowers,
much as it was with our old encampment at Brunnar;
at last these open out before us into a wider plain, and
we can see Skjaldbreid clear to his feet, and the grey
lava we journeyed over that other day, and the aforesaid
toothed screen of mountains, ending in a gap through
which show mountains a long way off, bright and intense blue under the now bright sunny sky; on the
other side of this gap rises a lumpier range gradually
drawing toward us, which is Armansfell: and through
this gap lies our way to Thingvellir.   We are now
come to our old camping stead of Brunnar, and there
we bait, not at our encampment on the hillside, but on
the grass meadow about the pools: we rest about an
hour and then set forward, I greatly excited by the warm
day and the thought of the Thingmeads before us.
Then passing by our old camp, we follow up a willowy
stream that runs under bents edging a sandy plain somewhat willow-grown also, with Skjaldbreid ever on our
left, looking no otherwise than when we saw it weeks
ago from the east side of it, for in short it is quite round.
Then over a neck of shale and rock called Trollahals
(Troll's-neck) into a great wide sandy valley, going
utterly waste up to the feet of Skjaldbreid, and with a
small stream running through it.   We are now turning
round Skjaldbreid, and can see on his south-west flank
two small hills lying that are perfect pyramids to look
at from here.   We are drawing near to the spurs of
Armansfell now, and the wide plain narrows as a hill on
our left shuts out the view of Skjaldbreid, and then we
are in a great round valley of dark brown sand, as flat
as a table and almost without a pebble on it: the
shoulder of Armansfell, the haunt of the Land-spirits,

rises on the south-west of the valley ; and in that corner
is a small tarn, for in fact in the wetter times of the year
the whole valley is a lake except these slopes on which
we are riding now.   The valley, open at the side we
rode into it, is quite shut in everywhere else, but at the
east corner the hills sink into a low neck, which we
make for, and scaling it, are in a pass with shaly sides
scantily grass-grown here and there.   My heart beats,
so please you, as we near the brow of the pass, and all
the infinite wonder, which came upon me when I came
up on to the deck of the ' Diana ' to see Iceland for the
first time, comes on me again now ; for this is the heart
of Iceland that we are going to see : nor was the reality
of the sight unworthy.   The pass showed long and
winding from the brow, with jagged dark hills showing
over the nearer banks of it as you went on, and betwixt
them was an open space, with a great unseen but
imagined plain between you and the great lake, that
you saw glittering far away under huge peaked hills of
bright blue, with grey-green sky above them, Hengill
the highest of them, from the hot springs on whose
flank rose into the air a wavering column of snow-white
steam.

" Down through the pass now, which gets so steep
that we have to dismount, and so narrow that its sides
hide the distant view as we get lower ; till where the
pass, still narrow, widens into Godaskörd, so called after
a witch-wife of ancient times, we can see the great grey
plain before us, though the nearer mountains now hide
the Hengill and those others beyond the lake : now as
we get toward the mouth of the pass there rises on our
left a little peaked hill, called the Maiden's Seat, because
the other side of it looks into the meadows of Hofmanna-
flötr (Chieftain's-flat), where the men returning from
the Althing used to hold games, the women looking on

from the hill aforesaid : the pass comes out presently on to grass and bush-grown banks above the meadow, which lies perfectly flat and green under grey cliffs on the other side, which fall away, as they sweep round to us, into grass-grown slopes : westward it opens into the great plain, which is hidden from us again by the slopes on our right : it was a beautiful and historical-looking place.

" We were now fairly in the plain of the Thingmeads ; the great round mass of Armansfell, scooped here and there into shallow dales (dal-verpi, dale-warps), with a bunch of snow lying on them in places, is the north boundary of it ; and opposite to that, on the other side of the now unseen lake, is the noble Hengill and its flanking mountain : these two change no more for us, but on the south-east we have at first a ragged toothed wall of clinker running down from the flank of Skjald- breid, which falls after a while into a gap through which pours the great sea of lava down the slowly sloping side of Skjaldbreid : as we ride along (over the lava now), we come opposite to a flat-topped hill some way down the lava-stream, and just below it opens a huge black chasm, that runs straight away south toward the lake, a great double-walled dyke, but with its walls tumbled and ruined a good deal in places : the hill is the Raven-burg, and the chasm the Raven-rift. But as we turn west we can see, a long way off across the grey plain, a straight black line running from the foot of Armansfell right into the lake, which we can again see hence, and some way up from the lake a white line cuts the black one across. The black and the white line are the Great Rift (Almanna-Gjá) and Axewater tumbling over it. Once again that thin thread of insight and imagination, which comes so seldom to us, and is such a joy when it comes, did not fail me at this first sight of the greatest marvel and most storied place of Iceland.

"When we first came into the plain it was on the edge of the lava, sandy but grown over with willow and grass; we are on pure lava now, which is also far from barren, being much grown about with grass and willow, but chiefly birch; everywhere, however, the bare molten rock shows in places, never tossed up in waves, but always curdled like the cooling fire-stream it once was, and often these strands or curdles are twisted regularly like a rope. Over this lava-plain we rode to a little stead called Hraun-tún that lay on a low mound of soft grass, with a few great boulders scattered about it, rising like an island from the much-riven lava-sea; there we struck the regular road from the south-east to Thingvellir, and hastened along it at about eight o'clock on the loveliest and clearest of evenings. On our way we crossed by a narrow bridge-like rock over a terrible chasm, deep, straight-sided, and with water at the bottom, into a little sunken plain nearly round, all grass-grown and smooth and flat, round which the lava has run without breaking into it: a small stream follows the inside of the lava wave nearly all round this strange place, and through its opening we ride into the lava again; over a wave-top and into the trough of it, as it seems, and then on to another wave—and lo, there we are on the lower side of the Great Rift, a grass-grown, shrub-grown slope, with a huge wall of grey rock rising on the other side of the chasm, as perpendicularly as though the plummet had ruled it. It was getting dusk when we got there, and we had hit the Rift rather high up, so we rode straight down toward the lake along the Rift-side, the great wall with a fantastic coping of clinker ever on our right, till we saw, at the end of a bight of the lake, an undulating bright green tún with a church and stead on their little mounds, and between us and them a flat green plain with Axewater winding about it most sweetly, till, straightening itself on the Rift-ward side of the stead, it ran straight for the lake, widening as it went.

"We got leave to encamp on the tún down by the side of Axewater, and soon had our tents up on a beautiful piece of mossy turf close to the water's edge, almost under the shadow of the Great Rift, whose wonderful cliff rose into the moonlit sky a few rods on the other side of the river, and was all populous with ravens that kept crying out and croaking long after we were settled there."

The next day, "a most beautiful morning, warm and soft like a fine day of latter May in England," he visited the famous Hill of Laws. "A deep rift in the lava splits into two arms having a little island in the midst, bridged by a narrow space on which two men could barely stand abreast. When you are in the island it widens and slopes upward higher and higher, till at last, where the two arms of the rift meet, there is a considerable cliff above the dark dreadful-looking rift and its cold waters: a dozen yards from this is a little mound rising from the surface of the island, which, if the Hill of Laws is the heart of Iceland, is the heart of the Hill of Laws, for here stood the Speaker at Law, and every year gave forth the law: the whole island is not a large church for the ceremony; it might hold some five hundred men close-packed; but surely 'tis one of the most dramatic spots in all Iceland, and Grim Goatshoe, who picked it out for the seat of the Althing (he had a penny for his pains from every householder of Iceland), must have been a man of poetic insight. It is a good deal raised above the level of the Valley of Axewater; the rift all round it is deep and wide, I should say sixteen feet wide at the narrowest, where you can see, many, many feet below, the rocks all blue and purple through the clearest water in the world; this is the place that they call Flosi's Leap; for the tradition (not the Njala Saga) says that Flosi the Burner leapt across it to join his men who were drawn up outside the Berg: and they say he was in all his arms when he leapt. The Hill of Laws is all covered with sweet deep grass, and the heath-berries grow all down the sides of its rift. As you stand here you look, as I said, across the grassy valley through which Axewater, having tumbled over the sheer height of the upper wall of the Great Rift, and cleft the lower wall through, wanders serpentine, making little sandy or grassy islets as it goes; the most obvious of which, a mere patch of turf, nearly level with the river, but in the very midst of the plain, is called the Battle-Holm, because there the judicial combats were held.

"You must suppose that only the Lawman and some of the chiefs, with the jurors of the courts, had their place on the Hill of Laws; the main body of the people were on the other side of the water-filled rift, which in fact made the Hill of Laws a fortress easily defensible in those days so lacking in good shot-weapons. Across the plain of Axewater, on the first slopes of the lower wall of the Great Rift, were set up the booths of the different districts, going all down the Rift-side right to the lake: just opposite where the stead now stands is a breach in this lower wall, through which runs the Reykjavik road; and the slope on the lakeward side of this is known as the site of the booth of Snorri the Priest, whereby he stood with his men in this very gap in the Rift-wall at the Battle of the Althing, prepared to help the winners moderately, and make peace if he could do so to his own advantage.

"Just in the very midst of the Hill of Laws rises a low mound regular in shape, and still having on it signs of the concentric rows of seats on which the jurors of the court sat.

" You must not forget, when thinking of all this, that the huge wall of the Great Rift does verily bar the whole plain from the slopes of Armansfell to the lake; so that no ordinary man could scale it except in that one place by Snorri's booth aforesaid : and the long line of it cuts clean against the sky with never a mountain rising over it till Armansfell thrusts up a broad shoulder at the further end."

The travels now were ended: nothing remained but the day's ride back into Reykjavik, and so home. Two days, clear and golden-soft, were spent at Thingvalla: then the weather broke in the night, and they struck their last camp and rode off in a downpour of driving rain.

" At last we came, with a great jump in my heart, to the sea, and riding past a creek or two, could see a long way off the beacon on the hill above Reykjavik, and very dimly the harbour and ships lying there; then we turned from the sea a little, and presently our road ran into the one that led to Bolavellir, our first camp in Iceland; thence away the road was almost like a road in England, and we swung along a great pace, keeping quite close together, the horses knowing well that they were coming near their journey's end. There we were past the beacon, and into the little town; and I, heeding not other people, galloped my best to Mistress Maria's house, jumping off my horse (Mouse, to wit) just six weeks to the minute since I had mounted him before, by the paling of the queer little weedy-looking garden before the black, white-windowed cottage that I have seen in night-dreams and day-dreams so often since. Well, Miss Sæmundson, who met me presently, told me that there were no letters for me there, so off I galloped for the post-office. Why doesn't one drop down, or faint, or do something of that sort when it comes to the uttermost in such matters? I walked in quite coolly in appearance and gave Mr. Finsen my name scribbled big on a piece of paper; be shuffled the letters and gave me eleven: I opened one from Ellis there and then, thinking that from him I should hear any bad news in the simplest form: though indeed the eleven letters at first glance did somewhat cure my terror, for there was no one dead at least.

"So home I went soberly to another lodging than last time, and thence, after reading my letters, with not more than the usual amount of disappointment and wondering at people's calmness I suppose, to Mrs. Maria's house again, where was dinner and the courtly old carle Sir Henry Holland, whose age (eighty-four) I thought was the most interesting thing about him. I was rather low after all, and cowed by the company, and a sense of stiffness after our joyous rough life just ended."

The "Diana" came in that night, and after three days at Reykjavik in the wind and wet, busy with selling the horses and seeing the museum and dining with the Governor, they sailed for home on the last day of August. As on the outward voyage, the "Diana" put in at Berufirth for a few hours. "At noon the signal gun was fired, and we were off presently, the pilot's boat towed alongside of us; I watched it going through the water, cold green under the shadow of our sides: the pilot's son sat in the stern, a tall, handsome-looking youth of about eighteen, 'wide-faced, grey-eyed, and open-eyed,' the very type of a northern youth, as he sat looking dreamily out to sea: his father went over the side into the boat presently, and they cast off, and soon even the shadows of the rocks faded into the mist, and I had seen the last of Iceland." The voyage back was uneventful. In the evening of the 6th of September, a soft warm grey day, the "Diana" came along the pier

at Granton in time for Morris to catch the night mail
for London. "I was curious to see," he writes on the
last page of his diary, "what effect the trees would have
on me when day dawned, but they did not have much.
I thought the houses and horses looked so dispropor-
tionately big for the landscape that it all looked like a
scene at a theatre."

"I think I should have plenty to tell you of my
travels if I saw you," he writes to Mrs. Baldwin a few
days after his return, "but I am the worst of letter
writers; besides I made a sort of journal which I intend
writing out, perhaps may manage to do so to part of it
in time to send Georgie while she is staying with you,
and then you can read it if you care to; anyhow you
shall see it when it is done if you like, though I believe
it will be but a poor specimen of its class. Moreover, I
confess to a dread of setting to work on it: it is true that
the journey was altogether successful, and that I think I
have gained in many ways by it: but it seems such a
long way off now, and there is a bit of one's life gone;
and the world so much the narrower to me because of
it: and when I look over it I am afraid of having to
grin sourly at this bit of enthusiasm, and be puzzled at
that bit of high spirits; and note here how I refused to
acknowledge a disappointment, and there how I pre-
tended not to be weary—and in short—all the rest of it;
something in its way like looking at a drawerful of old
letters—if anybody ever did venture on such a bold act,
which I doubt.

"I rather miss the mountains, I must say, which is
not what I expected, for I use to consider myself a hater
of them: to-day I had to go out on business to a place
near Wimbledon, and there was what people called a
pretty view there, and I thought how dull it looked, and
that after all people were right to build villas and plant

I.　　　　　　　　　T

red geraniums about it: my own little old house by
Lechlade though is sweet and innocent enough, and
though it has a sadness about it, which is not gloom but
the melancholy born of beauty I suppose, it is very
stimulating to the imagination. I am going down there
on Saturday, where I expect to enjoy making the acquaintance again of the little pony that carried me in my six
weeks' ride, the bravest and best tempered of little beasts:
you should have seen him picking his way in one of
those dismal bogs, where if you sneeze, the earth, or
rather the roots of the grass, trembles violently: they
say, however, that the Icelandic ponies get lazy among
the fat pastures and soft air of England—small blame to
them."

He had already been down to Kelmscott, where his
family, with Rossetti, had been living during his Iceland
voyage. On the 23rd of September he went there again,
stopping on the way at Oxford to buy a boat for the new
house, and driving over from Oxford up the beautiful
autumnal Thames valley. Early in October the long
summer came at last to an end. Mouse, the pony, was
left at Kelmscott, where he grew fat and lazy, and was
much loved by the children. The little biography which
one of them gives me, five and twenty years after, makes
a pretty picture of that peaceful home.

"He was gentle and quiet, though not without sly-
ness: for I remember there was one gate-post against
which, when I went out for a ride, he used often to try
to rub me off his broad back. I'm ashamed for my horse-
manship to think how often the rogue had his way.
Father used to ride him about the country a good bit at
first. Then I jogged about with him, and he used to be
put to a little basket-carriage, and go meandering along
in a meditative way. He got enormously fat on our
coarse thick plentiful English grass, with little to do;

and I used to imagine him lonely, and yearning for the
fun and clatter and hardships of his Iceland life among
his friends, as he stood there with his head stretched
forward looking intensely meditative.   One day, when
the hunt passed through our home-meadows, the excitement of horses and hounds was too much for the
lonely philosopher: he threw up his head and, fat as he
was, bundled over a hedge and actually followed the
hounds a good way.   I missed the gentle funny little
animal much when he died."

CHAPTER IX

LOVE IS ENOUGH: PERIOD OF ILLUMINATIONS:
DISSOLUTION OF THE FIRM
1871-1874

As soon as he returned to England, Morris resumed the work of illuminating which had already for about a year been one of the main occupations of his leisure, and which for between three and four years more held a foremost place in his interest. During these years he produced a number of books, some completed and others not, in very various styles and all of remarkable beauty. His earliest experiments in the art of illumination, made fourteen or fifteen years before, had been already remarkable not only for an all but complete mastery of colour, but for the genius with which they reproduced the tone and spirit of the earlier mediæval work, as he had studied it first in the painted books of the thirteenth and fourteenth centuries at the Bodleian Library, and afterwards in those at the British Museum. But they were full of technical defects in drawing; and their deficiency was most marked in the drawing of the letters of the text which is commonly known by the name of handwriting. Morris's own handwriting had been then, and for years afterwards continued to be, decidedly bad: while not illegible, it was slovenly, and had neither beauty nor distinction. When he took up the art of illumination in 1870, he began to study handwriting as a fine art. By practice he soon mastered it; and the texts of his painted books show a steady advance in skill of execution. The reaction on his own cursive hand was marked and immediate. The beautiful handwriting familiar to his friends for the last five and twenty years was directly due to his study and practice of the art in the period of his work as an illuminator. In the decoration of his painted books —as in everything which had to do with pattern and colour—there is also an advance in splendour of colouring and breadth of design, but the earliest are in their simpler treatment as faultless as the latest: the art of decoration seems to have been born in him and to come from his hands full-grown.

The "Book of Verses," a selection of his own lyrical poems, completed on the 26th of August, 1870, and given by him to Mrs. Burne-Jones, is the first, and though not the finest, perhaps on the whole the most beautiful, of all his painted books. In this book he broke completely away from the mediæval method. That method reappears, transformed through his own original genius, in the colour and design of the great manuscript Virgil, in which his art both as scribe and as illuminator culminates. But here there is a modernness which owes nothing to any tradition: and a freshness, a direct appeal to first principles and instincts, which (as in the case of his earliest wall-papers) charms by its simplicity and fitness even more than the later and technically finer work. If, as has been sometimes thought possible, ornamented handwriting should again take its place among the popular arts, it is in the direction indicated by this beautiful volume that its most hopeful way would seem to lie.

The book is on paper, and consists of fifty-one pages. It was not wholly executed by his own hand. One of the pictures was painted by Burne-Jones, and the remainder, including a portrait-head of the author on the first page, by Mr. Fairfax Murray; and the painted letters were coloured by Mr. George Wardle, who also drew in part of the ornament from Morris's designs. To produce a painted book in the full beauty of which it is capable, Morris considered that division of labour was advantageous: it was not likely that the scribe and the miniaturist would be found at their best in the same person, and here too, as in larger work, he found the excellence as well as the pleasure of art to lie in co-ordination of skilled workmen. Other books, however, were executed by him unaided. The next done after the " Book of Verses " was a manuscript, also on paper, of his translation of the Eyrbyggja Saga; a folio of 239 pages, slightly ornamented and without pictures. This manuscript, with the single exception, carefully noted by him upon it, of the laying on of the gold leaf on three pages, which was done by one of the workmen at Queen Square, was wholly written and ornamented by his own hand. It was finished in April, 1871; and before it was finished, he had begun a new book on vellum with continuous and elaborate ornament. This was a copy of FitzGerald's " Rubáiyát of Omar Khayyám."

This manuscript, given by him to Mrs. Burne-Jones, may take rank, by its elaborate beauty, as one of his chief masterpieces. It was finished on the 16th of October, 1872, after being a year and a half in hand. On its tiny scale—twenty-three pages measuring six inches by three and a half—it is a volume of immense labour and exquisite workmanship. On eighteen of the pages the illumination is confined to a central space of less than three inches by two, with a title in gold above each. In that central space, alongside and between the verses, is a running ornament of flowers and fruits. On the other five pages the margins are completely filled with floriated design, among which are minute but beautifully drawn and coloured figures, the lower half of the last page being also filled by a design of two figures holding a scroll. The treatment of the fruit and flower work is an admirable adaptation of an almost Pre-Raphaelite naturalism to the methods and limits of ornamental design : the raspberries on page 14 and the honeysuckles on page 21 may be specially instanced as unsurpassable in their truth to nature and their decorative effect.

The fine lambskin vellum for this, as for his other manuscripts, he procured from Rome. The English lime-dressed vellum used for a few special copies of " Love is Enough " had been found disagreeable in surface and almost useless for fine work. Owing to the continuous demand for vellum at the Vatican, the tradition of its proper manufacture had been preserved more fully at Rome than elsewhere. But sometimes the orders from the Vatican absorbed the whole annual output, and no skins were to be had. When the Kelmscott Press was started, a sufficient supply of Roman vellum could not be procured for it; and an English maker, after many unsuccessful trials, at last succeeded in producing sheets of a quality nearly equal to the Roman.

Before this Omar Khayyám was finished, he had begun another copy of the same poem for Burne-Jones on paper. This was executed more in the style of the " Book of Verses," but with somewhat more profuse ornament; and in it Burne-Jones himself painted six extraordinarily beautiful pictures, each in a different scheme of colour, and showing, although each is only slightly over four inches by two in size, his finest qualities of design and invention. The floral decoration which runs down the margins and between the verses is in pale colours, green, blue, yellow, pink, and crimson, with a preponderance of green. The initial letters of the lines are alternated in gold and colours, the page always beginning with a gold letter, and one colour being used down each page. The pictures are inclosed in gold frames, unburnished; and on the pages with pictures and those facing them the whole of the illumination is enriched with burnished gold throughout. This book was given by Burne-Jones to Miss Frances Graham (Mrs. J. F. Horner), and is now in her possession.

Immediately after his return from Iceland, Morris had also begun the composition of a new poem, with the origination and completion of which his work as an illuminator is intimately connected. " Morris has been here twice since his return," Rossetti wrote to William Bell Scott from Kelmscott on the 2nd of October, " for a few days at first and just now for a week again. He is now back in London, and this place will be empty of all inmates by the end of this week, I think. Morris has set to work with a will on a sort of masque called ' Love is Enough,' which he means to print as a moderate quarto, with woodcuts by Ned Jones and borders by himself, some of which he has done really very beautifully. The poem is, I think, at a higher point of execution perhaps than anything that he has done, having a passionate lyric quality such as one found in his earliest work, and of course much more mature balance in carrying out. It will be a very fine work."

The poem in its first form was finished by the beginning of winter, but it was afterwards very much altered. It gave him more real trouble than any other of his poems. " I have come down here for a fortnight," he writes from Kelmscott on the 13th of February, 1872, " to see spring beginning, a sight I have seen little of for years, and am writing among the grey gables and rook-haunted trees, with a sense of the place being

almost too beautiful to live in.   I have been in trouble
with my own work, which I couldn't make to march
for a long time; but I think I have now brought it out
of the maze of re-writing and despondency, though it is
not exactly finished."   For other reasons, to be mentioned presently, it was not published till the end of the
year.

"Love is Enough" is probably the least familiar to
most readers of Morris's longer poems; but apart from
any question of purely poetical quality, it is in some
technical respects much the most remarkable.   It re-
constitutes, under modern conditions, forms of later
mediæval poetry which had long fallen into disuse.   The
fluctuating contest between epic and romantic treatment
which is visible in " The Earthly Paradise " is here put
aside ; they are replaced by a dramatic form which com-
bines qualities taken from both, but is itself of a quite
distinct kind : a kind which was being gradually worked
up to in England during the fifteenth and sixteenth
centuries, when the Renaissance burst in with a crash
and produced the new world of the Elizabethans.   The
distinctively mediæval structure, with its carefully planned
architectural arrangement, is resumed in a manner which
dramatic poetry had abandoned for over three hundred
years.   In his use of receding planes of action which yet
do not lie in what might be called, by an easy metaphor
from another art, any real aerial perspective, he approxi-
mates dramatic poetry to the manner of treatment of
those late mediæval tapestries, the finest of which were
his ideal of decorative arrangement.   The outer frame is
given by the rustic lovers, Giles and Joan.   Within this
is a second plane, in which stand the Emperor and
Empress.   Within this again, in the central plane, is
Love as the interpreter of the action, both inwards and
outwards.   On the fourth plane is the main action itself,

the dramatic interlude of the Freeing of Pharamond: and on the last and inmost of all, subtilized out of any definite personality and charged with all the distilled emotion of the fourfold action, is "the Music," the final and interpenetrating spirit of the whole work. The detailed structure of this multiplex arrangement is worked out with an extraordinary ingenuity and elegance. Morris's best decorative designs have just such an ordered intricacy, such a free yet precisely adjusted pattern. Most notable of all is the instinctive art which keeps all these planes of action interlaced or interfused, so that the whole poem constitutes a single design. The problem was of the same kind as he had to face in designing for wall-papers or chintzes, that of so arranging the "repeat" that the pattern should flow continuously over the whole space to be filled and not fall asunder into patches. It is here further complicated by another condition, a fact of texture, as it would be called if the matter being dealt with were a textile fabric. To make the different planes of action distinct, each has its own metre. These metres are the short octosyllabic couplet, the heroic decasyllable, the alliterative unrhymed verse of the body of the play, and, for the "Music," an exquisite invention of rhymed dactylics. The way in which they are interwoven is a masterpiece of metrical device. In the two scenes of the induction (to use the appropriate term of the Renaissance dramatists) the ground is laid of the whole metrical system of the poem; in the first scene by a single phrase of the Music; in the second by a full period of the Music and a single phrase of the alliterative dialogue-metre. Thereafter follows the play itself, in five scenes, with the Music at the end of each, and before and after each the interpretation, in stately heroic metre, given by Love before the dropped curtain. But in the fourth scene, by an ingenuity the most elaborately simple, the whole of the elements of the fivefold play are interlaced. The scene has passed like the other three; the Music has followed; and Love, clad as a pilgrim, has spoken before the curtain. But now, instead of a fresh scene following, the curtain rises again on the same scene; and Love goes on to the stage, drops the heroic verse in which he has hitherto spoken, and holds a dialogue with Pharamond in the alliterative play-metre: during which, the Music, hitherto only sung between the scenes, mingles with the play from without, growing nearer and nearer till, at its last cadence, Azalais enters. And at the end of this scene, the dialogue-metre, without a check, becomes, for two couplets, the rhymed dactylic metre of the Music, as though the lovers, in the exaltation of their meeting, had become for a moment one with the central harmony of things.

The architectural instinct, the faculty of design in its highest form, which was the quality in which Morris's unique strength lay, was never applied by him with more certain and delicate a touch. And the ingenuities of the metrical treatment in which this design is worked out are almost equally striking. The rhymed iambic verse, whether of eight or of ten syllables, was his old familiar medium; nor is it used here with greater skill than he had used it in "The Earthly Paradise," though even here we may find subtle adaptations to the dramatic method. But the rhymed dactylics to which reference has been made—a metre at once one of the rarest, one of the most difficult, and if successfully used, one of the most hauntingly beautiful, which the English language uses—are a noble development of that single exquisite fragment, "Pray but One Prayer for Me," which had been one of his very earliest achievements in poetry. And the alliterative metre which he invented, or re-invented, for the body of the play deserves a more serious notice.

The fact that the whole of English poetry, from the sixteenth century downwards, is written in metres of foreign origin, only naturalized in English through the long and difficult practice of centuries, is one which, however familiar to students of mediæval literature, is little realized beyond the circle of historians and scholars. As was the case in Latin literature for a period of about the same length, the foreign metres, after a time of struggle during which the native metre produced its finest achievements, conquered it and drove it completely below the surface. But, as was the case in Latin literature, the native metre not only had a deep influence on the special development of the imported metres, but retained an affinity to the structure of the language which made it tend to reappear when the dominant metrical forms were exhausted from over-use. Here, at the present day, the parallel ceases. But if the argument from the Latin analogy were seriously pressed, it might be conjectured that the future forms of English poetry would be, not, indeed, the form of the mediæval English alliterative metre,—for the English language, like the Latin, has developed too widely and changed too deeply in structure to revert to its Saturnians,—but forms essentially based on the same metrical principles. Of the experiments in this direction—still no more than tentative efforts amid the overwhelming predominance of the normal rhymed iambic metres—" Love is Enough " is one of the first and the most successful.

It was not indeed from any such wide and general considerations that Morris was led to essay its use. He simply went by known facts. As he had followed the metres of Chaucer for his narrative poems, he followed the metres of the earliest English plays for this dramatic poem. In these he found the alliterative Middle English verse, freed from the rigid rules which had governed it up to the close of the fourteenth century, and adapted to the changed modulation of a language which had by that time dropped its weak vowel-endings; but at the same time cramped and slightly vulgarized by an attempt to add the foreign enrichment of rhyme. For this metre, he instinctively felt, rhyme was unsuited, unless where it was desired, for special occasions, to raise it by this additional ornament to a lyric tension. But rhyme was for the metre a purely artificial importation: the solution, then, was quite simple: do away with the rhymed endings, and there is left a verse as elastic and varied as the regular alliterative verse native to England, less difficult to write, and better adapted to modern vocabulary and intonation of speech. The experiment has remained an isolated one. He never repeated it himself; for his translation of " Beowulf," a *tour de force* executed for a special object, keeps as closely as possible to the original metre of early English poetry, with its rigid metrical laws, and its mouldings (if a metaphor from architecture be allowed) axe-hewn, rather than undulating under the chisel. Nor did he succeed in reconstituting the fine and flexible Middle English metre as a practical form of verse for modern poetry. Morris himself felt that this new poem was both tentative and difficult, and its failure to make any impression on a large audience was received by him with perfect equanimity. It was a thing he had done to please himself, and he thought highly of it, but he did not expect it to please other people to anything like the same degree.

Once more the attempt to produce a volume in a beautifully decorated outward form had to be abandoned. He designed, and cut on wood, borders for the pages of what would have been a very beautiful small quarto.

In some copies these were to have been filled in with colours and gilding, so that it would have been another illuminated book, with the text printed, not written. Besides the borders, there were to have been pictures, to which the whole scheme of the book lends itself with special aptness. Some of the scenes are written, as it were, directly for illumination. In the first scene of the play, there is a series of ornate comparisons—Nimrod carved on the high-seat in the hall, Argo woven on the hangings of the guard-room, Mars painted in the window of the council-chamber—which are introduced with exactly the decorative effect of pictures within the great initial letters of a painted book. The transitions, too, from one part of the poem to another call out to be made through some reinforcement of either music or pictures.

"Love is Enough" bears the marks of all the varied sources of romance from which its author had drawn in earlier work, perhaps with the effect of a structure too composite for easy apprehension. The story, at least in its main outline, the theme of a king who gives up his kingdom for love in the valley, is taken from the Mabinogion, and is in feeling intimately Celtic. The names of Pharamond and Azalais—Teutonic words made musical by the speech of Central or Southern France—carry the mind back to some dim Merovingian epoch in which the ox-wagons of Frankish kings rolled through the mountain gorges of Auvergne and the vineyards of Burgundy. The representation of the play before an Emperor and Empress brings it vaguely within the central current of European art towards the close of the Middle Ages: and touches of landscape here and there show that the author's mind was still full of Iceland.

It was the last complete poem of any magnitude which

Morris wrote for several years.   For some time he had been feeling about for new methods of literary expression : after this poem was written he became once more absorbed in handicraft and the productions of his workshops or of his own unaided hand.   Some months before, this feeling after new vehicles had led him to begin what is certainly the most singular of his writings, a novel of contemporary life.   The story dealt with the love of two brothers for the same woman, and was evidently going to take a tragic turn.   As far as the development of the story gives any indication, rather more than one-third of it had been written when it was abandoned.   The fragment was swiftly written and never revised.   But revision was, as has been already noted, at no time a thing much to his taste, or for which he had any aptitude.   No further criticism need be passed on the fragment than what was said of it by Morris himself a year later.   Mrs. Baldwin, to whom he had given sympathetic counsel in her own first efforts at narrative prose, had expressed a wish to see what he had done.   He sent her the manuscript with the following letter :

" Queen Square,
" June 22nd, 1872.

" Dear Louie,

" Herewith I send by book-post my abortive novel : it is just a specimen of how not to do it, and there is no more to be said thereof : 'tis nothing but landscape and sentiment : which thing won't do.   Since you wish to read it, I am sorry 'tis such a rough copy, which roughness sufficiently indicates my impatience at having to deal with prose.   The separate parcel, paged 1 to 6, was a desperate dash at the middle of the story to try to give it life when I felt it failing : it begins with the letter of the elder brother to the younger on getting *his* letter telling how he was going to bid for the girl in marriage. I found it in the envelope in which I had sent it to Georgie to see if she could give me any hope: she gave me none, and I have never looked at it since. So there's an end of my novel-writing, I fancy, unless the world turns topsides under some day. Health and merry days to you, and believe me to be

"Your affectionate friend,

"WILLIAM MORRIS."

Henceforth, but for a few lyrics, original or adapted from Icelandic and Danish ballads, his writing was confined to translation until he began his great epic of "Sigurd the Volsung."

The workshops at Queen Square had been slowly encroaching on the living part of the house. The manager was continually appealing for more room to carry on the work, which was cramped as it was, and which Morris was always, almost without his will, extending in one direction or another by fresh inventions or experiments. "I am going with Janey to-morrow," he writes on the 25th of November, "to look at a house in Hammersmith in Theresa Terrace: it is Mason the painter's house, who died about a month ago. We must, it seems, turn out of this house next spring, for Wardle wants it all for the business." Towards the end of 1872 the family removed from Queen Square. Morris himself kept two rooms for his own private use, and the rest of the house was turned over to the use of the firm, the drawing-room being made into a much-needed show-room, and the upper floors into additional workshops. The new house was not the Hammersmith one, but another not far from it, on the high road between Hammersmith and Turnham Green, in a rambling suburb of orchards and market-gardens, and with easy access to the Thames down

Chiswick Lane. Before the building of the District Railway it was a pleasant, if somewhat remote, suburb. The house itself was very small, "a very good sort of house for one person to live in, or perhaps two," as its mistress afterwards described it; but there was a large garden, and the quiet was complete. Here Morris lived for six years. The parting from Queen Square took place with little effusion of sentiment. Morris himself was too elated by the prospect of setting up a little dye-shop in the empty basement to care much about the abandonment of the house. It had never been more than a temporary home forced on him by disagreeable necessity.

On the 23rd of January, 1873, he writes, "We have cleared out of Queen Square as far as our domesticity is concerned: I keep my study and little bedroom here, and I daresay, as time goes on, I shall live here a good deal: for the rest, we have taken a little house on the Turnham Green road, about twenty minutes' walk from the Hammersmith Station; and otherwise easy to get at because of the omnibuses: it is a *very* little house with a pretty garden, and I think will suit Janey and the children: it is some half-hour's walk from the Grange, which makes it quite a little way for me; on the other hand, I can always see any one I want at Queen Square quite safe from interruption, so in all ways it seems an advantage—does it not? Withal I never have had any sentiment of affection for this house, though so much has happened to me while I have lived here. I have always felt myself like nothing but a lodger here. Nevertheless, there is something profoundly dismal about the empty rooms here that strikes a chill on one."

"I am going to have the little ones home," he writes the following day, "to Turnham Green to-day; 'tis a month since I have seen them. Jenny is twelve years old now: bless us, how old I'm getting. Except the work for the firm, in which I am rather busy, I am doing nothing now but translations: I should be glad to have some poem on hand, but it's no use trying to force the thing; and though the translating lacks the hope and fear that makes writing original things so absorbing, yet at any rate it is amusing and in places even exciting."

The following letter was written a few days later to Mrs. Coronio, who was then living at Athens. The friendship between her and Morris was affectionate and unbroken through life.

> "26, Queen Square,
> "Feb. 11th, 1873.

"My dear Aglaia,

"You see our letters crossed: and I'm glad I wrote to excuse myself before I got your letter taking me to task. I am in much better condition now than I was when I wrote last: I suppose the change has done me good: we are quite settled in our new house, and I find it very pleasant: my own room is particularly cheerful and pretty, and I can work in it with a much better heart than in the dingy room at Queen Square. I go most days to the Square though, and come back when I feel inclined, or not at all when I feel inclined: all this involves a good deal of walking, which, no doubt, is good for me: it seems quite a ridiculously little way to the Grange now, after the long way it used to be. Last Sunday, Ned came to breakfast with me, and we had a pleasant hour or two. I am very hard at work at one thing or another; firm's work for one thing. I should very much like to make the business quite a success, and it can't be, unless I work at it myself. I must say, though I don't call myself money-greedy, a smash on that side would be a terrible nuisance; I have so many serious troubles, pleasures, hopes and fears, that I have not time on my hands to be ruined and get really poor: above all things it would destroy my freedom of work, which is a dear delight to me. My translations go on apace, but I am doing nothing original: it can't be helped, though sometimes I begin to fear I am losing my invention. You know I very much wish not to fall off in imagination and enthusiasm as I grow older: there have been men who, once upon a time, have done things good or noteworthy, who have got worse with time and have outlived their power; I don't like that at all. On the other hand, all great men that have not died young have done some of their best work when they were getting quite old. However, it won't do to force oneself about it, and I certainly enjoy some of the work I do very much, and one of these days my Heimskringla will be an important work.

"Iceland gapes for me still this summer: I grudge very much being away from the two or three people I care for so long as I must be, but if I can only get away in some sort of hope and heart I know it will be the making of me. I am very much disappointed that you are not coming back before: I quite looked for you this month.

"Yes, truly, letters are very unsatisfactory; they would do very well if one could write them at our best times; but continually one has to sit down to them dull and cold and worried, with the thoughts all slipping away from us, till the sheet is filled up with trivialities—as this will be I fear—only there is something about the look of the writing of anyone one is fond of, that is familiar and dear and saves one from utter disappointment, and one feels that the stiff awkward sentences all about nothing or little have still something of a soul in them. Think what an excitement that day was for me when I

got letters after eight weeks in the Iceland journey: lord!
how my heart did go thump thump as I galloped up to
the post-office at Reykjavik!

"I wonder how you will feel at the changes in the
house here: Janey's room has already got the workmen's
benches in it: the big room is bare and painty; there is
hammering and sawing and running up and down stairs
going on; and all looks strange, and as yet somewhat
wretched.   It doesn't touch me very much I must say
though: for this long time past I have, as it were,
carried my house on my back: but the little Turnham
Green house is really a pleasure to me;—may all that be
a good omen!   Yet you must come and see me here
too when you come home, if you won't be too much
terrified at my housekeeper, who is like a troll-wife in an
Icelandic story: with a deep bass voice, big and O *so* ugly!

"We have had cold weather enough lately, snow and
a dreadful east wind; all of which I don't care a penny
about to say the truth.

"On Saturday I am going down to Cambridge, to
Magnússon, to do Icelandic: as stupid over the language
as you others who are such quick linguists would think
me, I am really getting on with it now: when I am
down there, which has been once or twice, we all talk
nothing but Icelandic together.

"Well, I had best make an end now before I get too
dull.   Once again forgive me for not writing to you
oftener: I have really had a hard time of it: but I hope
things have taken a long turn now, and that I shall be
something worth as a companion when I see you again;
which I look forward to very much indeed.   Write
soon again, please, and tell me how you are.

"Good-bye, then, with love and best wishes.

"I am your affectionate

"WILLIAM MORRIS."

With a mind still so full of his first journey to Iceland and so excited at the prospect of a second, it is not surprising that his first visit to Italy, which took place this spring, was something of an anti-climax. It was a very short one, and gave him little satisfaction. With the noble Italian art of the earlier Renaissance he had but little sympathy: for that of the later Renaissance and the academic traditions he had nothing but unmixed detestation. Some time in these years his old fellow-pupil, Mr. Bliss, then engaged on researches among the archives of the Vatican, met him in the Bodleian Library at Oxford, and pressed him to come with him to Rome. His reply was too characteristic to be forgotten. " Do you suppose," he said, " that I should see anything in Rome that I can't see in Whitechapel ? "

Even the earlier and, to his mind, the far more interesting and beautiful work of the twelfth and thirteenth centuries in Italy did not appeal to him in the same way as the contemporary art of England or Northern France. On this occasion he only saw Florence and Siena, and returned after a fortnight. Burne-Jones, with whom he went out, and who himself made a more prolonged stay, found him a rather exacting companion, and a little determined to make the worst of things. The interior of the Duomo at Florence depressed him with its chilly bareness: San Miniato was unfortunately in the death-agonies of a thorough restoration; and even the more unspoiled Siena failed to excite him. Indeed it was from the natural beauty of Italy, both now and on later visits, that he drew far more pleasure than from its art. The descent to Turin from the Mont Cenis " on the most beautiful of all evenings, going, still between snow-capped mountains, through a country like a garden, green grass and feathery poplars and abundance of pink-blossomed leafless peach and almond trees," roused him to real enthusiasm, as did also the passage of the Apennines between Bologna and Pistoja. In Florence, the cloisters of Santa Maria Novella were what he found most to his mind; at Siena, even the wonderful cathedral library, all as bright as a painted book, could not please him because he wanted it to have been painted by some one at least a century before Pinturicchio. The exterior of the Duomo of Florence he did indeed afterwards, a little grudgingly, admit to be the finest exterior of any building in the world.

Of the second journey to Iceland, which took place this summer, there is no need to give any detailed chronicle. Faulkner was again his companion. On board the mail steamer they found among their fellow-passengers that fine scholar and archæologist, John Henry Middleton. The acquaintance then formed was the beginning of a long friendship. As regards mediæval art of all kinds, Middleton, with a more contracted imagination, had a knowledge equal to Morris's own: in Greek and Persian art it was even greater, and when Morris later took up the manufacture of carpets and woven stuffs as part of his business, he found much help in Middleton's great knowledge of Oriental textiles. The article on Mural Decoration jointly written by them for the " Encyclopædia Britannica," ten years afterwards, is one surviving record of a long association in taste and sympathies.

The party started early in July and were away for a little over two months, sailing and returning, as in 1871, by the " Diana." Their journey through the interior was, however, longer and more adventurous than on their first visit. After a preliminary excursion of ten days to the more or less familiar ground in the southwest of the island, they started on the 1st of August to cross the great central wilderness in a north-easterly

direction.   From Dettifoss, the furthest point reached,
they made their way across the northern mountains to
the little seaport of Akureyri on Eyjafirth, and thence
back over the wilderness by a more westerly route,
reaching Reykjavik at the beginning of September.   It
was a journey which involved great physical endurance
—one day they were fifteen hours in the saddle—but no
one was the worse for it in spite of much cold and rain.
Except Lithend, no place famous in a Saga was visited,
though from a northern mountain they saw Drángey,
Grettir's island, lying below them down the long reach
of Skagafirth.   But the land itself, apart from the particular associations of places, had grown in his mind into
a strange fascination.   Even more now than two years
before, the touch of Iceland was something that stirred
him with an almost sacramental solemnity.   "The journey," he writes of it after his return, " has deepened the
impression I had of Iceland and increased my love for
it.   The glorious simplicity of the terrible and tragic,
but beautiful land, with its well-remembered stories of
brave men, killed all querulous feeling in me, and has
made all the dear faces of wife and children and love
and friends dearer than ever to me.   I feel as if a
definite space of my life had passed away now I have
seen Iceland for the last time : as I looked up at Charles'
Wain to-night, all my travel there seemed to come
back on me, made solemn and elevated, in one moment, till my heart swelled with the wonder of it :
surely I have gained a great deal, and it was no idle
whim that drew me there, but a true instinct for what
I needed."

In a lighter vein, but yet with a touch, at the
close, of the same feeling of awe and breathlessness, he writes to Mrs. Baldwin on the 14th of
September :

" Dear Louie,

"I came back safe and well last Friday, and I am
sorry to say without the pony for your little lad : this
was not laziness on my part, but was because I found
the price of ponies gone up so much since I was last
there that they are quite as dear there (for what they
are) as in England : I mean that a pony of any character,
and by no means first-rate, will cost from £8 to £10
there, and as it would cost £8 or so more to get it to
Wilden, the money, say £17, seemed enough to buy a
better beast than I could be reasonably sure of bringing
you : add to this that they will probably be cheaper
there next year, and that a letter from me to one or
other of my friends there would be enough to get an
average specimen at the current price there if you still
wish it.

"The old lady (age seventy-seven) turned out to be
an ungrateful and stupid old creature as ever came out
of Somersetshire (her native den). Yet one may be
grateful to her for the following scene.

"On the strand at Reykjavik a row of general shops
fronting the sea, Mr. Tomsen's shop in the foreground.

"Enter 1st, the Lieutenant of the 'Diana,' his hands
in his waistcoat pockets, and he whistling 'See the con-
quering Hero Comes' to keep up his spirit. 2nd, two
sailors from the 'Diana' carrying the old lady's bandbox
and bundle. 3rd, the skipper of the 'Diana,' arm in
arm with the OLD LADY. (Costume of her : a drawn
grey silk bonnet, a little white shawl, a purple chintz
scanty gown beautifully flowered, white stockings, and
shoes with 'sandals.') Captain a fat, red-faced, intensely
good-natured old naval officer. 4th, the whole of the
male population of Reykjavik who can spare time from
doing nothing, looking anxious as to whether they will
all be able to get into Mr. Tomsen's shop.

" Old Lady to Lieutenant as they come on to Mr. Tomsen's doorstep, who stands there (little, polite, red-haired man) looking anxious as to how many of No. 4 he can keep out of his shop:

" ' Mr. Lieutenant ' (says she, taking about 4d. in small Danish money out of her pocket), ' will you take this ?'

" Lieutenant. ' Thank you kindly ; what am I to do with it ?'

" O. L. ' Please to give it to the crew.'

" L. ' What will they do with it ?'

" O. L. ' I do not wish them to drink too much.'

" L. ' Shall they drink coffee with it ?'

" O. L. ' O yes, Mr. Lieutenant, that would be very nice.'

" L. grins and pockets the 4d. sterling, and the whole of 1, 2, and 3 disappear into Mr. Tomsen's shop, who manages to shut out No. 4, who takes its hands out of its pockets to take snuff and then settles itself to waiting till 1, 2, and 3 come out again.

" This is literal truth : also that the old lady wanted to be Guy Fawkesed about Iceland in a chair : also that she teased Mrs. Magnússon to buy her a lamb that she might cook it herself in her own private room, and scolded her heartily because she couldn't get her one at once : also that she slept on board ship with nothing over her but a sheet, though the thermometer was nearly at freezing point : also that she would hardly pay for anything, and (till the lamb came) was like to die of starvation (she told us she had £1,000 a year) if some one hadn't given her some plovers.

" I hear she went back by the return trip of the ' Diana ' and, the weather being rough, was not much seen upon deck on the voyage : I still think she was the flying Dutchwoman. And now she is out of the story.

"We had a very successful journey, did all we meant to do, and had fine weather on the whole: a great comfort, as wet weather makes daily riding little more than something to endure while it lasts, however amusing it may be to look back on, when it is well over. One day we rode through what we thought was a dust-storm mixed with drizzle, till a farmer told us that there must have been some eruption of the fire-mountains, as there was no sand thereabout, and that this was fine ashes. Skaptar Jokul has been very unquiet for years now, and the eruption in January last was a much more tremendous affair than one would have judged by the slight notice of it in our papers. One priest told me that they saw it for about a fortnight, gushes of fire ten times or so an hour, so that the long nights were quite light with it, and the short days all dark with the smoke. No one knows where the crater was among the unreachable ice of the great Jokul: the big river of Skeidara was nearly dried up by it for the time.

"Our guides were very pleasant, friendly fellows, as innocent of the great world as babies, and, apart from their daily labour, living almost entirely in the glorious past days of Iceland. One of them, Haldor by name, was born at Lithend, where Gunnar lived and died. I suppose I shall never see them again, and the days of these two journeys there have grown inexpressibly solemn to me.

"Please give my kindest remembrances to Baldwin, and believe me,

"Yours affectionately,
"WILLIAM MORRIS."

Icelandic literature in one form or another still filled the first place in his mind. The notion of rewriting the epic of the Volsungs in English verse, though it was not begun till a good deal later, was already much in his thoughts, and he went on translating the smaller Sagas and executing beautifully written copies of his translations. The illuminated manuscript of the Frithiof Saga, in the possession of Mr. Fairfax Murray, and that of the three Sagas of "Hen Thorir," "The Banded Men," and "Howard the Halt," given by Morris to Mrs. Burne-Jones, both belong to this period. The decoration of the former was never completed, but both are works of remarkable delicacy and beauty.

Even the transfusion of modern sentiment into an ancient story, as had been done with the Arthurian cycle by Tennyson, was a thing that Morris instinctively disliked. But the epic of the North was a thing that lay still nearer his heart; and what he thought a false or inadequate treatment of these great legends roused him into an agony of anger. On the 12th of November, 1873, he wrote from Queen Square to Mr. Forman, who had sent him a copy of his brother's translation of Wagner's libretto for "Die Walküre":

"Many thanks for your letter and the translation of Wagner: I have not had time to read it yet: nor to say the truth am I much interested in anything Wagner does, as his theories on musical matters seem to me as an artist and non-musical man perfectly abhominable: besides I look upon it as nothing short of desecration to bring such a tremendous and world-wide subject under the gaslights of an opera: the most rococo and degraded of all forms of art—the idea of a sandy-haired German tenor tweedledeeing over the unspeakable woes of Sigurd, which even the simplest words are not typical enough to express! Excuse my heat: but I wish to see Wagner uprooted, however clever he may be, and I don't doubt he is: but he is anti-artistic, don't doubt it."

The art of Wagner, indeed, with its lack of reticence,

its idealized appeal to the senses, its highly coloured and heavily charged rhetoric, was quite alien from all Morris's sympathies. Though, as he says in this letter, he was a non-musical man, the older music, the church music of the Middle Ages and that of the great English and Italian masters of the sixteenth and seventeenth centuries, appealed to him very deeply. Music was a thing that, on the whole, he put away from him as not belonging to his work; but from the early days of his singing plainsong at Oxford till, in the weakness of his last illness, he broke to tears over a few snatches of virginal-music, it was from no want of sensitiveness—rather perhaps the reverse—that he would not admit it into his life.

He was now preparing the volume of translations, new and older, from the Icelandic, which, for some forgotten reason, was not published till 1875. Of its contents he writes again to Mr. Forman, on the 8th of December:

"I would have answered your letter before (many thanks for it) but I had not quite made up my mind about the Stories in my translation book. It stands thus now as I intended at first: the Story of Gunnlaug the Worm-tongue, printed in the Fortnightly some years back; the Story of Frithiof the Bold, printed before in the Dark Blue; the story of Viglund the Fair, never before printed: these 'three Northern Love Stories' will give the name to the book, but to thicken it out I add three more short tales; Hroi the Fool, Hogni and Hedin, and Thorstein Staff-smitten; the first of these three a pretty edition of a 'sharper' story and the same as a tale in the Arabian Nights. The second a terrible story; a very well told, but late version of a dark and strange legend of remote times. The third simple, and not without generosity, smelling strong of the soil of Iceland, like the Gunnlaug."

He also worked a good deal at drawing from the model, "for my soul's sake chiefly," he quaintly said, "for little hope can I have ever to do anything serious in the thing." "I never," he says on the same occasion, "had the painter's memory which makes it easy to put down on paper what you think you see, nor indeed can I see any scene with a frame, as it were, round it, though in my own way I can realize things visibly enough to myself. But it seems I must needs try to make myself unhappy with doing what I find difficult, or impossible."

This unhappiness is not strange to the artistic temperament. But his practice in drawing now was not useless to him: and its effects may be seen, not indeed in any marked proficiency in drawing the human figure, but in a greater breadth and decisiveness of design in his decoration: a matter of no small importance when the designing of patterns for chintzes and woven tapestries became, as it did soon afterwards, one of his chief occupations. "I can't say that I get on with my drawing," he writes nearly a year afterwards; "but then I never expected I should: so I keep it up, dreading the model day like I used to dread Sunday when I was a little chap." At present, however, what he called the mood of idleness (his idleness was more productive than most men's work) was rather strong on him. "It is wet and wild weather," he writes one day during that winter, "but somehow I don't dislike it, and there is something touching about the real world bursting into London with these gales: it makes me feel lazy in the mornings though, and I feel as if I should like to sit in my pretty room at Turnham Green reading some hitherto unprinted Dumas, say about as good as the Three Musketeers." Another letter of a few months later shows very clearly all the strange thoughts that were revolving in his mind. He was now forty: and at this middle point of life the spreading and interlacing ways of the future rolled out before him, dark and entangled indeed, but showing clearer and clearer beyond them some goal to which they all tended.

" 26, Queen Square,
" March 26, 1874.

" My dear Louie,
　　" Many thanks for your kind and friendly letter: it was very nice of you to remember my birthday, which was solemnized by my staying at home all day and looking very hard at illuminations, now my chief joy. Yesterday, however, was May's birthday, mine was on Tuesday, on which sad occasion I was forty. Yet in spite of that round number I don't feel any older than I did in that ancient time of the sunflowers. I very much long to have a spell of the country this spring, but I suppose I hardly shall. I have so many things to do in London. Monday was a day here to set one longing to get away: as warm as June: yet the air heavy as often is in England: though town looks rather shocking on such days, and then instead of the sweet scents one gets an extra smell of dirt. Surely if people lived five hundred years instead of threescore and ten they would find some better way of living than in such a sordid loathsome place, but now it seems to be nobody's business to try to better things— isn't mine, you see, in spite of all my grumbling—but look, suppose people lived in little communities among gardens and green fields, so that you could be in the country in five minutes' walk, and had few wants, almost no furniture for instance, and no servants, and studied the (difficult) arts of enjoying life, and finding out what they really wanted: then I think one might hope civilization had really begun. But as it is, the best thing one can wish for this country at least is, meseems, some great and tragical circumstances, so that if they cannot have

pleasant life, which is what one means by civilization, they may at least have a history and something to think of—all of which won't happen in our time. Sad grumbling —but do you know, I have got to go to a wedding next Tuesday: and it enrages me to think that I lack courage to say, I don't care for either of you, and you neither of you care for me, and I won't waste a day out of my precious life in grinning a company grin at you two.

"And so good-bye again, with many thanks.

"Yours affectionately,

"WILLIAM MORRIS."

Yet his daily work went on with seemingly unabated energy. He kept writing again and again to Fairfax Murray at Rome for supplies of the fine Roman vellum for illumination. The vellum manuscript of the Odes of Horace was begun in March, 1874: about the same time he was planning another, of his own "Cupid and Psyche," with pictures from the designs which Burne-Jones had, five years before, made for the original scheme of the illustrated "Earthly Paradise." The Virgil was begun towards the end of the year, when he had at last obtained a sufficient supply of vellum of the larger size required for a folio.

Meanwhile the dye-house at Queen Square was occupying more and more of his attention. It had long been plain to him that the art of dyeing, fallen into a deplorable condition since the introduction of the anilines, lay at the foundation of the production of all coloured stuffs, whether printed, woven, or embroidered. A profound study which he made this year of all that could be gathered from books on the subject, supplemented by continual experiments in his own vats, left him still unsatisfied; and in the following year he resolved to learn the art practically and thoroughly among the

Staffordshire dye-works.   This was the beginning of a
fresh period in his life of renewed and strenuous activity.
Just at present, however, he allowed himself more holiday-
making than usual, often spending whole days fishing,
and, besides his stays at Kelmscott, going with his family
to Belgium in July, and to Mr. and Mrs. George
Howard's at Naworth in August.   On the 24th of July
he wrote to his mother from Bruges:

"We have had but little railway travelling, only from
Calais to Tournay, and from Tournay to Ghent: we
found it so terribly hot on the railway that we quite
gave up the idea of moving much, and so hired an omnibus at Ghent to take us here last Tuesday by road, and
a very pleasant drive we had on a beautiful day, with a
shower or two to lay the dust, through the ripe wheat
and rye.   I find Bruges scarcely changed at all; it is
really a beautiful place, so clean and quiet too."   A child
of the party remembers that long sunshiny drive, and
the halt for dinner at Eecloo, where, French and English
being alike useless, Morris made a desperate effort at
making himself understood by haranguing the amazed
inn-keeper in Icelandic.

The visit to Naworth, on which he was accompanied
by Burne-Jones, had the additional pleasure of a meeting
with Dixon and a renewal of the affection and enthusiasm
of Oxford days.   "I saw Ted and Morris," Canon
Dixon wrote to Price, "at the abode of splendour last
week—slept there, and we were most jolly.   Ned is in
poor health I grieve to find, and a little quieter in manner,
otherwise unaltered: Topsy genial, gentle, delightful;
both full of affection: it was a most happy meeting."

"I would like you to understand," Morris wrote to
Mrs. Howard after his visit to Naworth, "as well as my
clumsy letter-writing will let you, how very happy I was
these few days in the north.   I hope you will let me

come again some time: and that then you will think me less arrogant on the—what shall I say?—Wesleyan-tradesman-unsympathetic-with-art subjects than you seemed to think me the other day: though indeed I don't accuse myself of it either: but I think to shut one's eyes to ugliness and vulgarity is wrong, even when they show themselves in people not un-human. Do you know, when I see a poor devil drunk and brutal I always feel, quite apart from my æsthetical perceptions, a sort of shame, as if I myself had some hand in it. Neither do I grudge the triumph that the modern mind finds in having made the world (or a small corner of it) quieter and less violent, but I think that this blindness to beauty will draw down a kind of revenge one day: who knows? Years ago men's minds were full of art and the dignified shows of life, and they had but little time for justice and peace; and the vengeance on them was not increase of the violence they did not heed, but destruction of the art they heeded. So perhaps the gods are preparing troubles and terrors for the world (or our small corner of it) again, that it may once again become beautiful and dramatic withal: for I do not believe they will have it dull and ugly for ever. Meantime, what is good enough for them must content us: though sometimes I should like to know why the story of the earth gets so unworthy."

When the autumn holiday ended, worries awaited him which lasted through the winter and were not finally adjusted—so far as any adjustment was possible—till the following spring. The formation of the firm of Morris, Marshall, Faulkner & Co. in 1861 has been already recounted: and it has sufficiently appeared how, as the years went on, the business became one in which capital, invention, and control were supplied practically by Morris alone. The business, in which he had em-

barked all his means, had become not only the daily
work of his life, but the main source of his income; and
it became necessary, now that he was a man in middle
life with a growing family, to put things on a proper
footing, and secure a provision in case of need for his
children. On the other hand, his partners from their
side saw not without uneasiness the extension of a business in whose liabilities—for the firm, formed before the
passing of the Act of 1862, was not a limited company
—they might at any moment find themselves seriously
involved. On both sides, therefore, the dissolution and
reconstitution of the firm was indicated as desirable or
even necessary.

Under the original instrument, each of the seven
partners had not only an equal voice in the management, but an equal interest in the assets of the firm.
The profits had never, after the first year or two, been
divided: partly because for years there were none to
divide, partly because the legal rights of the partners
had since then practically been allowed to lapse. But
these legal claims now represented sums which involved
intricate calculation, and which, in any case, were a formidable drain on the resources of the business, that is to
say, on Morris's own fortune. It was plain that if they
were insisted on, he would be placed in a position of
great financial difficulty, if indeed he could continue to
carry on the business at all. It will be remembered that
the capital contributed by the partners at the inception
of the business, in respect of which these profits were
now claimable, was £20 each, and it seems uncertain
whether even this was in every case actually paid. In
respect of the £120 purporting to have been embarked
in the firm by the whole six, they had claims on the
business for some seven or eight thousand pounds.

The story is not wholly a pleasant one, but it is proper

that the truth should be told.   Three of the partners,
Burne-Jones, Faulkner, and Webb, refused to accept
any consideration in respect of their claims as partners.
The other three stood on the strict letter of their legal
rights.   The position they took up is given in the words
of Madox Brown's solicitor, at a meeting—one of many
during this winter—held on the 4th of November:
"that as in the inception of the firm no member in-
vested money, nor gave any time or labour without
being paid at an agreed rate, the position of the several
members ought to be considered as equal in respect to
their claims on the assets of the firm; and further, that
he, Mr. Brown, considers that the goodwill ought to be
taken at three years' purchase and ought to be included
in the said assets."   In other words, the terms of partnership were such that each of the other partners, who
had confessedly contributed nothing beyond a trifling
sum towards capital, and who had been paid at the time
for any assistance they gave towards the conduct of the
business, was entitled to an equal share of the value of
the business which had been built up by the energy, the
labour, and the money of Morris alone.

Such, however, was their legal claim if they chose to
stand upon it.   The calculations and negotiations were
long and intricate; it was not till March, 1875, that
they were complete, and the dissolution of the firm
finally effected.   On the 31st of March a circular was
issued announcing that the firm had been dissolved and
that the business would thenceforward be caried on
under Morris's sole management and proprietorship.   It
was added that Burne-Jones and Webb, though no longer
partners, would continue to help with designs for stained
glass and furniture as before.   The name of the business
remained Morris & Co., a name which had already for
some years practically superseded the longer title of

Morris, Marshall, Faulkner & Co., under which it had been originally registered.

This transaction finally snapped the chain of attachment between Morris and Rossetti, which had, for other reasons, long been wearing thin. "They never throve together," says an intimate friend who survived them both, "after the first year or two." In the previous summer Rossetti had finally left Kelmscott and given up his share in the tenancy, to Morris's great relief. From the first almost he had been "unromantically discontented" with it : "he has all sorts of ways so unsympathetic with the sweet simple old place that I feel his presence there as a kind of slur on it." The action which, together with Madox Brown and Marshall, he now took over the dissolution of the partnership, caused Morris intense pain and mortification. With Madox Brown the breach did not remain unhealed; in his last years he was again on cordial relations with Morris, and this trouble was forgotten. But from this time forward Morris was no longer to be seen in Rossetti's house at Cheyne Walk, and the estrangement between the two powerful and self-centred personalities was final.

CHAPTER X

PERIOD OF DYEING: THE ÆNEIDS: SIGURD THE VOLSUNG
1875-1876

On the 25th of March, 1875, when the dissolution and reconstitution of the firm was just completed, Morris wrote to Mrs. Baldwin from Queen Square :

" It was very kind of you and I thank you very much for remembering me and my birthday: I have been a happy man with my friends, nor do I think, as far as my constant affection and good wishes are concerned, that I have done otherwise than to deserve the good hap. I am in the second half of my life now; which is like to be a busy time with me, I hope till the very end: a time not lacking content too, I fancy : I must needs call myself a happy man on the whole: and I do verily think I have gone over every possible misfortune that may happen to me in my own mind, and concluded that I can bear it if it should come.

" You would like to see my babies: they are such big girls—and so good; and even so handsome. Me! what a boy I feel still to have that responsibility on me, for in spite of my forty-one years I really don't feel a bit older than when Ned and I were living within sound of those tin-pot bells of St. Pancras: well-remembered days when all adventure was ahead ! Nay, in some things I have run through a time when I was older—

but by no means wiser—than I am now, between those days and these.

"I shall be not very far from you next week: for I am going with Charley Faulkner, my inevitable travelling-fellow, to look at my fatherland. We are going to Shrewsbury, and thence to a college farm of his on the very head waters of Severn and Wye, where we are to have ponies and go over the hills and far away, only for about a week in all though: 'tis a short journey, but I think I shall love it. I think one sign of my increasing years is an increasing desire for travel, that I may see the wonders of the world before it is all gone from me: but I suppose I shall get less and less of that pleasure for some time to come: for I am very busy both with my bread and cheese work, and also with my pleasure work of books. I am publishing a little set of Icelandic stories very soon: also this summer a translation of the Æneids, which has been my great joy for months of late."

With such equanimity, even with such elation, it was that he entered on a fresh and crowded period of his life. Out of years of much restlessness and great emotional tension he had emerged, as a traveller might issue from some mountain gorge to a shining and fertile table-land lying broad under the sun. The brooding over death which had for years filled so much of his imagination seemed to fall quite away from him; and with it, as part of the same process, fell away the striving after things impossible. Before him now lay a life more equable in impulse and more rich in achievement; sweeter tempered, and yet more full than ever of the tears of things, of the desire to do good and to contend against evil, and of unquestioning pursuit of duty not without the courage of hope.

His "pleasure work of books" was still to issue in what

he himself regarded as his highest achievement in literature, the epic of " Sigurd the Volsung." But during the
year or eighteen months in which it was composed, his
principal daily occupation, on what he calls the bread
and cheese side of his activity, was the study and practice
of dyeing and the cognate arts. This was necessary in
order to lay a secure foundation for the production of
textiles of all kinds: and it was not till he had mastered
its processes that he was able to give his invention and
his manual dexterity full scope, and produce what he
wished, instead of being restricted to what he could make
out of the bad or imperfect material supplied to him by
the ordinary channels of commerce. From the very
beginnings, the work of the firm had been hampered
and often crippled by the difficulty of getting material,
either raw or manufactured, which came near Morris's
standard. " I remember," he said at the opening of the
Manchester Art and Industrial Exhibition in 1882,
" when I was first setting up house twenty-three years
ago, and two or three other friends of mine were in the
same plight, what a rummage there used to be for anything tolerable. On the whole I remember that we had to
fall back on turkey-red cotton and dark blue serge."
There was now indeed a noticeable improvement in some
directions. Industrial art was no longer, as it had been
in the fifties, absolutely debased. From centres of education at South Kensington and elsewhere there had been a
slow and partial diffusion of knowledge, and ugliness or
dishonesty, or both, did not now reign uncontrolled over
the whole field of decorative production. Adulteration
had been checked : but the traditions of the great age of
adulteration had become a fixed habit. On every side
Morris was confronted by the double barrier of material
that would not take good colour, and colour which
in its own substance was uniformly bad. The coarse

serges used in the early days of the firm as the ground for embroideries could only be had dyed in one of two ways, in bright anilines, or in colours which were quiet but muddy and without character. When it came to a question of carpets and woven hangings the difficulties were even greater. The dyes in use for carpet-work were both crude and fugitive. Those used in modern French silks he found almost as untrustworthy. "To-day we have bad accounts," is a doleful note of his about this time, "of another set of silk curtains of our selling : green this time, dyed at Lyons: as far as dyers are concerned I wish the days of Colbert back again : it was red last time, and Tours." "I am most deeply impressed," he writes at the end of 1875, "with the importance of our having all our dyes the soundest and best that can be, and am prepared to give up all that part of my business which depends on textiles if I fail in getting them so." All that could be done was to select the best and make the most of such combinations of them as were possible. "Mr. Morris showed his usual sagacity," Mr. George Wardle notes, "in adopting this system of colour so long as the production of the colours themselves was beyond his control. His skill as a colourist was shown in combining colours which, separately, were of but very mediocre character. This system of colour, which may be called provisional, marks very distinctly what may be called the first period of the history of the firm, when Mr. Morris had not yet a dye-house. The peacock-blues, rusty reds, and olive-greens of that period were not by any means his ideals, but the best he could get done. As soon as he was able to set up his own dye-house he turned at once to the frank full hues of the permanent dye-stuffs—indigo blue, madder red, weld yellow, etc.—and with these he produced the beautiful Hammersmith carpets and the Merton tapestries and chintzes."

It may be added that, like most great masters of colour, and following in this matter the best traditions of Oriental art, he used but few colours, and gained his effects by skilfully varied juxtaposition and contrast. In November, 1875, he wrote to Mr. Thomas Wardle, at Leek, giving a complete list of the steam-colours which he required for his own designs. They consist of two blues, one blue-green, two greens, two yellows, and one brown. " To these," he goes on, " one might add a black (if such a thing is to be got fast in steam-colours), and a shade or two of rust-yellows or buffs, which would present no difficulty, as they would be such as are ordinarily used. With the above colours I can carry out any design I should care for that did not need the madder colours, and setting indigo apart. As to the indigo, when we once get it, Prussian blues and greens will be things of the past with us."

Curiously enough, those provisional colours with their dull neutral tints were what clung to the minds of buyers and imitators long after Morris had been able to discard them entirely. The so-called peacock-blue, which he gave up at once when he had revived the use of the indigo vat, and the more appropriately named sage-green, which was one of his particular aversions, became obstinately associated with his name through ignorant imitation as much as by careless or malicious detraction. An incident which occurred in the Oxford Street show-room a few years later gives an instance of what he had perpetually to bear from this invincible ignorance, and of how he sometimes found it past bearing. A person of importance called to discuss the carpeting of his new house. The best specimens of the Hammersmith carpets, then produced in a complete range of pure bright colour, were submitted to his inspection. He gave to them a somewhat impatient and wandering attention. " Are these all?" he asked. He was told yes. "But I thought," he went on, "your colours were subdued?" At this Morris, who had been gradually boiling up during the interview, boiled over. "If you want dirt," he broke out, "you can find that in the street." To the street the offended customer turned, and that was the end of his dealings with Morris & Company.

In the beautiful little essay "Of Dyeing as an Art" which Morris contributed to the catalogue of the second exhibition of the Arts and Crafts Society in 1889, he gives an account, at once lucid and fascinating, of the processes which he himself had to recover from abuse or disuse through laborious researches and experiments. "The art of dyeing," he says there in summing up the matter, "is a difficult one, needing for its practice a good craftsman, with plenty of experience. Matching a colour by means of it is an agreeable, but somewhat anxious game to play." The theory for this practice he sought out of old books, mainly French of the sixteenth and seventeenth centuries, the ancient practice itself being almost extinct. Gerard's "Herbal," the old favourite of his boyhood, supplied useful information about certain disused vegetable dyes. He even went back to Pliny in the search after old methods. "I have sent you a copy of Philemon Holland's Pliny," he writes in August, 1875, to Mr. Thomas Wardle, "a most curious book in itself, and the translation a model of English: altogether one of the most amusing books in the world to my mind." Other old herbals which he acquired, both for their woodcuts and for the information they gave as to dyeing, were those of Matthiolus (Venice, 1590) and Fuchsius (Basle, 1543), the latter of which he notes as the best of all the herbals for refinement of drawing in the illustrations. "I have got a copy of Hellot (Paris, 1750)," he writes in June, 1876, "who is

only about wool-dyeing : he is very minute about the
management of the vats, and I think might be of some
use in that quarter, as he wanted to do with his vats as
we do, viz., make all the shades of blue to be used : he
has an interesting chapter on kermes, which he praises
as the best and fastest of colours.   I can't help thinking
that there might have been some foundation for the old
idea that pastel and woad were faster than indigo :
Hellot says that a vat of pastel only is better for the
light colours, as it is hard to get them evenly dyed in a
healthy indigo vat, and if they are dyed in an old and
weak vat they are apt to be dirty."   "We have been
trying the 'Cuve d'Inde' here after Hellot," he writes a
little later, "but cannot make much of it.   I was at
Kelmscott the other day, and betwixt the fishing, I cut
a handful of poplar twigs and boiled them, and dyed a
lock of wool a very good yellow : this would be useful
if fast, for the wool was unmordanted.   The fishing by
the way was so-so, no perch but one, but the pike rather
good : I got one of 5 lb. on the paternoster."   He
studied these treatises, "Le Teinturier Parfait" and others,
with such ardour and imagination that he felt himself quite
at home among the processes as soon as he got the
necessary vats and becks set up.   His first dyeings were
all done with his own hands, with no help beyond that
of a boy who had till then been employed as errand-boy
to the glass-painters' workshop.   "So well had he
prepared himself," Mr. George Wardle says, "that I do
not think a single dyeing went wrong, nor was any
appreciable quantity of yarn wasted."   But in the little
dye-house at Queen Square nothing could be done
beyond what might be called laboratory experiments :
to dye on the scale required for the firm's wants meant
falling back on regular dye-works.   For these he went to
Mr. Thomas Wardle at Leek.   He was the brother-in-

law of Morris's own manager at Queen Square, and was then already becoming known as one of the first practical authorities on dye-stuffs and the art of dyeing, chiefly as applied to silk and cotton. Morris found him full of interest in the revived methods which had long gone out of use, but which Mr. Wardle remembered as going on in his own boyhood, and which some of his older workmen had themselves practised. For about two years from the summer of 1875 Morris paid numerous and often protracted visits to Leek, where he and Wardle actually restored vegetable dyeing to the position of an important industry.

His first visit to Leek was made in July of this year. "I can't get back till this day week," he writes home when he had been there a few days. "I really can't come away without having come here for nothing; not that I haven't got on fairly well, but that I must see something more of results. The copper pots in the dye-houses, full of bright colours where they are dyeing silks, look rather exciting, but, alas! they are mostly aniline: our own establishment is very small, but I daresay will for some time to come turn out more goods by a great deal than we shall sell."

"The yarns dyed," Mr. George Wardle informs me, "were used for the pile carpets, for he began this business about the same time in Queen Square." The first of his carpet-looms was set up in the top story, and a carpet-knotter was got from Glasgow to teach the girls the method of working; she stayed a few weeks, by the end of which time the girls had learned all that she could teach. The first of his silk-looms, of which there will be more to say hereafter, was set up in Ormond Yard, a year or two later. It was not, however, till he was able to arrange a complete set of dye-shops and bleaching-grounds of his own at Merton Abbey that either carpet or silk weaving could be carried on by him except on a small and experimental scale.

What he worked at most assiduously at Leek was the lost art of indigo-dyeing. In itself this is one of the most delicate and uncertain vats in its due preparation and maturing. The experienced indigo-dyer is said to know when the fermentation has reached its proper point by an acute sense of smell, where no more scientific tests are found to answer. If the proper moment is not seized, the vat becomes useless. Even when the three days' preparation of the vat has been brought to a successful issue, the proper dipping of the yarn, so as to take the dye evenly, and not let any part of it touch the air for a moment, is a matter of the most delicate and accurate handling. " The setting of the blue-vat," Morris says in the essay on Dyeing, " is a ticklish job, and requires, I should say, more experience than any dyeing process." The decay of European indigo-dyeing, itself an art of late importation and not practised in Europe till the end of the sixteenth century, and its replacement by the so-called Prussian blue (ferro-cyanide of potassium, dyed on an iron basis) early in this century, and long before the invention of the anilines, was mainly due to the greater ease and certainty of the latter process. This very uncertainty and delicacy gave it to Morris an additional touch of fascination beyond that of the madder or weld vats. About this time his hands were habitually and unwashably blue, and in no condition to do fine work.

" We have come over here," he writes from Lichfield during one of his fortnights at Leek, " to spend Sunday. Such a dull town is Lichfield, in a dull landscape : the church elaborate and complete, but so small as to be even petty: the old houses here seem to have been pulled down gradually by prosperous dulness, there are scarcely any much older than Johnson's time left; I daresay it was a sweet place enough while ago, when the old wood houses were standing. They have had some history even of late too; there is a stone in a house looking up into the Cathedral-close to mark where Lord Brooke fell, shot through the head from the big tower of the church just as he was beginning the siege of it (he was a Parliamentarian) in 1642—what a little time ago!

"I shall be glad enough to get back to the dye-house at Leek to-morrow. I daresay you will notice how bad my writing is; my hand is so shaky with doing journeyman's work the last few days: delightful work, hard for the body and easy for the mind. For a great heap of skein-wool has come for me and more is coming: and yesterday evening we set our blue-vat the last thing before coming here. I should have liked you to see the charm work on it: we dyed a lock of wool bright blue in it, and left the liquor a clear primrose colour, so all will be ready for dyeing to-morrow in it: though, by the way, if you are a dyer, you must call it *her*.

"Leek, Monday. I was interrupted there, and had no time for more at Lichfield: we drove from there this morning about eighteen miles to a station on the Dove, not a bad drive, through the last remains of Needwood Forest. I have been dyeing in *her* all the afternoon, and my hands are a woeful spectacle in consequence: *she* appears to be all that could be wished, but I must say I should like not to look such a beast, and not to feel as if I wanted pegs to keep my fingers one from the other. I lost my temper in the dye-house for the first time this afternoon: they had been very trying: but I wish I hadn't been such a fool; perhaps they will turn me out to-morrow morning, or put me in the blue-vat."

It was this absorption in dyeing and dye-stuffs which stopped his work as an illuminator. In the earlier

The volume of translations from the Icelandic appeared, under the title of "Three Northern Love Stories," a month or so later. Its contents were those of which he had given the list already quoted when he began to think of preparing them for publication eighteen months before ; and it did not involve any further labour now. But at the beginning of November a new book appeared, which represented long-continued work of a high order, and challenged a wider and more informed criticism, his verse translation of the Æneid.

In departing from the sphere in which he was thoroughly at home and had recognized authority, to undertake a work which would be reckoned as one of scholarship in the narrower sense of that term, Morris took, so to speak, his life in his own hand. "A translator of Virgil into English verse," as Lord Bowen observes in the brilliant little introduction to his own version, " finds the road along which he has undertaken to travel strewn with the bleaching bones of unfortunate pilgrims who have preceded him." And on all the surrounding rocks are perched the severest and most highly educated of critics : men who have learned, if not to do original work of any material human value, at least to take a legitimate pride in their own domain and either to resent or to despise the incursions of amateurs in scholarship. Trained scholars are only too apt, in the words of the same fine and large-minded scholar on another occasion, to be "jealously and suspiciously mounting guard over their own educational blessings, as if they were keeping an eye on their luggage at a crowded railway station." Morris himself was not, in the proper sense of the word, a trained scholar. He had only taken a pass degree at Oxford, and had passed practically on the amount of scholarship with which he went up to Exeter. Since then, while his reading in mediæval Latin had been immense, he had hardly touched the classical authors. Of all the classical authors, Virgil is the one who demands the greatest knowledge from any one who would really understand him ; and it cannot be said that Morris brought to this task any adequate equipment.

Yet for his purposes the attempt was not only legitimate but successful. The earlier romanticists had decried the Æneid as an artificial epic (as though there were such things as natural epics) ; but their attack had recoiled on their own heads. By refusing to acknowledge the supremacy of Virgil in poetry, they had only thrown discredit on the soundness of their own canons and the truth of their own taste. In this translation Morris did not only indicate what Virgil's beauty and value were to a more sane mediævalism. He did more; he vindicated the claim of the romantic school to a joint-ownership with the classicists in the poem which is not only the crowning achievement of classical Latin, but the fountain-head of romanticism in European literature. In the Æneid, as in other works of supreme genius, the reader imputes his own qualities, but this is because Virgil's own genius is compounded of many subtly woven and far-ranging elements. For what in Virgil is most Virgilian we may go in vain to any translation : for some of his qualities, his stateliness, his rolling pomp of language, his intricate modulation, we need not go to this one : yet it sensibly, and often with great felicity, embodies certain other qualities which more fully trained translators have missed : his sweetness, his romantic melancholy, and something at least of his delicate and haunting music.

Morris took all the pains he could, short of writing a preface, which was a thing he scorned to do, to emphasize the fact that he approached Virgil from this romantic or mediæval side. The very title of " The Æneids " which he gave to the volume was a plain notice of the aim and end of his work. Still, it need not cause surprise that this view of the Æneid, though it represents a substantial element, not only of its true original value, but of that which has since accrued to it through the associations of many centuries, was only received with partial approval by an age more familiar, through habit and education, with the other side of Virgil's art.

Mr. Swinburne, writing to Morris on the 9th of November, 1875, a few days after the publication of " The Æneids," begged him to do a Homer, or at least an Odyssey. Just at the moment, however, anything of the kind was far from the poet's mind. On the day that Swinburne's letter was written, he wrote himself to Mrs. Morris from Kelmscott:

" It began to rain again before I got to Lechlade, at first to my infinite disappointment: however, when I got here and had had my lunch, and, as it were, made myself free of the river by an insane attempt to fish, I began to feel very comfortable, and took out my work and looked at it. The floods are already very high, and as it is certainly going to rain for the next 24 hours, I expect to see something curious. I don't think I shall come back before Saturday, as I really hope to do a pile of work here. I am rather short of victuals, as the booby Judd (female) only got me 1 lb. of bacon instead of 3, as I ordered her : however, there will be enough, I daresay, till we can send into Lechlade : there is also one tin of kangaroo meat. My hands are still somewhat stiff with my work on the river—Lord! how cold it was— wind E. or thereabouts. I am obliged to write by candlelight though 'tis only 4 o'clock.

" Best love to my one daughter—wouldn't she have

liked to have been out on the flooded river with me, the wind right in one's teeth and the eddies going like a Japanese tea-tray: I must say it was delightful: almost as good as Iceland on a small scale: please the pigs, I will have a sail on the floods to-morrow."

The birthday letter, which he never omitted to send to his mother, has in it this year a mention of another source of relief to him, the resignation of his Directorship of the Devon Great Consols Company.

"Dearest mother," he writes, "I send you my best love and many happy returns of the day: item I send you a flower-pot and saucer from some samples that they have just sent us from India, and which are still curiosities, as I suppose there are not two more in England at present out of the India House Museum. I have just come from the D. G. C. meeting, and, I suppose, ended my business there, except for receiving my £100 which they were once again kind enough to vote us. Stanley will tell you all about the meeting. I am much better than I have been. I went down (or up) to Oxford for two days at Whitsuntide, and I am going there about the middle of June again to take my M.A. degree; which is perhaps rather a fad of mine; but I thought I might indulge it for once."

The Leek dye-vats were busily at work all that winter and into the following spring. On Sunday, the 26th of March, 1876, he wrote from there to Mrs. Burne-Jones:

"My days are crowded with work; not only telling unmoveable Lancashire what to do, but even working in sabots and blouse in the dye-house myself—you know I like that. Your kind hope for my poem was vain I am sorry to say: T. Wardle rather insisted on my going out with him, so I yielded, not very loth, as I thought a country walk would not be amiss: so we took train to a station and then walked, first by a gim-crack palace of

Pugin's, Alton Towers to wit, then to a village where your friend the novel-writer came from (called Ellaston, I rather think), then to a village church, Norbury, with a strange very rich chancel to it, out of place in that queer way that things are in England, then up the valley of the Dove to Ashbourne, which I think Dr. Johnson had something to do with : a dull walk that last, I scarcely know why, but Ashbourne church very fine and rich ; and so home.

" Some time this week I am going to Nottingham to see the hot vat in operation for flock wool-dyeing : when I was a very youngster, my father's mother, then grown doting, used to promise me a journey to Nottingham, her home, if I were a *very* good boy.

" Meantime I trust I am taking in dyeing at every pore (otherwise than by the skin of my hands, which is certain). I have found out and practised the art of weld-dyeing, the ancientest of yellow dyes, and the fastest. We have set a blue vat for cotton, which I hope will turn out all right to-morrow morning : it is nine feet deep, and holds 1,000 gallons : it would be a week's talk to tell you all the anxieties and possibilities connected with this indigo subject, but you must at least imagine that all this is going on on very nearly the same conditions as those of the shepherd boy that made a watch all by himself."

The fortunes of the indigo vat are continued in a letter written two days later to Mrs. Coronio.

" Leek,
" March 28th.

" My dear Aglaia,
" I am at last able to write to you, and thank you for your letter : I have a huge deal to do in a very limited time, for I am trying to learn all I can about dyeing, even the handiwork of it, which is simple enough,

but, like many other simple things, contains matters in it that one would not think of unless one were told. Besides my business of seeing to the cotton-printing, I am working in Mr. Wardle's dye-house in sabots and blouse pretty much all day long: I am dyeing yellows and reds: the yellows are very easy to get, and so are a lot of shades of salmon and flesh-colour and buff and orange; my chief difficulty is in getting a deep blood red, but I hope to succeed before I come away: I have not got the proper indigo vat for wool, but I can dye blues in the cotton vat and get lovely greens with that and the bright yellow that weld gives.

" This morning I assisted at the dyeing of 20 lbs. of silk (for our damask) in the blue vat; it was very exciting, as the thing is quite unused now, and we ran a good chance of spoiling the silk. There were four dyers and Mr. Wardle at work, and myself as dyers' mate: the men were encouraged with beer and to it they went, and pretty it was to see the silk coming green out of the vat and gradually turning blue: we succeeded very well as far as we can tell at present; the oldest of the workmen, an old fellow of seventy, remembers silk being dyed so, long ago. The vat, you must know, is a formidable-looking thing, 9 ft. deep and about 6 ft. square: and is sunk into the earth right up to the top. To-morrow I am going to Nottingham to see wool dyed blue in the woad vat, as it is called; on Friday Mr. Wardle is going to dye 80 lbs. more silk for us, and I am going to dye about 20 lbs. of wool in madder for my deep red. With all this I shall be very glad indeed to be home again, as you may well imagine.

" I am glad you liked my work at the show, though I don't think it was much to make a row about; the silk piece I thought was the best. Mrs. Lewes came from this country-side, by the way: I went through the village where she lived, on Sunday : Ellaston, I think, it was called ; a dull village ; I seem to see a good few people about like the ' Aunts ' in the ' Mill on the Floss.'

"I hope you are well.

"I am your affectionate

"WILLIAM MORRIS."

The following words were written also from Leek, during this visit, to a friend who was passing through one of those darknesses in which the whole substance of life seems now and then to crumble away under our hands. They contain, in brief words that are free from either doubt or arrogance, the confession of his own faith : a matter as to which he was reserved of speech, and only revealed himself under the stress of some unusual emotion.

"Wherein you are spiritless, I wish with all my heart that I could help you or amend it, for it is most true that it grieves me ; but also, I must confess it, most true that I am living my own life in spite of it, or in spite of anything grievous that may happen in the world. Sometimes I wonder so much at all this, that I wish even that I were once more in some trouble of my own, and think of myself that I am really grown callous : but I am sure that though I have many hopes and pleasures, or at least strong ones, and that though my life is dear to me, so much as I seem to have to do, I would give them away, hopes and pleasures, one by one or all together, and my life at last, for you, for my friendship, for my honour, for the world. If it seems boasting I do not mean it : but rather that I claim, so to say it, not to be separated from those that are heavy-hearted only because I am well in health and full of pleasant work and eager about it, and not oppressed by desires so as not to be able to take interest in it all. I wish I could say something that would serve you, beyond what you know very well, that I love you and long to help you: and indeed I entreat you (however trite the words may be) to think that life is not empty nor made for nothing, and that the parts of it fit one into another in some way; and that the world goes on, beautiful and strange and dreadful and worshipful."

So much as I seem to have to do!—the words were in one form or another habitually on his lips all through his life: yet he never used them complainingly or grudgingly, but rather as one who felt the world perpetual in its interest and variety, and to whom no length of days could be long enough to exhaust either the work that there was for him to do or his own active pleasure in doing it. But to one of his own heroes, whether Greek or Northern, the wish to be once more in some trouble of his own, however lightly uttered, might have seemed a wilful provocation of fate, and only too certain to draw down its own fulfilment. Within the next few months trouble of his own came to him against which he could have made no provision. The form that trouble took was one which can only be briefly touched upon, but which had too profound an effect upon his whole life to be entirely passed over. His elder daughter, now a girl of fifteen, exceptionally bright, clever, and diligent, was already her father's chosen companion, and gave promise of a brilliant future. In the summer of 1876 her health broke completely down. From this distress his mind was never henceforth free. To all who had the privilege of a close knowledge, his tenderness and unceasing thought and care for her were the most touchingly beautiful element in his nature; but his anxiety over her was literally continuous for the remainder of his life.

On the 18th of July he wrote to Mrs. Morris, who was at Deal with the two children:

"I am so glad to hear that things go well so far: though of course I cannot help being anxious. Yes, I got the dear thing's letters, and answered them on Sunday (else I should have written to you), and very pretty letters they were. The news from here is little or none; *e.g.*, that I broke the strings of the Venetian blind in my room last night; that no water came into the cistern on Sunday, and very little yesterday, and so on. Item, I was *not* the man that threw the medicine bottles at the dog last Saturday, and was fined a shilling for that righteous indignation.

"I can't help thinking that you have not been so hot as we have been these last days; though last night and to-day it has been cooler: so much so, that, calling on Kate yesterday evening, I found her refusing to go out with her mother because the wind was so cold: nay, she durst not go near the window, for she said that the bitter north wind cut her in half. As for me, that the grumbling circle may be complete, I am longing for that tail of the glacier in Thorsmark, or our camp in the wilderness at Eyvindarkofarver under the snow mountains: in fact, though I don't feel unwell (and therefore ought to hold my noise, as you very truly say), I am depressed and languid (say lazy) and don't care for my work, at any rate not the bread and cheese part of it: though for want of finding any amusement in books on Saturday and Sunday I did manage to screw out my tale of verses, to the tune of some 250 I think. By the way the Athenæum has been very civil to me about that scrap of poem I published in it the other day, though it was not worth publishing either, and sent me £20: it seems, such is the world's injustice and stupidity, that it was a success—never mind; I shall pay for it when my new poem comes out. I cannot tell you how pleased I am to hear that you think so well of Jenny: you don't say

much about May : I suppose it can't fail to do her good :
I think it would be a great pity to hurry them away if
the place really seems to suit them, and if you can hold
out there : I will give you as much of my company as
work will let me : to-day week or to-morrow week I
hope to come down, and shall stay three days or so at
any rate : I am looking forward to it very much. Take
care of yourself, my dear, and tell me of anything you
want : I think we had better spend that £20 in carriages
at Deal ? "

In spite of the engrossing occupation of the dyeing
work and the unsettlement caused by his daughter's
illness, the composition of " Sigurd the Volsung " had
been advancing swiftly throughout the year. It was
published at the end of November. What reception he
anticipated for it may be gathered from the letter just
quoted : and, in fact, for one reason or another, it was
but languidly received. In his own judgment, it stood
apart from the rest of his poetry, less because it showed
any higher perfection in craftsmanship than because the
subject was the story which he counted the first in the
world, and because he was convinced that he had treated
this story with a fidelity and a largeness of manner for
which he could answer to his own conscience. The
Volsunga Saga had for long seemed to him almost
too great a story to be re-told, and too perfectly set
forth in the noble Icelandic prose of the twelfth century
to gain, or not to lose, from fresh handling. " This is
the Great Story of the North," he had written six years
before, " which should be to all our race what the Tale
of Troy was to the Greeks : to all our race first, and
afterwards, when the change of the world has made our
race nothing more than a name of what has been, a
story too, then should it be to those that come after us
no less than the Tale of Troy has been to us." When

at last he resolved to attempt the re-telling, he was
bound by an almost impossible loyalty to his original.
For the purposes of an epic it is almost obvious that the
story begins far too early, and has epic unity only from
the point at which Sigurd's own conscious life begins.
The Icelandic Saga is a chronicle which the genius of its
tellers has almost against their will converted into an
epic, but which retains much history that the limits of
an epic reject.   The whole of the life of Sigmund, which
fills the first of the four books of the poem, is a separate
story, containing a strange and savagely magnificent
epic of its own, centring round the three colossal figures
of Sigmund and Signy and their son Sinfiotli.   No art
or skill can make this earlier epic either subordinate to,
or coherent with, the epic of the After-born; of Sigurd,
only born after Sigmund's death, and of those with whose
lives an inextricable fate enwound his.   It is as though the
epic of Troy opened with a recital of the epic of Thebes.
Both in the Greek and in the Scandinavian cycle the
story that comes earlier in the history is also earlier in
its structure; more primitive, more colossal, less fully
human.   The cannibal savagery of Tydeus, the incest
of Œdipus and Jocasta, the living burial of Antigone,
rouse a greater horror than anything in the Trojan
story, but it is not one based on the same universal
human sympathy.   And so it is with the story of
Sigmund: the wolf-change of the Volsung, the cruel
purposeless slaughter of Signy's children, the strangely
inhuman life and death of the son of that awful brother
and sister, are tragic indeed, but with such tragedy as
belongs to the dim and monstrous reign of the older
gods.   With what skill Morris effects the transition,
with what genius he drives the story through into its
destined channel, is hardly to the purpose: the fact
remains that what he tried to do was wrong, and that

no skill can set it wholly right.   Indeed when he came
to the end of the story he was obliged to confess as
much.   The Volsunga Saga does not end with the epi-
sode of Gudrun casting herself into the sea while the
palace of Atli roared up in flame.   Here Morris stops.
But the Saga-writer goes pitilessly on : and after it has
lost Gudrun as well as Brynhild the story relapses into
something of its earlier horror and savagery.   The death
of Swanhild, her head tied in a bag because " when she
opened her eyes wide, then the horses durst not trample
her," is followed by the dismal ending of Gudrun's
sons : nor will the Saga-writer stay his hand till he can
set down the destruction of that whole kin, root and
stem.   To pursue the Saga to its end, in a fifth book,
Morris no doubt felt to be impossible.   To continue
after the main interest is gone would be a grave fault
of art.   But it is a fault of art scarcely less grave to an-
ticipate that interest, and excite it at the opening of the
tale in disparate matter, and, as it were, on a false issue.

Yet the main story, as it is told in the other three
books of the poem, is undoubtedly unsurpassed in the
world for epic grandeur and tragic tension ; and in his
version, the most Homeric poem which has been written
since Homer, Morris felt that he had given it no inadequate treatment.   It is a story at once deeper-search-
ing into human nature and more universal in its view
of human life than that of either the Iliad or the
Odyssey.   To cool reflection it must be plain that
the story of the Iliad is in itself one of the second
order : one that had to be filled up with episodes of
extraneous interest, and is raised to its rank, as, on the
whole, the greatest poetical achievement of mankind,
only by the prodigious genius of its final author.   The
story of the Odyssey, as it is summed up in the well-
known words of Aristotle—" a certain man being in

foreign lands for many years, and watched jealously by
Poseidon, and alone, and things at home being likewise
in such case that his substance was spent by suitors and
plots laid against his son, arrives after a tempestuous
voyage, and discovering himself to certain persons, attacks
his enemies and destroys them, but is saved himself"—
is a Saga of the simplest order without any dramatic
motive of great depth or complexity, but told with in-
comparable skill, and brought into a wider atmosphere
by the Phæacian romance and the Arabian tales of
miraculous adventure incorporated with the original
story.   Had the luminous intelligence to which we owe
the Iliad and Odyssey been applied to a story in
itself so tremendous as that of Sigurd, Brynhild, and
Gudrun, it is difficult to imagine to what unscaled
heights the epic might have risen.   As it is, for want of
that Greek intelligence, the story is not fully humanized.
Grimhild's witch-drink, for instance, is not, like the cup
of Circe, the mere embroidery of a fairy-tale: it is
essential to the tragedy, and is a type of that savage or
inhuman element which lingered through the literature
as well as the life of the North.

To Morris's mind, at any rate, the philosophy or
religion that lived under these half-humanized legends
was something quite real and vital: and it substantially
represented his own guiding belief.   In a summarized
statement of the northern mythology which he wrote
out about this time, he concludes with the following
striking sentences :

"It may be that the world shall worsen, that men
shall grow afraid to 'change their life,' that the world
shall be weary itself, and sicken, and none but faint-hearts
be left—who knows? So at any rate comes the end at
last, and the Evil, bound for a while, is loose, and all
nameless merciless horrors that on earth we figure by fire

and earthquake and venom and ravin. So comes the great strife; and like the kings and heroes that they have loved, here also must the Gods die, the Gods who made that strifeful imperfect earth, not blindly indeed, yet foredoomed. One by one they extinguish for ever some dread and misery that all this time has brooded over life, and one by one, their work accomplished, they die: till at last the great destruction breaks out over all things, and the old earth and heavens are gone, and then a new heavens and earth. What goes on there? Who shall say, of us who know only of rest and peace by toil and strife? And what shall be our share in it? Well, sometimes we must needs think that we shall live again: yet if that were not, would it not be enough that we helped to make this unnameable glory, and lived not altogether deedless? Think of the joy we have in praising great men, and how we turn their stories over and over, and fashion their lives for our joy: and this also we ourselves may give to the world.

" This seems to me pretty much the religion of the Northmen. I think one would be a happy man if one could hold it, in spite of the wild dreams and dreadful imaginings that hung about it here and there."

In this spirit it was that Morris approached the story of Sigurd. Nor need it be matter of surprise that the strength of the poem no less than its weaknesses, its unity of spirit and motive no less than the complexity of its scheme, made it pass over the heads of a public little accustomed to the strenuous task of embracing and taking in any work of great scope and organic structure. Whether or not it be true, as is often lightly said, that the age for epics is over, the time when " Sigurd " appeared was emphatically an age of the idyl, and unresponsive to the appeal of the larger poetic architecture. Morris himself never concealed his own opinion of the merits of the poem. To a petulant, but not wholly unjustified, criticism which Rossetti made on the dragon-transformation of Fafnir, as an element in the story which was not merely barbarous, but silly, he made a reply which can scarcely be quoted here, but which no one who has heard it is ever likely to forget. But he did not let the tepid welcome which "Sigurd" met with weigh on his spirits. Two months after its publication he writes from Leek, where he was again busy among his dye-vats and ordering three hundredweight of poplar-twigs for experiments in yellow dyeing (the colour they gave did not turn out sufficiently fast to satisfy him):

" My ill temper about the public was only a London mood and is quite passed now: and I think I have even forgotten what I myself have written about that most glorious of stories, and think about it all (and very often) as I did before I began my poem."

" I had been reading the Njala," this letter goes on, "in the original before I came here: it is better even than I remembered; the style most solemn (Dasent now and then uses a word too homely I think, which brings it down a little): all men's children in it, as always in the best of the northern stories, so venerable to each other, and so venerated: and the exceeding good temper of Gunnar amidst his heroism, and the calm of Njal: and I don't know anything more consoling or grander in all literature (to use a beastly French word) than Gunnar's singing in his house under the moon and the drifting clouds: or do you remember the portents at Bergthorsknoll before the burning, and how Skarphedinn takes them? or Skarphedinn's death; or how Flosi pays the penalty for the Burning, never appealing against the due and equal justice, but defending himself and his folk stoutly against it at every step. What a glorious outcome of the worship of Courage these stories are."

His position as a poet was in any case secure among those best qualified to judge; and popularity with any large mass of thoughtless opinion was not a thing he very much cared for. The element of aristocratic fastidiousness in his nature rather shrank from it, and it was not till later, when he became the exponent of an active creed, that he felt any of the discouragement that comes of appealing to averted ears. Sir Francis Doyle was now vacating the Oxford Professorship of Poetry, in which he had succeeded Matthew Arnold. Morris was at once thought of by his friends as (at all events if Mr. Swinburne were excepted) the most eminent of other living Oxford poets; and though his want of orthodoxy alike in politics and in religious belief made it certain that he could not be an unopposed candidate, inquiry seemed to justify them in thinking that he might be asked to stand with fair prospects of success. The offer was one which tempted him greatly. His love for Oxford, in spite of his hatred of the typical Oxonian, was very deep-seated, and the position was one which, without involving any serious labour, was both influential and distinguished. But finally he made up his mind against it.

"I am afraid," he wrote on the 16th of February, 1877, to Mr. Thursfield, who had approached him on the subject on behalf of the members of Convocation who were anxious that he should consent to stand, "you must think I have been a long while answering your letter; I beg you to excuse my apparent neglect on the grounds that I found it hard to make up my mind what was right to do. In the first place I thank you personally very much for moving in the matter, and I must say that nothing hardly would please me so much as such a recognition from my University, apart from considerations of fitness on my side : nor would laziness or the various heavy business on my hands prevent me from coming forward if I thought I could be of any real use: neither would a contested election frighten me, though I don't like such things. It is therefore with the greatest regret that I find I must needs say ' no '; and this simply because I feel that I am not the man to fill the post: I suppose the lectures a Poetry Professor should give ought to be either the result of deep and wide scholarship in the matter, or else pieces of beautiful and ingenious rhetoric, such, for example, as our Slade Professor could give; and in both these things I should fail and do no credit either to the University or myself. It seems to me that the *practice* of any art rather narrows the artist in regard to the *theory* of it; and I think I come more than most men under this condemnation, so that though I have read a good deal and have a good memory, my knowledge is so limited and so ill-arranged that I can scarce call myself a man of letters: and moreover I have a peculiar inaptitude for expressing myself except in the one way that my gift lies. Also may I say without offence that I have a lurking doubt as to whether the Chair of Poetry is more than an ornamental one, and whether the Professor of a wholly incommunicable art is not rather in a false position: nevertheless I would like to see a good man filling it, and, if the critics will forgive me, somebody who is not only a critic. I ask your pardon for writing so much about myself, but your kindness has brought it on your head."

Shairp was elected without a contest to the professorship: and the chair was dignified by an occupant of unimpeachable orthodoxy, of a most kindly and courteous nature, and of some merit both as a critic and as a poet.

CHAPTER XI

ALMOST without knowing it, Morris was now beginning to take a part in public action and political life. From both he had hitherto, in common with the circle of artists to which he belonged, kept apart as from matters that did not concern him. As regards the arts of life, he had been content to labour in his own field, and trust to good work producing its influence, without any active attempt to inculcate first principles or to stem the tide of competition and industrialism by organized teaching. In politics, he was a passive, rather than an active Liberal; voting with his party, and even occasionally attending public meetings, but not a name known in the press or on the platform. In active civic duties, any more than in active political work, he had probably taken no share since his illness in 1864 had made him retire from his Volunteer corps. But this abstention was not natural to him, as it often is to artists and men of letters. His innate Socialism—if the word may for once be used in its natural sense and not as expressing any doctrine—was, and had been from his earliest beginnings, the quality which, more than any other, penetrated and dominated all he did. In this year it forced itself out in two different channels, which would by ordinary people be distinguished from one another as belonging to the fields of art and politics, but which to Morris himself, to whom both art and politics, except in so far as they bore directly on life, were alike meaningless, only represented two distinct points at which the defence of life against barbarism could be carried on. One of these movements he originated, or at least put into active existence, by the formation of the Society for the Protection of Ancient Buildings. The other he aided with all his power by work and money spent in the service of the Eastern Question Association. The Society for the Protection of Ancient Buildings has had a long, a quiet, and not a useless life: and has, directly or indirectly, saved many remnants of the native art of England from destruction. The Eastern Question Association was formed to meet a passing political crisis and broke up when its object had ceased. But from Morris's work on the former grew the whole of his later activity as a lecturer and instructor in the principles of art, and as founder and leader of a guild of craftsmen who exist now as the permanent result of his influence. From his work on the latter was developed, by a process of which every step can be clearly traced, his conversion to a definite and dogmatic Socialism.

The destruction of ancient buildings which, throughout the whole of Morris's life, he had seen going on almost unchecked, whether from mere careless barbarism or under the more specious and ruinous pretext of restoration, had been a thing against which it seemed hopeless for any one to fight. It had hitherto been attacked only in isolated instances, by individuals, without any clear statement of principle or any certainty of continuous action. It could only be combated with any hope of success through some permanent and organized body, to whose representations some attention would have to be paid, and who would have time and money to spend on their work. The formation of a society wholly devoted to this purpose seems first to have occurred to Morris's mind in the autumn of 1876, and in connexion with two definite instances of restoration which then came under his own eyes. One was that of Lichfield Cathedral, which he and Wardle had been visiting from Leek. The other was near Kelmscott. On the 4th of September, 1876, a party drove from Kelmscott to pay a visit of a few days to Cormell Price at Broadway. On the way, as usual, they stopped to bait in the pretty little town of Burford on the Windrush. The alterations going on in the beautiful parish church there roused his horror; and at Broadway Tower he drafted a letter urging the formation of a Society which might deal with such cases, and, if the destruction done by the restorers could not be stopped, might at all events make it clear that it was destruction and not preservation. But for some reason or other no immediate action was taken for several months after. At the beginning of March, 1877, an account of the proposed restoration of the splendid Abbey church at Tewkesbury roused him to take practical steps. Mr. F. G. Stephens had for some years been upholding the cause of ancient buildings in the Athenæum newspaper with much courage and persistency, singling out for special attack the wholesale operations carried out in so many cathedral and parochial churches by Sir Gilbert Scott. To the Athenæum Morris now turned for aid in realizing his project. On the 5th of March he wrote to it as follows:

"My eye just now caught the word 'restoration' in the morning paper, and, on looking closer, I saw that this time it is nothing less than the Minster of Tewkesbury that is to be destroyed by Sir Gilbert Scott. Is it altogether too late to do something to save it,—it and whatever else of beautiful and historical is still left us on the sites of the ancient buildings we were once so famous for ?   Would it not be of some use once for all, and with the least delay possible, to set on foot an association for the purpose of watching over and protecting these relics, which, scanty as they are now become, are still wonderful treasures, all the more priceless in this age of the world, when the newly-invented study of living history is the chief joy of so many of our lives ?

" Your paper has so steadily and courageously opposed itself to these acts of barbarism which the modern architect, parson, and squire call ' restoration,' that it would be waste of words to enlarge here on the ruin that has been wrought by their hands ; but, for the saving of what is left, I think I may write a word of encouragement, and say that you by no means stand alone in the matter, and that there are many thoughtful people who would be glad to sacrifice time, money, and comfort in defence of those ancient monuments : besides, though I admit that the architects are, with very few exceptions, hopeless, because interest, habit, and ignorance bind them, and that the clergy are hopeless, because their order, habit, and an ignorance yet grosser, bind them ; still there must be many people whose ignorance is accidental rather than inveterate, whose good sense could surely be touched if it were clearly put to them that they were destroying what they, or, more surely still, their sons and sons' sons, would one day fervently long for, and which no wealth or energy could ever buy again for them.

" What I wish for, therefore, is that an association should be set on foot to keep a watch on old monuments, to protest against all ' restoration ' that means more than keeping out wind and weather, and, by all means, literary and other, to awaken a feeling that our ancient buildings are not mere ecclesiastical toys, but sacred monuments of the nation's growth and hope."

The train caught fire. A fortnight after this letter appeared, the Athenæum announced that his proposal was likely to take effect, and within another fortnight the Society for Protection of Ancient Buildings had been constituted and had held its first meeting, Morris acting as secretary. The eminent men in many walks of life who at once joined it were sufficient to protect it from either contempt or ridicule; and if it has not stayed destruction, it has at all events saved much that would otherwise have been lost, and has had an immense though quiet influence in raising the standard of morality on the subject of ancient buildings throughout England. Architects and owners alike now take a wholly new and wholly beneficial sense of their responsibility. The principles of the Society are given by Morris with unsurpassed lucidity and force in the statement issued by it on its foundation.

"Within the last fifty years a new interest, almost like another sense, has arisen in these ancient monuments of art; and they have become the subject of one of the most interesting of studies, and of an enthusiasm, religious, historical, artistic, which is one of the undoubted gains of our time; yet we think that if the present treatment of them be continued, our descendants will find them useless for study and chilling to enthusiasm. We think that those last fifty years of knowledge and attention have done more for their destruction than all the foregoing centuries of revolution, violence, and contempt.

"For architecture, long decaying, died out, as a popular art at least, just as the knowledge of mediæval art was born. So that the civilized world of the nine-

teenth century has no style of its own amidst its wide
knowledge of the styles of other centuries.   From this
lack and this gain arose in men's minds the strange idea
of the Restoration of ancient buildings; and a strange
and most fatal idea, which by its very name implies that
it is possible to strip from a building this, that, and the
other part of its history—of its life, that is—and then to
stay the hand at some arbitrary point, and leave it still
historical, living, and even as it once was.

"In early times this kind of forgery was impossible,
because knowledge failed the builders, or perhaps because instinct held them back.   If repairs were needed,
if ambition or piety pricked on to change, that change was
of necessity wrought in the unmistakable fashion of the
time; a church of the eleventh century might be added to
or altered in the twelfth, thirteenth, fourteenth, fifteenth,
sixteenth, or even the seventeenth and eighteenth centuries; but every change, whatever history it destroyed,
left history in the gap, and was alive with the spirit of
the deeds done amidst its fashioning.   The result of all
this was often a building in which the many changes,
though harsh and visible enough, were by their very
contrast interesting and instructive, and could by no
possibility mislead.   But those who make the changes
wrought in our day under the name of Restoration,
while professing to bring back a building to the best
time of its history, have no guide but each his own individual whim to point out to them what is admirable
and what contemptible: while the very nature of their
task compels them to destroy something, and to supply
the gap by imagining what the earlier builders should
or might have done.   Moreover, in the course of this
double process of destruction and addition, the whole
surface of the building is necessarily tampered with; so
that the appearance of antiquity is taken away from

such old parts of the fabric as are left, and there is no laying to rest in the spectator the suspicion of what may have been lost; and in short, a feeble and lifeless forgery is the final result of all the wasted labour.

"Of all the Restorations yet undertaken the worst have meant the reckless stripping a building of some of its most interesting material features; while the best have their exact analogy in the Restoration of an old picture, where the partly perished work of the ancient craftsmaster has been made neat and smooth by the tricky hand of some unoriginal and thoughtless hack of to-day. If, for the rest, it be asked us to specify what kind or amount of art, style, or other interest in a building, makes it worth protecting, we answer, Anything which can be looked on as artistic, picturesque, historical, antique, or substantial : any work, in short, over which educated artistic people would think it worth while to argue at all.

"It is for all these buildings, therefore, of all times and styles, that we plead, and call upon those who have to deal with them, to put Protection in the place of Restoration, to stave off decay by daily care, to prop a perilous wall or mend a leaky roof by such means as are obviously meant for support or covering, and show no pretence of other art, and otherwise to resist all tampering with either the fabric or ornament of the building as it stands; if it has become inconvenient for its present use, to raise another building rather than alter or enlarge the old one; in fine, to treat our ancient buildings as monuments of a bygone art, created by bygone manners, that modern art cannot meddle with without destroying."

Among the celebrated names whom the newly-founded Society was able to announce as members was that of Carlyle. The story of how he was induced to join it is highly characteristic: I owe it to Mr. William De Morgan, through whom, as a neighbour and friend, living in Cheyne Row a few doors off, Carlyle was approached.

"I sent the prospectus to Carlyle," Mr. De Morgan tells me, "through his niece Miss Aitken, and afterwards called by appointment to elucidate further. The philosopher didn't seem in the mood to join anything—in fact it seemed to me that the application was going to be fruitless. But fortunately Sir James Stephen was there when I called, and Carlyle passed me on to him with the suggestion that I had better make him a convert first. However, Sir James declined to be converted, on the ground that the owners or guardians of ancient buildings had more interest than any one else in preserving them, and would do it, and so forth. I replied with a case to the contrary, that of Wren's churches and the Ecclesiastical Commissioners. This brought Carlyle out with a panegyric of Wren, who was, he said, a really great man, 'of extraordinary patience with fools,' and he glared round at the company reproachfully. However, he promised to think it over, chiefly, I think, because Sir James Stephen had rather implied that the Society's object was not worth thinking over. He added one or two severe comments on the contents of space.

" I heard from his niece next day that he was wavering, and that a letter from Morris might have a good effect. I asked for one, and received the following:

'Horrington House,
'April 3.

'My dear De Morgan,
'I should be sorry indeed to force Mr. Carlyle's inclinations on the matter in question, but if you are seeing him I think you might point out to him that it is not only artists or students of art that we are appealing to, but thoughtful people in general. For the rest

it seems to me not so much a question whether we are
to have old buildings or not, as whether they are to be
old or sham old: at the lowest I want to make people
see that it would surely be better to wait while architecture and the arts in general are in their present experimental condition before doing what can never be
undone, and *may* at least be ruinous to what it intends
to preserve.

' Yours very truly,
' WILLIAM MORRIS.'

"Next day," Mr. De Morgan goes on, " I received
from Miss Aitken a letter from Carlyle to the Society,
accepting membership. It made special allusion to Wren,
and spoke of his City churches as ' marvellous works,
the like of which we shall never see again,' or nearly
that. Morris had to read this at the first public meeting
—you may imagine that he didn't relish it, and one heard
it in the way he read it—I fancy he added mentally,
' And a good job too !' "

Morris's prejudice against the seventeenth and eighteenth centuries was indeed carried to a pitch that amounted
to pure unreasonableness: and in the work of Wren and
his successors he steadily declined to acknowledge either
fitness, or dignity, or elegance.

The rather lumbering title of the Society was at an
early date replaced for familiar usage by the more terse
and expressive name of the Anti-Scrape, a word of
Morris's own invention. Two months after its formation
he writes to a friend : " By the way you have not yet
joined our Anti-Scrape Society: I will send you the
papers of it: the subscription is only 10/6, and may save
you something if people ask for subscriptions to restorations by enabling you to say, 'I am sorry, but be damned
—look here.' "

Meanwhile Morris had been swept into politics by an impulse no less powerful and sincere against barbarism. If ancient buildings were all but alive to him, and he felt their ruin and defacement as a kind of physical torture, his sympathy with oppressed fellow-creatures rather gained than lost in force from this feeling.   The collapse of the Turkish Government in its European provinces during the year 1876 had been accompanied by massacres and torture on a prodigious scale in Bulgaria, the news of which in England, at first received with incredulous apathy, gradually roused an overpowering horror and indignation.   The armed intervention of Russia, though it did not take place till the following April, had been long foreseen ; and feeling in England was torn violently asunder between traditional jealousy of Russia and sympathy with the oppressed Christian populations.   For long the former feeling was predominant both in the Government and in the nation ; and the group of persons who towards the end of 1876 founded the Eastern Question Association were at first a minority, trifling in number, however powerful in the justice of their cause and the strength of their convictions.   Into this work Morris flung himself heart and soul : he was treasurer of the Association, and through the Russo-Turkish War, and the confused and hostile negotiations which followed, worked hard for it with tongue and pen.

On the 15th of November, when the first steps were being taken towards organizing the movement, he wrote to Faulkner at Oxford :

"I am very willing to receive you as a convert if you must needs ticket yourself so, though I don't see the need, as both your views and mine being interpreted meant declaring ourselves enemies of that den of thieves the Turkish Government.   As to the Russians, all I say is this : we *might* have acted so that they could have had no pretext for interfering with Turkey except in accordance with the unanimous wish of Europe: we *have* so acted as to drive them into separate interference whatever may come: and to go to war with them for this would be a piece of outrageous injustice. Furthermore if we came victorious out of such a war, what should we do with Turkey, if we didn't wish to be damned? 'Take it ourselves,' says the bold man, 'and rule it as we rule India.' But the bold man don't live in England at present I think; and I know what the Tory trading stock-jobbing scoundrel that one calls an Englishman to-day would do with it: he would shut his eyes hard over it, get his widows and orphans to lend it money, and sell it vast quantities of bad cotton. For the rest, I know that the Russians have committed many crimes, but I cannot accuse them of behaving ill in this Turkish business at present, and I must say I think it very unfair of us, who freed our black men, to give them no credit for freeing their serfs: both deeds seem to me to be great landmarks in history. However, I repeat, to finish, that my cry and that of all that I consider *really* on our side is 'The Turkish Government to the Devil, and something rational and progressive in its place.' If people say that latter part is difficult, I can only say that it is difficult to make a pair of shoes, or even a poem; and yet both deeds are sometimes done;—more or less ill 'tis true."

"I do not feel very sanguine about it all," he adds, after giving details as to the action which it was proposed to take: "but since it is started and is the only thing that offers at present, and I do not wish to be anarchical, I must do the best I can with it."

Into the details of the historic controversy this is no place to enter: it is one long ago judged by time. But the manifesto which Morris issued in May, 1877, when

the recent declaration of war by Russia had brought the
Eastern Question into a very acute and dangerous stage,
is remarkable, less for any unusual insight into what is
called the political situation, than for the body to whom
he addressed it, and the tone it took on political action
in the largest sense.   It contains his later socialist teaching as yet folded in the germ.

" To the working men of England " this manifesto is
headed : and it contains this remarkable passage :

" Who are they that are leading us into war ? Greedy
gamblers on the Stock Exchange, idle officers of the
army and navy (poor fellows !), worn-out mockers of
the clubs, desperate purveyors of exciting war-news for
the comfortable breakfast-tables of those who have
nothing to lose by war ; and lastly, in the place of
honour, the Tory Rump, that we fools, weary of peace,
reason, and justice, chose at the last election to represent
us.   Shame and double shame, if we march under such
leadership as this in an unjust war against a people who
are not our enemies, against Europe, against freedom,
against nature, against the hope of the world.

" Working men of England, one word of warning
yet : I doubt if you know the bitterness of hatred
against freedom and progress that lies at the hearts of a
certain part of the richer classes in this country : their
newspapers veil it in a kind of decent language ; but do
but hear them talking among themselves, as I have often,
and I know not whether scorn or anger would prevail
in you at their folly and insolence.   These men cannot
speak of your order, of its aims, of its leaders, without a
sneer or an insult : these men, if they had the power
(may England perish rather !), would thwart your just
aspirations, would silence you, would deliver you bound
hand and foot for ever to irresponsible capital.   Fellow-
citizens, look to it, and if you have any wrongs to be

redressed, if you cherish your most worthy hope of raising your whole order peacefully and solidly, if you thirst for leisure and knowledge, if you long to lessen these inequalities which have been our stumbling-block since the beginning of the world, then cast aside sloth and cry out against an Unjust War, and urge us of the middle classes to do no less."

Throughout this period his letters are full of the same excitement, and of the same feeling that it was to the working classes that the only useful appeal could be made. " I was at the working-men's meeting at the Cannon Street Hotel on Wednesday," he writes on the 4th of May; " it was quite a success; they seem to have advanced since last autumn. Some of them spoke very well, nor would the meeting so much as listen to George Potter on the other side. Burt (M.P. for Morpeth and who is, or was, a working man) was chairman, and spoke excellently though shortly, with a strong Northumbrian tongue: he seemed a capital fellow. Meantime the Liberal party is blown to pieces, and everything is in confusion."

As summer passed over, the shadow of imminent war lifted: but in autumn Morris was once more eagerly at work on the Committee which, under the presidency of Lord Lawrence, strove unavailingly to prevent the Afghan campaign, which was accepted by the war-party in England as an equivalent for open hostilities with Russia. At the beginning of 1878, when the Russian troops had forced the Balkans, the crisis became acute again. " This is terrible news," he writes on the 5th of January, when war seemed all but certain. " I confess I am really astounded at the folly that can play with such tremendous tools in this way; and more and more I feel how entirely right the flattest democracy is." At a meeting held in Exeter Hall on the 16th to protest against the threatening attitude of the Government, Morris appeared for the first time as a writer of political verse. "Wake, London Lads!" a stirring ballad written by him for the occasion, was distributed in the hall and sung with much enthusiasm. Here, as in the manifesto of the previous year, the appeal is to the "political working man," as Morris calls him in a letter describing this meeting, and is made in the name of the future and its hope. When the crisis in the East was finally past, it left Morris thoroughly in touch with the Radical leaders of the working class in London, and well acquainted with the social and economic ideas which, under the influence of widening education and of the international movement among the working classes, were beginning to transform their political creed from an individualist Radicalism into a more or less definite doctrine of State Socialism.

Morris's absorption in wider interests during this period was accompanied by a fresh development of energy in his own professional work. The dyeing and calico printing industry, still mainly carried on at Leek, was now established as an important branch of the business, and the designing of patterns for chintzes and figured silks was part of his daily work. Weaving both in silk and wool had also taken its place alongside of dyeing in his own workshops. "I am dazzled," he writes in March, 1877, "at the prospect of the splendid work we might turn out in that line." A French brocade-weaver from Lyons, M. Bazin, was brought over in June to set up the first silk-loom. As to this and other work begun or projected, Morris wrote to Mr. T. Wardle on the 13th of April:

"Thank you for getting me news of the brocader. We are willing to agree to his terms of 3,000 fr. for the year, and think it would be prudent not to guarantee for longer : but if he suits us, no doubt the situation will be a permanent one for him. I think before we strike a bargain we should see his specimens of work : meantime we send a parcel of examples of cloth such as we are likely to want as far as the weaving is concerned. We shall have to find him standing-room for the loom : what space and height is wanted for this? we should by all means want it big enough to weave the widest cloth that can be done *well* without steam-power : and it ought to be such as could weave a design 27 inches wide. We should certainly want to weave damask. I hope that your correspondent understands that we want a really intelligent man : if he turn out such, his position with us will be good, as we should surely be wanting more looms, and he would be foreman over the others. As soon as we are agreed, he must let us know when he can come, and send us some proper paper for pointing, in order that we may get a design ready for him without delay. So much for the brocader, when I have thanked you again very much for getting me on so far, and confessed that I am prodigiously excited about him.

" The tapestry is a bright dream indeed; but it must wait till I get my carpets going; though I have had it in my head lately, because there is a great sale now on in Paris of some of the finest ever turned out : much too splendid for anybody save the biggest pots to buy. Meantime much may be done in carpets : I saw yesterday a piece of ancient Persian, time of Shah Abbas (our Elizabeth's time) that fairly threw me on my back : I had no idea that such wonders could be done in carpets.

" We met again last night and are getting on I think : are going to expostulate with Ormskirk, Halifax, and Cherry-Hinton (*young* Scott's this last) at once. As for the old bird, all I can say is that he is convicted out of his own mouth of having made an enormous fortune by doing what he well knows to be wrong."

Early in that summer, the premises which have since then been the sale and show rooms for the firm's work had been opened in a newly-built block of buildings at the corner of Oxford Street and North Audley Street. The expanding business and the inaccessibility of Queen Square to the ordinary purchaser forced on this step. "I can't say I am much excited about it," was Morris's own comment, "as I should be if it were a shed with a half-dozen looms in it." The Queen Square premises were now wholly set free for the manufacturing part of the business, and the increased business filled up the free space at once. It cannot be denied that Morris looked on the political situation, as he was bound to do, from the point of view of the manufacturer, as well as that of the politician and social reformer. "Picture to yourself," he writes in May, "a three years' war, and the shop in Oxford Street, and poor Smith standing at the door with his hands in his pockets!"

During this year, Morris had as secretary and general helper at Queen Square a son of his old tutor Canon Guy. In October he left in order to go to Oxford, having made up his mind to take Orders. A diary which he kept during the last few months of his employment at Queen Square has been preserved, and gives a lively picture of the common course of work there as it went on from day to day. By Mr. Guy's permission I give a few typical extracts. The multifariousness of the master's energy, and the many difficulties that had to be contended with when any new kind of work was being started, are alike noticeable.

"18 May. Mr. Morris slept last night in town, and was up on the move when I arrived. He had been downstairs and set the new dye-pot at work, ready for him to set an indigo vat in the afternoon. Kirby's man came and finished fixing the ciphering tube. G. W. and W. M. talked over Mrs. Baring's house in Devonshire : the work we have proposed to do will certainly take two or three years before all completed : we have to get our Lyons silk-weaver at work for one thing. W. M. did a little work to a piece of embroidery in his room during the morning. I went down into the dye-shop with W. M. between 1 and 2 o'clock and helped him to set his vat. He dyed some blues which he will green on Tuesday next, if all is well, for Dimarco's carpet stuff. Mr. Broadhurst called and saw W. M. about the Eastern Question.

" 5 June. Mr. Wardle away at Richmond in morning. Mr. Morris came at midday : he dyed some blue silks in cochineal and madder to get purples : he has not yet learnt the real upshot of this dyeing; it is hard to get the colour on. Some of McCrea's wool was also dyed in the cochineal bath. Our clients are slow to pay their bills, this leads us into nasty difficulties. Mr. Morris spent the whole of this afternoon dyeing. Adams called about the Baptistery windows in All Saints, Putney; the two windows were ordered. Marlborough College window is ready to be sent.

" 7 June. Dyeing was madder. Mr. Morris wished to get a ply of blood red such as was dyed at Leek in February last, for a hanging pattern. He used 2 lb. of madder for $2\frac{1}{2}$ lb. of wool (3 hanks of weft and 2 hanks of warp). The colour in the end was not quite as deep as was wanted, owing to there being not a sufficient quantity of madder. When he was at Leek he used 80 lb. of madder for 100 lb. of wool, but you have to force the quantity a little when dyeing a small quantity of wools. In the spent bath other wools were dyed.

No news from Bazin yet about the pointing. There was a meeting at 264, Oxford Street, in evening, of the Society for Protection of Ancient Buildings. The Dean of Canterbury has written a letter on the subject of restoring the Cathedral; it was rather a cut against W. M., but however he will answer it no doubt.

"21 June. A letter came from Bazin saying that he leaves Lyons to-night for England. Murray came and saw G. W. in the afternoon; he has just returned from Italy. He showed G. W. some of his sketches. While he was there, W. M. came in; he has finished his work at the South Kensington Museum, which he did not care for much: he could not say anything for the designs which were produced by the students; he considered his time as having been wasted I believe. It is quite true about our red carpet having faded. W. M. is astonished at it. We had the cards down from the window to see the results of light and air upon the reds; they really have not much effect, but still a little; but the wools have been exposed to the light nearly a year, and had moreover to stand through all that strong sun of last year, as well as that of this year: no carpet is ever exposed so much to the light. The weld greens have gone, and W. M. is very lamentable over them. There are many secrets yet to be found out about dyeing. W. M. thinks that the Indian vat is the best for silks, and perhaps he will find out that it is the best for yarns; he intends setting one again soon. The blues (yarns) seemed to have stood a good deal, and W. M. is almost inclined now to say that they are the fastest of our dyes.

"25 June. The Heckmondwike Company sent up a woven pattern of the 3-ply green tulip carpet. W. M. called it dove-like, and so it is, the colours are very nice and well toned down. Bazin and a friend made their arrival in the afternoon; W. M. did not feel as if he wished to face Froggy at first, but said to G. W. (who went to receive the weaver) that he would be up in his room, if wanted ; but G. W. did not wish to exercise his French alone, but took the two new arrivals up into W. M.'s room. The Frenchmen went round to Ormond Yard with W. M. and G. W. to see what cards we have (these are the cards which we had from Lyons). Froggy says they will do for his purpose, and we shall have to set him at work at once on the silk willow pattern, using these cards. He will take some time in setting up the loom, which will give us time to get silk and to dye it perhaps.

" 12 July.   Mr. Lendon called about Bazin's work ; he gave us some instructions about the point paper, etc. He went round to Ormond Yard and saw the loom; the carpenter finished his work at midday. W. M. dyed a few silks in cochineal. He says that he cannot get on at all with this dye : he cannot make it out, he is unable to get a deep colour on. It will dye the deepest colour in a few minutes, and after that the colour will not get deeper, no matter how long you keep your goods in the decoction. I mordanted a few hanks of wool for to-morrow's experiments, which are to be in the fustic line.

" 23 July.   I tried to get the Indian vat set to-day, but the indigo, which has to be ground, prevented me. I hope to do so to-morrow.

" 24 July.   I was hard at work with the vat and managed to get it set by 5 p.m.   W. M. helped, and as he slept in town he was able to look at it before going to bed.   Silks were alumed for to-morrow's dyeing (weld and walnut, also madder).

" 25 July.   The vat was coming round all day ; she seemed to be doing well at 6.30, when I left ; a coppery scum was coming on the surface.

"27 July. The vat seemed to be doing well to-day; a little silk dyeing was done for experiments. A brevet was given her at 5 p.m.   Not very much business done.

"28 July.   The hopeful Indian vat brought W. M. up to town (an unusual thing for him to do on a Saturday): the vat had come round very well by this morning ; she was in a fit state for dyeing, and W. M. tried some wool in her, which proved to be successful. Still she was not quite come round to her proper form. A little cochineal dyeing was done; blues were dyed purple.

"20 Sept. Bazin began to weave, but the machinery (Jacquard) not being in very good order, he was unable to get on very far.   I prepared an estimate for east end window, All Saints, Putney.

"21 Sept.   Mr. Morris turned up from Kelmscott early, and as soon as he did so I went round to Ormond Yard with him, to see how Bazin had got on. He had got on better in working the machine than yesterday, but yet the (willow) pattern did not seem to be coming right, and it seemed as if the cards had got misplaced somehow or other.   The cards were making an absurd pattern, and W. M. did not know what to make of it. W. M. returned to Kelmscott by the 6.30 train.

"8 Oct. W. M. had to see about his packages, which he has to take to Ireland. He started by 8.25 mail train to Holyhead from Euston. He goes to the Countess of Charleville, Tullamore, King's County, to advise her as to the doing up of her house. He had to take with him patterns of carpets, silks, chintzes, etc. He goes to Leek on his way back from Ireland, and will stay there some while, making Tom Wardle look to his dyeing, etc., helping a good deal in it too."

This was Morris's first visit to Ireland.   In a letter he wrote from Leek after his return, there is the old keen eye for scenery ; but there is also a new tone, that of the social observer, one might almost say of the political theorist.

"I slept on board," he says, "for about two hours, and then stirred myself to get up and look, and when I came on deck we were just well in sight of land. It was much more beautiful than I expected to see : a long rather low cliffy coast on the right with a rocky steep island in front of it ; and on the left a long line of mountains rather than hills going on and turning the corner, and casting up points a long way inland : the said mountains very lovely in outline. The sky was grey and sulky, but not unfit for the scene, and a thickish mist hid all the feet of the mountains, while a cloud or two was lying on the tops of them : it looked very like Iceland and quite touched my hard heart.

"Dublin is not altogether an ugly town ; the Liffey runs through the chief street much like the Seine at Paris, which is good : yet a dirty and slatternly city is Dublin, and Guinness seems the only thing of importance there. I set off at about midday for my aristocrats ; the train running through a very flat country with the aforesaid Dublin mountains on the left ; you pass the Curragh, where our army of occupation sits, a fine moorland swelling up toward the Dublin mountains : then you see Kildare, with a great ruined mediæval church and a tall round tower beside it. Then the Dublin mountains die away, and the Slievh Bloom hills rise up on the left of the great plain ; which is to say the truth nothing but bog, reclaimed, half-reclaimed, or unreclaimed : in Elizabeth's time thick forest covered it, but the oaks and all are gone now. The villages we passed were very poor-looking, the cotters' houses in outside appearance the very poorest habitations of man I have yet seen, Iceland by no means excepted.

"Tullamore, my town, lies a little without the old Pale : my employers told me that it used to be the very centre of ribbonism ; even last year a man was slain there for 'agrarian' reasons. They told me that an old man had told them how he had seen in the rebellion 20 miles of country burning in a straight line, the cabins and villages fired by the Orange yeomanry : the grandfather of the present young lady who owns the estate commanded the troops of that district in the war, and his banners hang up very little the worse for wear in the hall of the house now—and these unreasonable Irish still remember it all, so long-memoried they are ! "

In November, 1877, Mrs. Morris and the two girls had gone to spend the winter at Oneglia on the Italian Riviera, where Morris himself was to join them in spring and make a tour with them through Northern Italy. His letters to Oneglia during these months give an unusually full account of his life and work during the winter. They are full of the Eastern Question, and the work of the Anti-Scrape, and the progress made by Bazin at the silk-loom in Ormond Yard, where "a poor old ex-Spitalfields weaver" had been found to help ; and also of a new and at first to him very laborious employment, that of composing and delivering lectures. The first lecture he ever gave in public was on the Decorative Arts. It was delivered before the Trades Guild of Learning, in what he calls "a dismal hole near Oxford Street," on the 4th of December. It was published immediately afterwards by Messrs. Ellis and White as a pamphlet ; and was reprinted, under the title of " The Lesser Arts," as the first of the collected addresses published in the volume of " Hopes and Fears for Art." The writing of prose was as yet as difficult to him as the writing of verse was easy, and he ruefully recognized that it was a thing he must work at unassisted.

"I should be glad to be out of Horrington House," he writes on the 29th of November, "'tis rather a doleful abode at present. I was thinking last Saturday of having Sarah up to read scraps of my lecture to her after the example of Molière, but refrained, lest I should kill her with surprise. I went with Wardle to the place and read 'Robinson Crusoe' to him to see if I could make my voice heard, which I found easy to be done."

"I gave my lecture on Tuesday," he continues on the 7th of December; "it went off very well, and I was not at all nervous. I have been having an afternoon with Froggy, the loom, and our Coventry 'designer' so-called: the loom was the wisest of the four of us and understood much more of what the others said than anybody else did—at least I think so."

"I am just come back from Kelmscott," a week later, "where I was two days with Webb: it was rather melancholy after our jolly time of last summer: we had two fine, but very cold days; this morning brilliant but white-frosty. The river had been much flooded, but was lower the first day, and I caught two good pike: I should like to have sent you one in a letter. The blown-down tree *is* that one by the causeway gate: it makes a sad gap, for it was a fine branchy tree."

From his mother's house in Hertfordshire he writes to the children on Christmas Day:

"I have been much agitated for the past week by the goings on of an August Personage and Lord Beaconsfield; but we hope to agitate others in our turn next week. On the whole our side has got weaker, and many people are sluggish and hard to move who thoroughly agree with us. The E. Q. A. met in committee yesterday and agreed to do something, though not as dramatically as I could have wished: however, we meet again next Monday, and then I hope we shall arrange to have a big meeting before Parliament. So much for politics: 'tis a fine Christmas Day to-day, though there has been a little snow. We have just had a peppering little snow-shower, item, a cock-pheasant has been on the lawn just now: these are bits of Hadham news you know, my dears."

On the 19th of January he gives an account of the Eastern Question Meeting at Exeter Hall the night before. " The evening meeting was magnificent, orderly and enthusiastic, though mind you it took some very heavy work to keep the enemies' roughs out, and the noise of them outside was like the sea roaring against a lighthouse. You will have seen about our music: wasn't it a good idea? I think Chesson suggested it first, and then they set me to write the song, which I did on the Monday night. It went down very well, and they sang it well together: they struck up while we were just ready to come on the platform, and you may imagine I felt rather excited when I heard them begin to tune up. They stopped at the end of each verse and cheered lustily."

" I am full of shame and anger," he writes to Faulkner on the 5th of February, " at the cowardice of the so-called Liberal party. A very few righteous men refuse to sit down at the bidding of these yelling scoundrels and pretend to agree with what they hate : these few are determined with the help of our working-men allies (who all along have been both staunch and sagacious) to get up a great demonstration in London as soon as may be, which will probably be Saturday week. There will certainly be a fight, so of course you will come up if you can."

The collapse came a week later. " To-morrow I am going to Cambridge," he writes on February 20th, " to give an address at the School of Art for Colvin. As to my political career, I think it is at an end for the present; and has ended sufficiently disgustingly. After beating about the bush and trying to organize some rags of re sistance to the war-party for a fortnight, after spending all one's time in committees and the like, I went to Gladstone with some of the workmen and Chesson, to talk about getting him to a meeting at the Agricultural Hall: he agreed, and was quite hot about it, and as brisk as a bee. I went off straight to the Hall, and took it for to-morrow: to work we fell, and everything got into train: but—on Monday our Parliamentaries began to quake, and they have quaked the meeting out now. The E. Q. A. was foremost in the flight, and really I must needs say they behaved ill in the matter. Gladstone was quite ready to come up to the scratch and has behaved well throughout: but I am that ashamed that I can scarcely look people in the face, though I did my best to keep the thing up. The working men are in a great rage about it, as they well may be: for I do verily believe we should have made it a success, though I don't doubt that there would have been a huge row. There was a stormy meeting of the E. Q. A. yesterday, full of wretched little personalities, but I held my tongue—I am out of it now; I mean as to bothering my head about it: I shall give up reading the papers, and shall stick to my work."

That work indeed was just then as engrossing and exciting to him as ever: and he was really glad to get back to it from the unfamiliar field of politics, work in which he took too seriously for his own comfort, and perhaps even for real effectiveness.

The project of reviving the art of high-warp tapestry-weaving, as it had been practised in its great days, was beginning to shape itself in his mind as something more than the bright dream of the previous spring. To Mr.

T. Wardle, who had continued to press the matter on him as a practicable scheme, and suggested its being undertaken by them as a joint enterprise, he wrote on the 14th of November, 1877, a long and interesting letter, which not only lays down the scope and difficulties of the work, but incidentally sets forth very clearly his own principles regarding this and other branches of decorative manufacture.

"I shall probably find one letter's space," he says, "not enough for going into the whole matter of the tapestry, but I will begin. Let's clear off what you say about the possibility of establishing a non-artistic manufactory. You could do it, of course; 'tis only a matter of money and trouble: but *cui bono?* it would not amuse you (unless I wholly misunderstand you), and would, I am sure, *not* pay commercially: a *cheap* new article at once showy and ugly, if advertised with humbug enough, will sell, of course: but an expensive article, even with ugliness to recommend it—I don't think anything under a Duke could sell it. However, as to the commercial element of this part of the scheme, 'tis not my affair, but on the art side you must remember that, as nothing is so beautiful as fine tapestry, nothing is so ugly and base as bad: *e.g.*, the Gobelins or the present Aubusson work: also tapestry is not fit for anything but figure-work (except now and then I shall mention wherein presently). The shuttle and loom beat it on one side, the needle on the other, in pattern-work: but for figure-work 'tis the only way of making a web into a picture: now there is only one man at present living (as far as I know) who can give you pictures at once good enough and suitable for tapestry—to wit, Burne-Jones. The exception I mentioned above would be the making of leaf and flower pieces (greeneries, *des verdures*), which would generally be used to eke out a set of figure-pieces: these would be within the compass of people, work-folk, who could not touch the figure-work. It would only be by doing these that you could cheapen the work at all.

" The qualifications for a person who would do successful figure-work would be these:

" 1. General feeling for art, especially for its decorative side.

" 2. He must be a good colourist.

" 3. He must be able to draw well; *i.e.*, he must be able to draw the human figure, especially hands and feet.

" 4. Of course he must know how to use the stitch of the work.

" Unless a man has these qualities, the first two of which are rare to meet with and cannot be taught, he will turn out nothing but bungles, disgraceful to every one concerned in the matter : I have no idea where to lay my hands on such a man, and therefore I feel that whatever I do I must do chiefly with my own hands. It seems to me that tapestry cannot be made a matter of what people nowadays call manufacturing, and that even so far as it can be made so, the only possible manufacturer must be an artist for the higher kind of work : otherwise all he has to do is to find house room, provide the frame and warp, and coloured worsteds exactly as the workman bids him. In speaking thus I am speaking of the picture-work : a cleverish woman could do the greeneries no doubt. When I was talking to you at Leek I did not fully understand what an entirely individual matter it must be : it is just like wood-engraving : it is a difficult art, but there is nothing to *teach* that a man cannot learn in half a day, though it would take a man long practice to do it well. There *are* manufacturers of wood-engraving, *e.g.*, the Dalziels, as big humbugs as any within the narrow seas. I suspect you scarcely understand what a difficult matter it is to translate a painter's design into material: I have been at it sixteen years now, and have never quite succeeded.

"In spite of all these difficulties, if in any way I can help you, I will: only you must understand fully that I intend setting up a frame and working at it myself, and I should bargain for my being taught by you what is teachable: also I see no difficulty in your doing greeneries and what patterns turned out desirable, and I would make myself responsible for the designs of such matters. With all this, I have no doubt that we shall both lose money over the work: you don't know how precious little people care for such things.

"To recapitulate: Tapestry at its highest is the painting of pictures with coloured wools on a warp: nobody but an artist can paint pictures; but a sort of half-pictures, *i.e.*, scroll-work or leafage, could be done by most intelligent people (young girls would do) under direction.

"I am sorry if in any way I appear to have wet-blanketed you: but the matter is such an important one that it is no use avoiding the facing of the truth in all ways, and I have accordingly given you my mind without concealment."

He began to make designs for greeneries forthwith, and studied pieces of old tapestry with minute care. In March, 1878, he writes again to Wardle:

"I inclose a warp from a sixteenth-century piece of tapestry, which as you see is worsted: the pitch is 12 to the inch: nothing in tapestry need be finer than this. In setting up your work you must remember that as tapestry hangs on the wall the warps are horizontal, though of course you weave with them vertical. If you send me the space of your loom I will make a design for it.

"Thanks for sending me Arnold's lecture,"—this was the address on "Equality" delivered at the Royal Institution in the previous month and afterwards reprinted in the volume of Matthew Arnold's "Mixed Essays" —"with the main part of which of course I heartily agree: the only thing is that if he has any idea of a remedy he durstn't mention it. I think myself that no rose-water will cure us: disaster and misfortune of all kinds, I think, will be the only things that will breed a remedy: in short, nothing can be done till all rich men are made poor by common consent. I suppose he dimly sees this, but is afraid to say it, being, though naturally a courageous man, somewhat infected with the great vice of that cultivated class he was praising so much— cowardice, to wit."

The strain and excitement of the political campaign of that winter ended in a severe attack of rheumatic gout, which seized and quite crippled him when he went out to join his family in Italy towards the end of April. It prevented him from being much more than a passive participator in the long-planned and eagerly awaited Italian tour. The machinery had been taxed beyond its power: he never quite regained his old strength, and in the following year there can be traced in his letters the first shadow of advancing age: not indeed a surprising thing in a man who had accomplished work so immense in its mass and so high in its quality by the age of forty-five.

From Genoa he writes on the 27th of April to Mrs. Burne-Jones:

"We entered this ancient city yesterday evening by no means triumphantly: we had a lovely drive on Thursday morning to a hill town with an ancient stone or two in its buildings, which are now nothing but tatters of disorder: yet it was agreeable and not very dirty. Diano

Castello it is called : people used to run there when the
Saracen Vikings burnt Diano Marina and the shore in
general : unhappily, though that drive was pleasant, and
the evening wandering among the olives was pleasant, I
felt the seeds of gout in me all day, and woke yesterday
morning with that plant flourishing vigorously : but I
didn't like to keep them stuck at Oneglia, as all preparations had been made for departure : so about midday we
got away, and I found myself in a carriage somehow
along with my dear Jenny, and a very pleasant ride we
had to Genoa with my gout seemingly decreasing : but
when we all met at the station there was a long way to
go to the omnibus, and the octroi objected to the box of
medicines (thinking them syrops), and I could not walk
or even hop well, so I got stuck, till a chap took me up
on his back : but even then I behaved so ill as this, that
when he set me down against a wall (lacking nothing of
Guy Fawkes but his matches and lanthorn) things began
to dance before my eyes, my knees went limp, and down
I went, thank you, and enjoyed a dream of some minute
and a quarter I suppose, which seemed an afternoon of
public meetings and the like : out of that I woke and
found myself on the ground the centre of an admiring
crowd, one of the members of which held a brandy bottle
to my lips which I had the presence of mind to refuse
and call for water.   Poor May, who was with me, was
very much frightened, but was very good : even then I
had to be Guy Fawkesed upstairs at the Hotel, chuckling
with laughter, till they landed me in this present palatial
suite of rooms : so I'm not likely to be able to tell you
much of Genoa, I fear.   Murray, who is still with us, has
taken the two girls out for a walk ; I can't help thinking
that they will enjoy the port and the streets of a big town
after the quiet of Oneglia, though I, for my part, when
I wandered among the olives above the sea the other

day, felt as if I should be well contented to stay there always; it really was a most lovely spot: and it was pleasant to have the high road close by it and to hear the jingle of bells as the carts went by, though when you were among the olives you could not guess of any road near: the trees went on terrace after terrace right up to the top of the low hill: you could see nothing else: nothing can be imagined more beautiful and soothing.

"This confounded gout and Guy Fawkesing of mine has of course put off our journey to-day, but I am much better now, and I hope we shall get on to Venice to-morrow: we shan't attempt stopping at Verona, where we can easily put up on our return: you see if we were once at Venice Janey and the girls could amuse themselves in any case; and as for me 'tis clear that Venice must be the hobbler's Paradise. Can't you imagine what a time it was for me when I looked out at the window at Oneglia, and saw those three all standing together?"

On the way to Venice the first view of the Lago di Garda gave him a shock of delight more powerful than anything else he saw in Italy. "What a strange surprise it was," he says, "when it suddenly broke upon me, with such beauty as I never expected to see: for a moment I really thought I had fallen asleep and was dreaming of some strange sea where everything had grown together in perfect accord with wild stories." At Venice itself he was so lame that he could only crawl into a few churches. In his letters it is difficult to distinguish the depression of his illness from his pain at the decay, and his horror at the restorations, going on all round him: "It is sad to think," he sums the matter up, "that our children's children will not be able to see a single genuine ancient building in Europe." A visit to Torcello ("it was a great rest to be among the hedges and the green grass again, and to hear the birds singing; swifts are the

only songsters in the city ") he speaks of as almost his one unmixed pleasure there.

Indeed he was always uneasy away from the earth and the green grass; and when they left Venice for Padua and Verona his spirits began to rise. " What a beautiful and *pleasant* place it is," he writes of Padua, " with the huge hall dividing the market place, and the endless arcades everywhere : or the Arena Chapel in the midst of the beautiful garden of trellised vines, all as green as the greenest just now. Yesterday was a stormy day, and in the afternoon the girls and I were caught in a shower as we were wandering about; however, it was but wandering in an arcade till it was over, and as the pavement was clean and dry I sat down with great content with my back to the wall. A dyer's hand-cart took refuge by us with a load of blue work (cotton) just done : I was so sorry I could not talk with one of the men, who looked both good-tempered and intelligent. In the evening we went to a queer old botanic garden and heard the birds sing, and then we were driven along the road outside the walls. The rain had cleared off but left great threatening clouds that quite hid the Alps, but the small mountains to the west of Padua were quite clear and blue, and set me longing to be among them. It was a beautiful evening, but damp I doubt; but how sweet the hay smelt ! "

From Verona he writes a little later : " 'Tis a piping hot day, not a cloud in the sky. I have just been into Sta. Anastasia, which is hard by: a very beautiful church, but appeals less to the heart than the head, and somehow don't satisfy that : also though 'tis meant to be exceedingly Gothic and pointed, it is thoroughly neo-classical in feeling. S. Zeno is not quite what I expected : 'tis a round-arched Gothic church, just as S. Anastasia is a pointed-arched Renaissance one. I am more alive again, and really much excited at all I have seen and am seeing, though sometimes it all tumbles into a dream and I do not know where I am.   Many times I think of the first time I ever went abroad, and to Rouen, and what a wonder of glory that was to me when I first came upon the front of the Cathedral rising above the flower-market. It scarcely happens to me like that now, at least not with man's work, though whiles it does with bits of the great world, like the Garda Lake the other day, or unexpected sudden sights of the mountains.   Even the inside of St. Mark's gave one rather deep satisfaction, and rest for the eyes, than that strange exaltation of spirits, which I remember of old in France, and which the mountains give me yet.

"I don't think this is wholly because I am grown older, but because I really have had more sympathy with the North from the first in spite of all the faults of its work. Let me confess and be hanged : with the later work of Southern Europe I am quite out of sympathy.   In spite of its magnificent power and energy I feel it as an enemy; and this much more in Italy, where there is such a mass of it, than elsewhere.   Yes, and even in these magnificent and wonderful towns I long rather for the heap of grey stones with a grey roof that we call a house north-away."

Almost immediately afterwards a fresh attack of gout hurried him to the North again.   "I am still plaguy lame," he writes the day after his arrival in London, " a very limpet, but am not so devil-ridden as I was.   I think that came of that infernal furnace-heat we were in, the last few days of Italy: it was such a relief when the cool mountain breezes woke me out of a doze as the train laboured up the last slopes before the great tunnel: and going through that merry Burgundy country with a fine windy sunny day I got quite merry myself."

Before going out to Italy he had arranged to take a new house in London, that one in which he lived for the rest of his life, on the Upper Mall at Hammersmith. It is a large Georgian house, of a type, ugly without being mean, familiar in the older London suburbs. It is only separated from the river by a narrow roadway, planted with large elms. The river indeed was so near a neighbour that at exceptionally high tides it occasionally brimmed over the sill of the water-gate in the low river wall, crossed the roadway, and flooded the cellarage of the house. The parapet along the edge had afterwards to be made continuous to avoid this danger. On bright days the sunlight strikes off the water and flickers over the ceilings : many barges and sailing boats go by with the tide, and the curve of the river opens out two long reaches, up by Chiswick Eyot with the wooded slopes of Richmond in the background, and down through Hammersmith Bridge. Behind the house a long rambling garden, in successive stages of lawn and orchard and kitchen-garden, still preserves some flavour of the country among the encroaching mass of building which is gradually swallowing up the scattered cottages, low and roofed with weathered red tiles, that then lay between the river and the high road. The house had some little history ; in its garden the inventor of the electric telegraph, Francis Ronalds, had in 1816 laid eight miles of insulated wires charged with static electricity, and worked by electrometers and synchronized rotating discs at either end. Fragments of his apparatus, the first electric communication ever practically worked, are still preserved in the South Kensington Museum. When Morris took it, it had just been vacated by Dr. George Macdonald, and was known as The Retreat ; this name, as rather suggestive of a private asylum, he at once changed, and called it Kelmscott House, after his other home on the bank of the same river. The hundred and thirty miles of stream between the two houses were a real, as well as an imaginative, link between them. He liked to think that the water which ran under his windows at Hammersmith had passed the meadows and grey gables of Kelmscott; and more than once a party of summer voyagers went from one house to the other by water, embarking at their own door in London and disembarking in their own meadow at Kelmscott. "The situation," he wrote of it to his wife at Oneglia, "is certainly the prettiest in London (you may mock at this among the olives beside the Midland Sea): the house could easily be done up at a cost of money: the long drawing-room, with a touch of my art, could be made one of the prettiest in London: the garden is really most beautiful. If you come to think of it, you will find that you won't get a garden or a house with much character unless you go out about as far as the Upper Mall. I don't think that either you or I could stand a quite modern house in a street: I don't fancy going back among the bugs of Bloomsbury."

Kelmscott House was taken from Midsummer, and the Morrises moved into it at the end of October. Under his skilful hands, the long drawing-room of which he speaks above—a handsome room with a range of five windows, filling the whole width of the house and looking out through the great elms over the river—had been made into a room quite unique in the quietness and beauty of its decoration. It was sufficiently out of the London dirt to admit of being hung with his own woven tapestry. The painted settle and cabinet, which were its chief ornaments, belonged to the earliest days of Red House; the rest of the furniture and decoration was all in the same spirit, and had all the effect of making the room a mass of subdued yet glowing colour,

THE DRAWING-ROOM, KELMSCOTT HOUSE, HAMMERSMITH.

into which the eye sank with a sort of active sense of rest. Morris's own study on the ground floor was severely undecorated. It had neither carpet nor curtains; the walls were mostly filled with plain bookshelves of unpolished oak, and a square table of unpolished oak scrubbed into snowy whiteness, with a few chairs, completed its contents. One of the first things he did after taking possession of the house was to have a tapestry-loom built in his bedroom, at which he might practise the art of weaving with his own hands. He was often up and at work at his loom with the first daylight in spring and summer mornings. Among his few fragments of diaries is one which he kept of the first complete piece he wove there. It is headed " Diary of work on Cabbage and Vine Tapestry at Kelmscott House, Hammersmith. Begun May 10th, 1879, after Campfield about a week's work getting in, also after weaving a blue list." A table of the number of hours spent daily on it follows, up to the 17th of September, when it was finished. Except for three intervals during which he was out of London, there are only two blank days on the list, and there are a good many days on which he worked at it for nine, and even for ten, hours. The total is 516 hours in the four months; and this was the work of a man who had a hundred other things to attend to, and who was never in a hurry! This tapestry-loom was for his own private use. The coach-house and stables adjoining the house were converted into a large weaving-room, the room afterwards used as the meeting-place of the Hammersmith Socialists. Carpet-looms were built there, and were soon regularly at work producing the fabrics which became known under the name of the Hammersmith carpets and rugs from this accident of their first origin.

During the winter of 1878-9, in fact, weaving in its various forms—on the Jacquard loom for figured silks, on the carpet-loom for pile carpets, and on the tapestry-loom for Arras tapestries—replaced dyeing as the chief object of Morris's interest. The regular work in examining at South Kensington, which he had begun two years before and which he continued till his last illness, had contributed to an increased interest in textiles. He had undertaken that work partly out of a feeling of gratitude for the immense service which the collections at the South Kensington Museum had been to him personally as a designer and manufacturer: "perhaps," he said incidentally in his evidence before the Royal Commission of 1882, "I have used it as much as any man living." The national collections there owe very much to him. For the last fifteen years of his life no important purchase of either textiles or embroideries was ever made without consulting him. "He never failed me," the Director of Art at South Kensington tells me, "and cheerfully put aside his own business when he knew that we had urgent need of his services. On one occasion he went with me to Paris at a few hours' notice and in very bad weather, to attend a sale, and when there offered to advance a considerable sum of money for the benefit of the Department, as in the hurry of our departure from London it had been impossible for me to get sanction for such expenditure."

The embroideries, no less than the woven stuffs, produced at Queen Square, took a fresh start from the introduction of home-dyed silks. This is a point on which all the embroiderers who worked for him lay special emphasis. "There was a peculiar beauty in his dyeing," says Mrs. Holiday, one of the most highly qualified of his later pupils in the art of embroidery, "that no one else in modern times has ever attained to. He actually did create new colours; then in his amethysts and golds and greens, they were different to anything I have ever seen; he used to get a marvellous play of colour into them. The amethyst had flushings of red; and his gold (one special sort), when spread out in the large rich hanks, looked like a sunset sky. When he got an unusually fine piece of colour he would send it off to me or keep it for me; when he ceased to dye with his own hands I soon felt the difference. The colours themselves became perfectly level, and had a monotonous prosy look; the very lustre of the silk was less beautiful. When I complained, he said, ' Yes, they have grown too clever at it—of course it means they don't love colour, or they would do it.'"

"I am writing in a whirlwind of dyeing and weaving," says a letter of March, 1879, "and even as to the latter rather excited by a new piece just out of the loom, which looks beautiful, like a flower garden." Even at Kelmscott he missed the daily fascination of his work. "Somehow I feel," he wrote from there a few months later, " as if there must soon be an end for me of playing at living in the country: a town-bird I am, a master-artisan, if I may claim that latter dignity." And again that same autumn, when he was much worried by work for the Society for Protection of Ancient Buildings, " Lord bless us," he breaks out, "how nice it will be when I can get back to my little patterns and dyeing, and the dear warp and weft at Hammersmith!"

END OF VOL. I.

CHISWICK PRESS : CHARLES WHITTINGHAM AND CO.
TOOKS COURT, CHANCERY LANE, LONDON.